BA88

W9-BCU-791

Skylark

Other Books by Howard Mansfield

Cosmopolis: Yesterday's Cities of the Future

In the Memory House

Skylark

The Life, Lies, and Inventions of Harry Atwood

Howard Mansfield

University Press of New England
Hanover and London

University Press of New England, Hanover, NH 03755
Printed in the United States of America   5 4 3 2 1

LIBRARY OF CONGRESS CATALOGING-IN-PUBLICATION DATA
Mansfield, Howard.
    Skylark : the life, lies, and inventions of Harry Atwood / Howard
Mansfield.
        p.   cm.
    Includes bibliographical references.
    ISBN 0–87451–891–1 (cl : alk. paper)
        1. Atwood, Harry.   2. Air pilots—United States—Biography.
    3. Inventors—United States—Biography.   I. Title.
    TL540.A74M36   1999
    629.13'092—dc21
    [B]   98–38960

Once again for Dr. B. A. Millmoss

The next generation will all fly. They will possess the instincts of birds. General knowledge of aerodynamics will be a conversation topic and far exceed our present developments. One dominating idea exists in the minds of our boys. They desire to fly. Nothing can stop them.

—CAPT. FRANK M. HAWKS (1930)

For me it seems that *all life flies*—protons, planes or people.

—RUTH NICHOLS, *Wings for Life* (1957)

We shall be journeying through interstellar space before the advent of another generation. We shall find it the most perfect roadbed we have ever traversed. We shall learn that it is a universal transmission line of energy and substance.

—HARRY NELSON ATWOOD, speech (1936)

Contents

Illustrations follow pages 82 and 194.

Skylark

ᔕ Introduction

Always in Flight

Katrina Atwood Copeland is lost in her father's house. She is seventy-seven years old. She had last lived in this house when she was twenty. This was a house unlike any other, as her father's life had been unlike any other.

When her father bought the house in the 1930s, it was a two-story farmhouse from 1820, such as you would find any place in New England. On a back road in a small New Hampshire town, the house faced the mountains. Her father loved mountains.

He covered the house in stone. He hired six young men, some of whom were living in a small cottage up the road, trying to ride out the Great Depression. One was a mechanic, another an engineer, talented men with an eye for stone. They labored for groceries, quarrying the old stone walls on the farm and laying the stone up until the clapboards disappeared behind a fortress.

Inside, he covered the floors with concrete, covered everything with layers of concrete, including the dining room table. Good china, passed down for generations, scraping on concrete. He built a tower to watch airplanes at a landing strip he had in mind, and also to watch lightning. He had ideas about lightning. Out front he built a pool—a concrete pool, which was unheard of in New Hampshire then—and fed a spring into it. He had a fear of fire and a love of experiment.

He tried all sorts of things: He flooded the basement with four feet of warm water to heat the house. He threw chicken wire and old bed frames into the concrete, and for insulation, layers of sawdust. He made it up as he went along.

This was the house that Harry Nelson Atwood had built.

Years after, folks who knew of the odd house would say, "the man who once lived there built an airplane, put it in a pool one winter; and then took it out and flew it to the White House—landed it right there—and the president came out to greet him."

Like all fables it was true and false at once. All that had happened, but not quite that way.

He had left this house in a hurry more than fifty years ago, even as he was still building up new stone walls by the barn. He hid his beloved grand piano from the creditors and buried his airplane—the airplane that was once proclaimed in the headlines, the hope of so many: the Airmobile, the Model T of aviation, one in every garage. "We'll Soon Be Skylarking in a Wooden Plane," read a headline. "The original Airmobile may eventually find its way to some museum along with the first locomotive, the original Wright biplane and the first sewing machine," the local newspaper speculated.

Amelia Earhart and other celebrity aviators, Ruth Nichols and Clarence Chamberlin, had come to see and to promote the Airmobile. Many in these small towns had never seen an airplane, and very few had even left the earth for a moment, and yet here in person were some of the heroes of the day, the thrill and glamour of the newsreels in a town of four hundred dragging itself through hard times. "It was like a gold rush," said one. Harry Atwood was the genius with the wonder-working invention that would lift them all out of the Depression. He had been a famous aviator himself back before World War I, when the pilot sat out on the wing and felt his way across the countryside. He was like no one they had ever met. He talked of space travel and future wars. "He had eyes that would look right through you," said one.

But underneath the headlines, there was an implosion, a failed contract negotiation, creditors and bills.

This was not the first time Harry Atwood had left town in a hurry. A few years before his arrival in New Hampshire, he had hidden his grand piano, declared bankruptcy at the local jail, and left a small Massachusetts town stirred up like an angry hornet's nest; creditors were after him, from the bank president to the undertaker, and the FBI was investigating. That time he had also left behind his three daughters, the eldest of whom was Katrina, then fifteen.

The Atwood girls were coming home from school when the bus was halted not far from their house. Their father sent them directly to a hotel in a nearby city, and then on to their grandmother's in Pennsylvania. The girls had no warning and no explanation. Their mother had died when Katrina was five, and now they were exiled from their father.

Though the girls did live with him again for a year or so in New Hampshire, they hated him for sending them away, for the hurt of that one afternoon. Later they would lose track of him for years at a stretch, not knowing if he was in Canada or Arkansas or the Midwest, not knowing if he was alive. He attended none of their weddings.

For a long time the stone house stood empty, then the concrete roof fell in. Several owners struggled mightily to reclaim the house; the first spent three years just carting out loads of caved-in concrete and rebuilding the roof. The walls and rooms had been moved and moved again until the inside of the house was as mercurial as a stage set under construction weeks before the opening of a show.

Her father's house was there in stone and yet it remained elusive. Harry Atwood could not have chosen a more fitting monument: unfinished, abandoned, collapsed, each room an experiment, a plan that was always changing.

Katrina follows a thread of memory through the house. Her host leads the way, presenting the vanished floor plan as he knew it. "This was the dining room, this was the bathroom, there was a fireplace. The kitchen would have been here—"

"No—wait," says Katrina. "This looks like the breakfast room."

Her host pulls out an old photo and they enter into a long discussion about a row of large square windows that were once there. They stand like two hikers over a map, trying to orient themselves. They reshuffle rooms, give new assignments to the old pattern, and resume the memory chase.

They make their way to the narrow front stairs, one of the only surviving details from 1820. The stairs are steep and the last step was made steeper by more than two inches of concrete, a small grey dam, the old balusters resting right on top. "The problem is your father poured concrete up here," the host says to Katrina as she pulls herself up the stairs.

"Father was always the problem," Katrina says good naturedly.

Katrina is a marvelous storyteller. She has a sharp intellect, a ready curiosity, and a demeanor like a brisk fall day—sunny and bright with passing clouds swiftly obscuring the sun. She can be engaging and outgoing, but she can quickly withdraw.

Her room upstairs is one of the few still in its old location. "And here's where I used to look out at my mountain and paint it," she says. And she remembers how she and her sisters would stay up all night talking and playing with their dogs sometimes.

Back downstairs, as her host leads her to her father's laboratory, her mood darkens. She rests on her cane, declining to look at the lab. She has seen it enough, she says. "Father made me mad one time. I remember standing here getting hysterical," she says. And then quietly to herself, "I was so angry with him."

She is done touring the past. She heads outside and sits down on the steps to smoke. She has emphysema, but smokes with religious zeal. Katrina is wiry and determined—tough you'd say with admiration, or stubborn, if you were annoyed. Her host catches up with her, and they sit awhile swapping stories; Katrina talks about her father, and the host about the labors of the past owners to tame this house, which has no foundation. It rides the heaving winter earth like a boat. The homeowner has to move the door latch plate four times each winter as the front door rises up. She gets up and thanks her host.

For a moment, Katrina stands across the road and looks at the house. This might be the last time she will ever see it. After all these years, she is still sorting out her father. "Good on invention. Getting things done the quickest, cleverest way. But a child his whole life. And the worst kind of *liar.*"

The word hangs in the air as she leaves: liar.

Katrina was seventy-seven—still young enough to change her mind.

I

He rises and begins to round,
He drops the silver chain of sound,
Of many links without a break . . .
As up he wings the spiral stair,
A song of light, and pierces air
With fountain ardour, fountain play,
To reach the shining tops of day . . .
As he to silence nearer soars,
Extends the world at wings and dome,
More spacious making more our home,
Till lost on his aerial rings
In light, and then the fancy sings
—GEORGE MEREDITH, *The Lark Ascending* (1883)

⬭ The Lark Ascending

The summer of 1911 was one of the hottest on record. Boston hit 104 degrees. Five thousand people slept outside on the Boston Common one night. There was an "ice famine." An ice cartel had created a shortage to drive up prices. People crowded into Atlantic City, the White Mountains, all pools and beaches. The news carried stories of death by drowning, heat stroke, and arguments and shootings provoked by the great heat. London recorded the warmest July in forty years and Paris had a drought—not one cloud was seen over Paris for the first three weeks in July.

In Washington, D.C., Alexander Graham Bell invented a way to stay cool. He set up his study in an empty indoor pool and hooked up an "ice stove," a fan to blow air over ice and pump it into his pool-bottom room.

That hot summer was the beginning of Harry Atwood in the world. He was twenty-seven.

In the spring he was a college dropout running a car repair garage in a town north of Boston. He had a daughter and a failing marriage. He had made two attempts to get a degree at the Massachusetts Institute of Technology, but had failed. He did own one success: he had patented two designs for electric meters and sold the patents to General Electric. He would use that money to free himself. He was going to fly.

The second aviation meet to be held in America took place near Boston. Some of the great aviators were at the Harvard-Boston aero meet. Wilbur Wright was a judge and President William Howard Taft handed out the prizes. An Englishman, Claude Grahame-White, won the top prize of ten thousand dollars. He flew out to the Boston Lighthouse and back—thirty-three miles. Harry Atwood was there early each day and stayed late. His head was full of the "science and gossip of aviation," his father said.

In the decade after the Wright brothers had triumphed at Kitty Hawk, each flight was an experiment, a leap into the unknown that had about it the feel of a kitchen-table science project. When you flew, you sat on the edge of the wing, suspended in space on a web of spruce and wires and fabric. The aeroplane was still more idea than machine, a tentative sketching in the blue sky, a da Vinci drawing come to life.

"The inventors up to that time had been hopeful rather than precise," a friend of the Wrights, Griffith Brewer, said of the earliest efforts.

Atwood yearned to join this great experiment and it had led to despair at MIT. "How well I recall one beautiful spring morning when I was obliged to call upon Physics Professor Dr. Comstock to explain my delinquencies in physics," he said.

"I carried a little bundle with me. It contained a homemade model of my idea of a possible flying machine. I figured that it might cause Dr. Comstock to dispose of my case with an attitude of sympathy rather than harshness. It did. He treated me with profound sympathy. In fact he treated me as a psychopathic doctor treats a patient. He talked to me about mental lapses and disorders. He suggested remedies. He gave me a fatherly talk about the dire future of young people who persist in cluttering their minds with fantastic junk. He climaxed his remarks by informing me that I was in the wrong institution, if I was unable to engage my mind upon the concepts of sanity. He paid no attention to my flying machine creation.

"I left Dr. Comstock's office a frustrated and 'flunked' freshman, and went straight to 237 Beacon St.," the home of his fraternity, Phi Beta Epsilon, known on campus as Phi Beta Cash because of its wealthy members, including Duponts and an heir to the Kodak fortune. Some students were assigned three rooms, one for a study, a bedroom for themselves, and a room for a servant. The son of an accountant, Atwood had grown up in Roxbury in modest circumstances. One summer before college he washed windows in his neighborhood, cleaning the storefronts that sat under the elevated trains. To speed his work he invented a squeegee-like device. But at college he adopted the Phi Beta Cash style. He traveled first class, even though he didn't have a return fare. He'd find a way home.

"The fraternity chef assisted me in burning the model in the kitchen fire, without asking questions. He seemed to fathom my dejection. The noon hour arrived and I was silent through the luncheon period. Then I paid a visit to the piano, and immediately gave a new rendition of my 'flying ditty,' 'Shall We Ever Be Able To Fly.'

"I played it again and again, and played nothing else. Each rendition was made with an acceleration of tempo, crescendo, and modulation. My thoughts were far away in the realm of the skies. I was clearing my mind from the clutter of fantastic junk, and trying to determine whether Dr. Comstock or I was in the wrong institution. When I had finished, the boys overwhelmed me with unusual applause. They did not know that they were applauding a 'coroner's inquest.'

"I did not graduate."

He went on to the most exclusive school in the country, the Wright brothers flying school in Dayton, Ohio. There were only two dozen aviators in the country, and the Wrights had trained about a dozen. The school was out on the trolley line at the Simms Station stop, in a farmer's cow pasture, Huffman Prairie. Clearing the field of cow pies was one of the student chores. The Wright brothers had made their second greatest flight here back in 1905. They had flown in a circle; the practical aeroplane was born. At the time, only a reporter from a small journal, *Gleanings in Bee Culture*, thought it noteworthy. When Wilbur Wright performed the same feat three years later in France, he caused a sensation: the French had been flying for two years, but no one had done that.

Atwood arrived in Dayton in May 1911, joining two army officers, Lt. Henry H. "Hap" Arnold and Lt. Thomas "Dashing" Milling. Arnold would later lead the air force in World War II. At this moment the army had but one aeroplane and no qualified pilots. Among the other students were Howard Gill, who would join the Wright Exhibition Team, and Cal Rodgers, who would be the first to fly from coast to coast. Both would be killed in plane crashes within two years.

Though the Wrights had been running the school for only a year, already there were many established traditions and stories. Most of flying was waiting. ("Aviwaiters" in one phrase.) A wind much more than ten miles an hour kept the aeroplanes on the ground and twenty minutes aloft was a long flight. A cross-country flight of eight miles was noted in the press. In addition, the Wrights did not fly on the sabbath. There was plenty of time for talk and pranks.

"The Atwood legend was the top," recalled Grover Loening, an airplane designer who worked for the Wrights and was the first to receive a master's degree in aeronautics, at Columbia in 1912.

When Atwood arrived at school he was "pretty confident of himself," said Loening. He was a perfect target for Hap Arnold and the others. They "picked on his zeal to do everything to be a perfect aviator as a swell chance for some first-class kidding," said Loening. "They explained to him carefully how important it was to develop a sense of balance, and that the way they had all practised was by mounting a two-wheeled handling truck and, standing at the center of the truck with a long board across the shoulders, proceed to balance the board and all on the two wheels. Atwood got to work at this practically impossible task, with Cal Rodgers sitting at a table checking Atwood's skill on a score pad they had rigged up, which would tell whether or not Atwood would be good enough at balancing to fly.

"Then, not content with the immense success of this episode, they told him that to be a really good aviator one had to learn to fly in a straight line and that it was the custom at the school for a new pupil to make his own line to practise on. So they presently had Atwood with his whitewash pail and brush painting a white line several hundred feet long on the grass field. Intensely serious, Atwood took a long time to catch on."

The joking was not much different from the actual course, which included hours of learning to balance a trainer the Wrights had devised. Wright training began with a tour of the factory and included thorough instruction in the assembly of the aeroplane and the engine. An aviator's life depended upon it. He would have to oversee the reassembly of planes after shipping, rebuilding after crashes, and before every flight would have to check each wire and rib. The mechanical instruction came easily to Atwood; as a boy he had worked on motorcycles and boats.

Then the students practiced the controls in the Wrights' trainer, an old plane set up on sawhorses. The Wrights' system used three controls, by far the most unnatural set-up. Their rival, Glenn Curtiss, had controls close to the modern—pull a wheel back to make the plane climb, push it forward to dive. To turn right, lean to the right in your harness.

Flying a Wright aeroplane required some thinking—too much thinking and not enough reacting and you were in trouble, the aviators said. One lever controlled the elevator and moved in the expected manner: push it forward to dive, pull it back to climb. The other control lever was of two parts, controlling both the rudder and the wing warping. The Wright wing was controlled by warping, the trailing edge of the wing flexed much like the tips of a bird's wing. To turn right, for example, the pilot had to pull the lever back to lift the left wing, while also turning the top of the lever the correct number of degrees to move the rudder.

Students worked at this for days. Sometimes Orville Wright would walk up behind them, unseen, and pull down on a wing to test their reactions.

Once off the trainer, students flew with an instructor, as passengers first, then gradually taking over the controls—the shared, central wing-warping and rudder lever, and one of the dual elevator levers. Students and instructors sat side by side, but not as they do today with the pilot on the left. The Wright system produced pilots who flew from the left seat and others who flew from the right, depending on how they were trained. Atwood was a left-handed Wright pilot.

After about a two dozen flights, and two or three hours in the air, a student soloed and realized how little he knew and how many questions he had. The sky was an uncharted ocean and he had just been given a rowboat and two oars.

"All those early aviators knew more than they could tell anybody. But what was it they knew, or knew they didn't know?" Hap Arnold said. "Things happened, that was all. The air was a tricky place. The best laws, discovered and formulated by the best aeronautical brains, could still be upset, it seemed in a second."

There was "serious, mysterious talk of 'holes in the air,'" said Arnold. Each crash, each flight was dissected. The students and the instructors joined in the birth of an aviation tradition, "hangar flying." "The best times of all in that Simms field 'hangar' were when the Wright brothers joined us," said Arnold. The Wrights would say little and listen as everyone had their say. "They were usually so courteous, almost diffident, really. Wilbur, for example, often hesitated to give an opinion without first consulting the little black notebook of aeronautical data he always carried with him.

"Once, I remember well, a loud argument was in progress about just how the loop would be accomplished—a time we hoped was not far off. Opinions differed as to whether it would be done from 'the inside' or 'the outside' . . . The Wright brothers listened with interest, never saying a word. Then, as everyone was laying down the law about this or that approach, Wilbur quietly attracted our attention and pointed overhead. In the slightly windy air far above the shed, a lark was fighting hard to fly straight upward, and as we watched, the bird struggled over on its back and curved down again, coming out in level flight from a crude but indisputable loop."

After two weeks of training, talking, and flying, Harry Atwood graduated. He had completed eighteen lessons and flown for a total of one hour and fifty-five minutes. In later years he told a different story: "Orville had gone to town one day and I decided I'd fly the machine. I had never been up but one time and then it was only for a few feet. But this time I got the thing off the ground and into the air.

"I had to learn how to maneuver the stick and make the airplane fly. I simply got the thing into the air and didn't know how to get it down. It took about two hours for me to get the feel of it and to know just how to make it do what I wanted. After that it was easy and I landed and found I'd been in the air longer than any other person.

"Everybody thought I was a hero."

He said he had been aloft longer than Orville Wright. He had broken Orville's record. That was a story for later years, a good tale for hangar flying. Just then the record showed no trace of his claim. But he did learn to fly, and in a few weeks he would be a hero.

With less than two hours in the air, Harry Atwood was now qualified for his new job: chief instructor at a new aviation school south of Boston in Squantum. The school was located at the Harvard Aviation Field where Atwood had watched the aero meet the previous fall. His new boss was a yacht designer, Starling Burgess. He had a contract to build Wright aeroplanes under license and he had sent Atwood out to Dayton.

Burgess had designed more than two hundred yachts by this time and would go on to design three America's Cup winners, just as his father had done. He had left Harvard in his senior year, at age twenty-two, started his business, and published a book of poetry, *The Eternal Laughter and Other Poems.*

Early on, in 1908, he saw Orville Wright fly. "As the beautiful creature left the rails and with a low bound cleared the earth, tears came unbidden to my eyes. Shall I ever forget that moment?" he wrote in his unpublished aviation memoir, *Take Off.* It was, he said, "the most exciting day of my life." He later signed on as the Wrights' first civilian student.

But Burgess also saw the dangers of flying, as a Harvard classmate recalled. "I well remember asking Starling if aeroplanes would be of value in war, to which he replied, 'Yes, but how can the enemy be persuaded to go up in them?'"

In his years of flying, his one serious crash was due to a moment of speculation. He was demonstrating a recently completed Wright-licensed aeroplane for the army. After a thirty-minute demonstration flight, the plane would be delivered. Something caught his attention below: a series of small canals crisscrossing the land, just like the ones on Mars. The newspapers had lengthy stories about the Martian Canals. Burgess flew over to have a better look, stalled and crashed. He walked away, but he had just wrecked a five-thousand-dollar machine. He had been looking at a goldfish farm.

The early Burgess aeroplane designs were crude. One was the first to fly in New England—a short hop in February 1910—and a later design, the Model B, was so unstable Burgess couldn't get a good flight out of it. He sought out an experienced aviator and convinced Glenn Curtiss to take it up. He flew, gratefully landed and pronounced it the most dangerous thing he had ever flown.

This left the young company a little short on accomplishment. An early advertisement in 1910 put in a few claims:

OUR AEROPLANES ARE SAFE
They fly well, too.
Our Model A flew successfully
but our Model B
beats it.

Our new Model C is
even better.

The designs may have been crude (and the Model C probably never flew) but the yacht builder's workmanship had impressed Wilbur Wright at the Harvard-Boston aero meet. "One fact could be noticed at a glance," said Burgess. "Every detail in the construction of my ship, each strut, each turnbuckle, each finely wrought socket and metal part showed reasonable preparation and the work of master craftsmen. A sailor would say, 'All was shipshape and Bristol fashion.'"

Burgess became the sole American licensee of the Wrights, paying them one thousand dollars for each plane built and a further royalty of one hundred dollars each time one was used in an exhibition. He built a modified Wright Model B, a reinforced, 163-pound heavier version he called the Burgess-Wright Model F. This was the only deal in town: his own designs were foundering, and the Wrights were about tie up all aircraft design in America with a court injunction.

The Burgess School of Aviation opened on May 30, 1911, with an instructor—Harry Atwood—just a week or so out of school himself. Tuition was five hundred dollars for twenty-four lessons each lasting about twelve minutes, four hours of actual flying. The school assumed "the cost of all breakage" during instruction.

Three students had enrolled. Atwood was not much interested in the actual chore of instruction—the day hemmed in by twelve-minute lessons, yelling at students over the noise of the engine. All this was relieved only by taking up paying passengers and answering the same fool questions all day. Teaching was a dull and potentially dangerous occupation.

He set about adding to his flying time. The first day he flew 104 miles in sixteen flights, the following week 385 miles. The students languished, but the school, and Atwood, were getting noticed, even for the smallest flight. One evening Atwood missed the trolley car to go to the inn for dinner, so he flew. "This is the first time anyone has flown to dinner in an aeroplane in New England," reported the *Boston Herald*. Another first. The press was getting to like this new invention.

In the school's opening week, Atwood flew with a student twenty-five miles to a country club. They had some fun along the way, coming in low over a beach, scattering the bathers, and diving down to within fifteen feet of a locomotive for a race. (Atwood said he was trying to keep his hands warm.)

This may not have been what Burgess had in mind for the role of his chief instructor, but his school was in the news. He dispatched Atwood to fly to Boston for the Dorchester Day celebration. The school would receive "considerable inducements" for the flight and a thousand-dollar bonus if Atwood cut "fancy figures."

As part of the show, Atwood proposed that Boston's mayor, John F. Fitzgerald, take a ride with him. The mayor declined for the good of the Commonwealth. "Personally I would not mind flying with him a bit, but it is a question of propriety," the mayor said. "The people would probably not care to have their chief executive taking risks of this sort, and my family certainly would not care to have me risking my life."

Understand, the mayor said, that "an over-city flight is different from a trip around an aviation course," which he had done the year before at the Harvard-Boston aero meet. "If weather and other conditions are ideal I might be induced to take a little spin over the field, but it would be improper for the mayor of a city to tempt fate by a dangerous over-house trip."

On Dorchester Day, "Honey Fitz" led the opening march, gave a speech, helped stop runaway horses, made three more speeches, drove a horse to victory in a race, and then led three more marches. He didn't fly.

Boston's reporters were, out of necessity or curiosity, more willing. At-wood arranged to fly a relay of reporters from an airfield outside Boston, at Waltham, north into New Hampshire. He wanted to break the American record for long-distance passenger carrying, then 116 miles. He had been flying three weeks. It would be the first extended flight into New Hampshire, and to each city and farm he flew over, he would bring the news of the aeroplane.

The aeroplane Atwood was flying had been named the "Moth," but as Atwood flew into New Hampshire, the moth was transformed into a "scor-pion." From the state line to the lakes in the north, newspapers praised the flight of the scorpion. And Atwood was transformed into the latest "daring young aviator."

He flew reporters from six of Boston's leading newspapers: the *Post, Globe, American, Herald, Transcript,* and *Journal.* For their entire careers, the reporters never forgot the trip—some remembered the terror—but all admired Harry Atwood and a few became friends, ready to report any-thing he would dream up.

Thomas A. Luke, a photographer for the *Boston Post,* was the first in the relay. "I think I'm lucky after all, to be standing around alive after my trip with Harry Atwood," Luke reported. "I've had some interesting experiences, but none anything like that voyage, and for cool chaps this boy from Lynn takes all the ribbons. Atwood is nothing short of a wonder."

Luke joined Atwood at the Waltham field late in the day, the favored time to fly because it was usually the calmest. Atwood made the photogra-pher leave his camera behind. "If you take that thing it will mean your death as well as my own. If that camera touches one of the warping wires while we are flying in this wind we will both go down to an awful smash," Atwood said. Another aviator and three mechanics standing nearby echoed Atwood's warning, and Luke, after some pleading, surrendered his "self-focussing beauty." He was soon glad that he had both hands free to hang on.

They took off, and Luke had a few moments to enjoy the odd sensa-tions of his first flight—"I could see people running about below us, the tops of their heads presenting the funny appearance of a lot of marbles rolling around on the ground"—then "things began to happen."

They flew into a strong head wind. At thirty-five hundred feet, the "first bad squall struck us. The machine plunged and dived until I thought it would fall apart.

"'Now, don't you feel glad you left that camera behind?' shrieked Atwood into my ear. I replied with a look—I could not speak—and the diving continued.

"The biplane shook and wavered like a piece of tissue paper in a breeze." Atwood was flying in winds much stronger than aviators would have chanced just a few months earlier.

"'Ain't this awful?' Atwood yelled at me. I gasped and lost my breath before I could nod. I was clinging on then with both hands clutched about the uprights of the machine and wondering just when the grand dive would come."

Over the Merrimack river, Atwood yelled "Hold on, now," as the aeroplane dropped "down, down, until the river seemed to be rushing up to meet us. I was firmly convinced we would never be seen again until someone dug us out of the mud of the river bed, but that boy on my left with his face calmly set, thrust the control lever, juggled the warping wire a bit, and we soared out straight again after dropping 1000 feet."

The worst was to come. The wind was forcing them down into the river. "Not all the jockeying of Atwood could rise us an inch." They were only fifteen feet above the water. "He turned his head to say, 'Can you swim?' I nodded in reply . . . just as a fierce squall of wind caught the planes of the machine and threw us almost out of our seats."

They flew up until they were over the tree tops and soon were near the landing site, which was marked with big tablecloths. They set down, but Luke was not free yet. "'No landing here,' he yelled. "'If we drop here we will never get out again.' And just as the machine struck the grass with a slight shock, he manipulated the elevator lever and we shot up again at a long angle straight into the tops of some high trees.

"We missed the trees by a horse hair and flashed over them into the sky again. Atwood calmly circled about and with one hand pointed out to the crowd in the field beneath that he was going to land further along." Atwood circled several more times as he studied the terrain, picked out an open farm field, and made a perfect landing. "I stepped out of the machine with a tingling sensation running all through me under my skin. I imagined that my face must have seemed to those who saw me like the face of a man whose execution has been stayed by a last minute pardon.

"I looked at Atwood. He had not turned a hair, and shook hands with me as cordially as if I had been the hero of the flight instead of himself."

As Luke was leaving the field, the next reporter saw him. "The first thing Tommy said was: 'Never again!'" Luke had ridden the Scorpion for thirty-eight minutes and covered twenty-three miles.

The next stages were a little easier. A. J. Philpott of the *Boston Globe* joined Atwood. They sat on the ground for fifteen minutes while Atwood studied the winds. He would make a run at taking off, but if that failed he might have to leave the reporter behind. They rose two-hundred feet and hit a pocket that dropped them fifty feet, then they were "struck with ter-rific force by a gust of wind. Atwood applied the full force of the lever on the warping device and righted the machine. We were struck on the other side and he was quick with the lever again." They climbed to fifteen hun-dred feet. "We both looked at each other a moment and grinned for we were now going along like a sled over the smooth ice."

Philpott was a veteran of one other flight and told his readers: "You know how a moving picture looks when it is first flashed on the screen? Well, that is about the way you feel. You seem to be part of a moving pic-ture. You feel free and easy and the whole harbor and islands and the big aviation field seem like one of those raised maps over which you are sim-ply floating, not in the least conscious of the fact that you are traveling between 40 and 50 miles an hour."

The crowd waiting in Nashua saw the approaching aeroplane and shouted: "There he is! There he is!" After the mayor greeted the first aeroplane in Nashua, Atwood was off with his next reporter, Joseph P. Toye of the *Boston American*, to fly the seventeen miles up the river to Man-chester. "The wind was fine," reported Toye. "Once in a while we would strike a puff that would slap us broadside. The big biplane would quiver from end to end." Toye also reported a "delightful sensation of floating along in a chair high in the air. The only disturbing element is the terrific coughings and barkings of the unmuffled engine."

Once again as Atwood came in to land, he saw there was no room for his aeroplane—people really had no idea what was required. They had never seen an aeroplane before. Wherever Atwood flew that summer there were crowds, hanging out of windows, on roofs, in trees, filling the field where he was supposed to land. Town after town would select a courthouse lawn or a baseball diamond—no bigger—and everyone would crowd in expecting him to "alight," as they said, as if he were in a balloon.

Atwood tried to wave the crowd away, but they thought he was just wav-ing. He "skimmed over the roof of a tenement house" and landed at the edge of the field. "That was the worst and most dangerous landing I ever made," he said. The crowd pressed in and delayed Atwood for an hour. He was running out of daylight. He tried to take off, but had to abandon his run after one hundred yards. The crowd was blocking him. He pleaded for the police and three officers arrived to clear a way.

By the time Atwood and his next passenger arrived in Concord, the streetlights were on and the few stores that were still open "looked like caves of light." It was eight in the evening. He dropped in a spiral dive toward the golden statehouse dome, and circled it twice "within fanning distance," fifty feet away. A group on the top of the dome were too shocked even to wave. Others, seeing an aeroplane dive for the first time, thought he was falling "like a bird with a broken wing."

His passenger, Phillips Ward Page of the *Boston Herald*, delighted in his first flight. "We could look down between our knees at the factories of the Amoskeag mills skirting the river bank," he said. But he was struck at how unbird-like flying really was. It is surprising, he said, "that motor driven flight is not like flying after all. Perhaps it cannot be called anything better than an exquisite translation through space."

It was too late to finish the last two legs of the flight; the delay in Manchester had cost Atwood the record. He was in Concord for the night and Concord was thrilled with its visitor. "The aviator vainly begged his admirers to keep at least three feet away from the aeroplane. Everyone wanted to touch it, as if there were no other way of being convinced that the thing was real," said the *Concord Monitor*.

The Wright Model B in its Burgess edition were glorious machines, silver ghosts. All the woodwork, the struts, and supports, were painted using an old sign painter's technique. They were dusted with aluminum powder over a wet varnish giving a slick silver look. The wings were a light gray cotton muslin fabric. The brass radiator gleamed. There were wires and nickel-plated fittings seemingly everywhere—you had to climb between some of the support wires to get into the two seats up front on the lower wing. And just behind the wings were twin five-foot tall propellers. No one had ever seen anything like it and people fumbled for descriptions. It's like a noisy reaper in the sky, one observer said. But it was like no machinery on the farm, like nothing in the mills. It was the greatest thing since the train and the automobile, maybe, but that didn't describe it either. So they stood and stared. People came by to be with the aeroplane until two thirty in the morning.

The next morning, Atwood and his new passenger tried to slip away two hours early to avoid the crowds. Even so, two hundred people caught word of the flight. After one false start when the motor quit, Atwood flew to Tilton in rough winds. There he took on his last passenger and headed north toward Laconia in a thirty-mile-an-hour gale. The winds were so strong he could not make headway and had to turn with the wind, blown along on a wild ride. "We are going up, old man, and only God knows how we will get down. We are rising because I can't help it," he told his passenger. The wind forced him first west, then back east.

"Five times on the trip I tried to make a landing, despairing of getting back to Concord," said Atwood. For miles the land was rocky or wooded, offering no chance to land. "I failed every time 'till I got to Pittsfield. Then when I tipped my machine and began to descend, the air currents caught me and forced me into the air again." The wind caught him at fifty feet and forced him up one thousand feet.

On the ground, people dropped their work and came running, looking up to the see the aeroplane. "Chickens fled as if before a monster hawk, while some horses in the field exhibited the wildest fright."

The aeroplane came down hard, just skimmed past a stone wall, and bounced thirty feet back into the air, slammed down again, bounced up and slammed down again and again, until it rolled several hundred feet through wheat eighteen inches tall, spun sideways, and came to rest, undamaged. They had covered forty-two miles in only thirty minutes, at a rate of eighty-four miles an hour, nearly double the trip's average speed of forty-five miles an hour.

Atwood called it "the roughest [time] I ever had in the air." They were lucky to escape without injury, he told his passenger, O. G. Draper, a reporter for the *Boston Journal.* Draper was thrilled, if maybe a little addled. His feelings on landing, he said, were a sort of "mental salad combining some trepidation, with more awe and still more exhilaration." His confidence in Atwood never wavered, he said.

Atwood immediately caught a train for Boston. He had to compete that afternoon in an aero meet. He would return for his aeroplane. Atwood had set a New England record for cross-country flying and an American record for relay flights. Over the next few days, Atwood took the aero meet by storm, winning the ten-thousand-dollar first prize, outdistancing the others in cross-country flying. On one flight he carried his father. "Let it suffice to remark," reported *Aero, America's Aviation Weekly,* "that Atwood in his Burgess-Wright biplane surpassed both in skill and daring the work of Brookins or Johnstone at the Harvard-Boston meet of 1910," when Atwood was a spectator longing to join the flying.

Back in New Hampshire, the editorial writers at the *Concord Monitor* pronounced the cross-country flight a "herald of a new epoch, the era of man's dominion of the air.

"Among those who witnessed our first aviator's arrival were a few who saw the first locomotive come puffing into town in September of 1848; there were many in the crowd who remembered the first bicycle and the first trolley car; while the first automobile was within the experience of all save the youngest."

Editorials in other papers assessed this new invention and the people crowded in for a look, but no one said it as well as a farmer in Pittsfield. He looked up from where he was hoeing a field and saw Atwood landing. "For God's sake," he exclaimed, "I've hearn' tell of 'em, but I never expected to see one."

What was it like to fly in 1911? We want to be told it was like the birds—the "man-birds" as they said—like the eagle and the skylark. We want to hear talk of air ruffling feathers, of floating along dreamily among the clouds. We want poetry. But flying was something altogether different. It was struts and wires, engines and oil, wind in the face, and crowds that rushed an aeroplane eager to sign their names on it or tear it apart.

For centuries people had looked at birds and dreamt of flight. That is the line in all the aviation histories. But to take flight at last, people had to leave behind the birds. Serious papers of bird studies were presented, ornithopters were built, but no amount of flapping would get anyone up in the air.

All the bird poetry and metaphor exist for the earthbound. Wordsworth, Keats, and Shelley kited their aspirations on the wings of the lark. They remained on the ground. Flying was so unbird-like, one of Atwood's passenger's had said. Once airborne, the pilot is not the "man-bird" of early aeronautics, no more than a man in the woods is a "man-deer" or a "man-fox." He is a man in his machine in the air. His poems and stories are about his machine—his ingenuity—and all that presses in on it: the night, the weather, the things that go wrong. He has "conquered" the air.

And for all that, flying was wonderful. It wasn't poetry as the world knew it, delivered from the English Lake District to the parlor sitting room. It was something at once joyous and terrifying, something that in 1911 was part circus, part science, and a hint of things to come.

"I assure you, learning aviation lacks poetry," said Lt. J. Conneau, a Frenchman who had won three big European cross-country races in 1911. "Before a pilot flies, he must needs lay up a store of physical endurance; his nerves must be perfectly steady." In winning his three races—circuits of Britain and Europe and a race from Paris to Rome—Conneau flew against great winds, through hot sun and the chill of storms, arriving at each stage exhausted and muscle-sore, desiring only a warm meal, a bath, and sleep. The uncertainty itself was tiring: the difficulty of judging the weather aloft while on the ground, the danger of getting lost or being turned around in the clouds, the unpredictability of the motor, the worry of running out of fuel and having to find quickly a field for landing. Three aviators had been killed and two others injured at the start of the European circuit.

"The conditions of a flight are seldom—one might say never—normal. The easiest aerial trips are accompanied by the most extraordinary surprises," said Conneau. "In fact, is not aviation a mere succession of unforeseen incidents?" This could serve as a definition of early flight. As one of Atwood's Dayton classmates, Thomas Milling, said, "Everybody expected to be killed."

There were collapsed wings, jammed controls, broken support wires, collisions with trees while taxying on the ground, hard landings that threw the pilot, killing him, or threw the motor on the pilot, crushing him. Motors quit, caught fire, misfired, lost compression, choked on bad gas, bad oil, dirt, and faulty spark plugs.

Aviators had little knowledge of turbulent winds, dives, and stalls. Aeroplanes folded up in the sky, they stalled, they pitched over on the ground. A steep bank or a steep dive might be too much. Things happened in the air that no one had the words for—an entire vocabulary was lacking. In a stall or a dive or a tail spin, aviators would instinctively try to fight the aeroplane, often hastening the plane's break-up and collapse. Most accidents occurred at low altitudes, two hundred to fifteen hundred feet. There was little room to recover, even if the aviator had known what to do. In one accident, a spectator counted seven seconds as a plane dived to a crash. The aviator, at a loss in his last moments, stood up as if pulling back on the reins of a horse.

Almost anything taken for granted today was lacking. There were only a few rough airfields, sketchy weather forecasts, few flying instruments (the Wright-trained pilots had a piece of yarn tied to a strut—it was a turn and stall indicator), no standard octane ratings for gasoline, no maintenance procedures to prevent failure from fatigued and stressed materials, no brakes for landing, and only recently wheels. Construction varied widely, from flimsy planes of bamboo and linen that could barely support their own weight at rest on the ground to the careful work of the yacht-builder Burgess.

The biplane Harry Atwood flew was underpowered and had no inherent stability. The pilot was always working to keep the plane in trim and only a few miles an hour separated the top speed from stall speed.

Earle Ovington, who flew a Bleriot monoplane in 1911, faced similar

problems: "If a plane is left for a second to its own devices it tips and begins to shoot sideways instead of going forward. Then you get into the
deadly side-slip. To keep the machine from tipping, that is to preserve its
lateral stability, you must move this same lever to the left or the right,
which warps the wings and keeps the machine on a horizontal keel. It
isn't as easy as it sounds, and requires a lot of agility on the part of the
driver—both mental and physical. If I should move the lever a bit to the
right when it should go to the left, it would mean a sideslip or a side som-
ersault. In either case it might easily be the end of me."

A pilot's license was optional. A pilot needed a license to compete and
to have records recognized, but not to fly. There were only a few aviation
schools. To some, flying was a backyard outing: they would acquire an
aeroplane and learn by trial and error.

The first known flight manual was issued in 1911 with one of Glenn
Curtiss's biplanes; it was six paragraphs long. After instructions for starting
the motor and facing into the wind, came step four: "When sufficient
speed has been attained the device will leave the ground and assume the
position of aeronautical ascent." Landing, "should the aeronaut decide to
return to terra firma," was covered in the last two paragraphs, with instructions to glide in, "causing the mechanism to alight more or less gently."

Hangar flying was marked by talk of the unknown. Aviators kept flying
into "holes in the air." One minute they would be on a level flight and the
next drop down suddenly as if they'd hit a "boulder." The air was "cheesy,"
they said, trying to explain, like "Swiss cheese." The word for "tailspin"
didn't exist. The first time Frank Coffyn went into a tailspin, he "didn't
know what in thunder to do. I just fiddled around with the controls and finally, within about fifty feet of the water, I got it out of the tailspin and
landed it on the ocean." He drifted in shark-infested waters for six hours
before he was rescued. "I didn't know what the hell it was till a year or two
later—that you could get into a tailspin." As Hap Arnold had said,
"Things happened, that was all. The air was a tricky place."

When aviators were killed in dives, medical experts theorized a collapse of the heart from such great, swift descent (altitudes from one thousand feet to as much as seven thousand feet or so). Other experts said aviators were falling victim to "Aerial Drowsiness." "There is a spirit of
daring, not to say of recklessness, consequent upon high flight which our
medical contemporary ascribes to the fatally tonic influence of the upper
atmosphere," reported *Current Literature*.

"After one is accustomed to being up high he in large measure loses
his fear of gravity," said Atwood. At "a thousand feet or more he feels

comparatively safe when he is as low as two or three hundred feet, as if he could step into the air at that height without experiencing so much as a jar when he hits the ground. This forgetfulness of gravity, I think, accounts for some of the fatal jinks which some aviators attempt."

Few of the most active early-bird aviators died a natural death. In 1911 the hundredth person was killed flying; the first had been killed in 1908. There were "bad accidents almost daily," said *Scientific American*. "We are a fearless generation," said Henri Lavedan, a French playwright. "Aviation intoxicates us. It has already advanced so quickly that it lures us on, perhaps more rapidly than it ought."

Aviation, said the *New York Times*, was "a business that requires a constant tempting of death" and "a certain degree of recklessness." This was a favorable view. Other newspapers and public leaders called for an end to flying. One study of the "martyrs of aviation" said flying was actually getting safer. There were many more aviators. You had to look at the ratio of accidents compared to the number of people flying. In 1909 there were fifty aviators and three were killed; in 1910, five hundred and twenty-nine died. In 1911, the number of flyers in the world had tripled to one thousand five hundred, and seventy-eight were killed. If you looked at how many miles were being flown, things looked even better. Consider deaths per mile:

1909   one killed for 14,000 miles of flight
1910   one killed for 32,000 miles of flight
1911   one killed for 40,000 miles of flight

By 1912, deaths per mile had decreased three-fold (one for 120,000 miles). "At this rate," the study concluded, "aviation will soon be less dangerous than automobiling." (If the 1912 rate prevailed today, 833 airline passengers would be killed for each 100 million miles flown. The 1993 rate was .01 deaths. On average, you would have to fly twenty-one thousand years before dying in a crash.) Flying was already safer than automobiling had been in its early days. There were 33 fatalities for every ten thousand registered vehicles; a total of 3,100 fatalities in 1912. And Claude Grahame-White, the English aviator, said that in 1910 mountaineering had claimed 90 lives, three times the toll from flying. At the same time, the Interstate Commerce Commission was studying railroad deaths. More than 165,000 had been killed and more than 1.3 million injured in the twenty-four years since 1887.

But the public wasn't convinced, and that was partly what kept them coming to see the exhibitions. "The crowds gaped at the wonders," said

Hap Arnold, "secure in the knowledge that nowhere on earth, between now and suppertime, was there such a good chance of seeing somebody break his neck."

The *Boston Globe*'s daily puzzle for July 10, 1911, had this caption:

> Let us, then, be up and flying,
>   With a heart for any fate;
> Still a-flying, though we're dying . . .

In the puzzle, a drawing, the reader was supposed to find the hidden aviator, a face in the clouds, ready to blow down the aeroplane.

Flying was a circus show (even Houdini had taken it up), and the promoters demanded that the show go on, no matter the wind or the condition of the field. The crowd had paid and would not accept excuses. Many did not believe till they saw it. Flyers had been forced to fly in blizzards to satisfy crowds.

At Ontario Beach, near Rochester, New York, Beckwith Havens' flying was part of a show with ten polar bears, a clown, and fireworks. Farnum Fish, the eighteen-year-old "boy flyer," would elaborately hook a fishing line to his aeroplane, take off, fly out of sight and return with a big fish dangling down. (No wonder a Sandusky, Ohio, newspaper mistakenly called Glenn Curtiss's aviation business "The Curtiss Amusement Company.")

Lincoln Beachey was the greatest showman. He would dress up as a woman, emerge out of a crowd, and "steal" his own aeroplane. He would fly in an upside down dive to thrill the crowds. (They couldn't fly upside-down level then—this was a controlled upside-down dive.) Beachey flew over Niagara falls, pit his biplane against a car in a race around a track, and in 1913 he mastered the loop-the-loop. Twenty-one pilots died trying to imitate his tricks, and Beachey quit for a time. He returned and was killed in a crash.

Eugene Ely was known for his "Ely Glide." He died the death of an exhibition flyer. Ely was a skilled aviator, who had made the first landing and take-off from an aircraft carrier. But he knew what some in the crowd wanted. "I see the crowd below me looking upward, and I know every man who watches me start downward half expects to see me killed. I suppose they all figure how they'll help pick up my bones some day," he said. Later that day he crashed and was taken to the hospital unconscious. He survived.

At the Georgia State Fair, a month later, twenty-thousand people watched him die. "Before making his ascent this afternoon, Ely told his attendants that he feared something would happen and asked them to notify his wife immediately if it did," reported the *New York Herald.*

Ely circled the track at three hundred feet and began "a spectacular dip" down to about seventy-five feet. Then the crowd saw him try to rise in his seat and jump from his aircraft as it turned upside down.

"He and the aeroplane struck the ground at the same time, and he rolled probably 30 feet, so terrific was the impact. The machine was demolished, bits of timber and metal flying many yards. The crowd rushed over the track and into the field, and when they reached Mr. Ely's side they saw he was dying. His body was literally broken to pieces, and the physicians were astonished that he had lived as long as he did.

"He died 11 minutes after the fatal fall, regaining consciousness, just before the end, long enough to murmur, so low that his words could hardly be heard: 'I lost control; I'm going to die.'"

Thousands swarmed the aeroplane, overwhelming the few police. "Many fought for souvenirs, and soon the littered field was cleared of the fragments of the machine. One man even unbuttoned the dying man's collar and pocketed it. The aviator's gloves, tie, and cap similarly disappeared. Ambulances soon reached the scene, but not until the spark of life had gone out."

The spirit of the Roman Coliseum pervaded these aero meets, said the *Scientific American.* With the public demanding dives and spirals "and other aerial gymnastics that are performed at imminent peril to life and limb" and promoters threatening aviators, "the death of an aviator under such conditions comes very near to being homicide of the most atrocious character."

Newspapers ran editorial cartoons with variations of the grim reaper beckoning: in the *Boston Herald,* the angel of death waits below aeroplanes with a large net marked by a dollar sign; in the *New York Herald,* the grim reaper stood wearing a sandwich board advertising "sensational acrobatic aerial performances for the amusement of the public." It was a universal sentiment. A German publication showed death sitting at a table as aeroplanes were drawn into a sticky fly trap.

"A disconcerting feature of last year's death roll is that it includes so many of the most skilled among the airmen," the *Scientific American* said in January 1911. "This fact might seem to suggest that we have not advanced as far as was supposed in our understanding of the conditions that govern the flight of heavier-than-air machines. On the other hand, it should be remembered that many if not most of the accidents have occurred when the airmen were attempting spectacular performances for the entertainment of the race-going public or winning large prizes."

This was not the way to advance aviation. The Wright brothers got out of the exhibition business. Their team had flown for a year and a half. Five of the nine team members were dead.

In the nation that was home to the invention, flying was a plaything, a circus trick. America trailed Europe in serious aviation. By 1911, no American held an important record. "What's the matter with America?" asked *Aeronautics* magazine in 1911. "Americans returning from abroad have expressed themselves as astounded at the progress and activity there . . . we have changed places from the head to the foot of the procession." The Europeans were doing some real flying, cross country, city to city.

Harry Atwood disdained the exhibition circuit. "I do not intend to die entertaining a crowd," he said. He would not join in any attempt to try to be the first aviator to loop-the-loop. "The only place for a loop-the-loop is over a graveyard," he said.

Atwood would fly his own way.

In the summer of 1911, American aviation had birdmen and stuntmen and daredevils and native geniuses. It took one twenty-seven-year-old flying in a straight line to make headlines.

A Summer's Hero

One morning over breakfast Harry Atwood decided that he would go see the Harvard-Yale crew races. He had not slept well—he was nervous, he said—and was up when the newspaper was delivered at 6:00 A.M. "I couldn't see anything in the paper except this boat race," he said. "I never saw a boat race before and I wanted to see this one. They told me I couldn't get a seat on the observation train, and there wasn't any other way to see the race."

He would fly there. The race was more than a hundred miles away, farther than any American had flown in one continuous flight. Without any special preparation, he took off with a mechanic from the Burgess company. Usually before any cross-country flight, the aviator drove the route, studying landmarks and places to land. Atwood had done that in New Hampshire, but he said that he knew the country around Boston pretty well. He pasted a map on a card to use as a reference, called his parents, and took off.

He flew toward the races in New London, Connecticut, flying at five hundred feet, low enough to read the map of the landscape directly, low enough for many towns to have a good look at their first aeroplane. In Middleboro, Massachusetts, a small boy was the first to see Atwood, and shouted, "See the big bird!" Atwood could hear the applause below.

In two hours and ten minutes, Atwood and James Fleet were over the races, surprising a crowd of fifty thousand. "In an instant every eye was focussed on the machine," said the *Boston Post*. "In another instant, bedlam broke loose. From a thousand whistles, from the heavy sirens of the large steam yachts to the diminutive toots of fog horns, bellowed forth a greeting.

"For five minutes the tooting and cheering kept up. The yachts and the crowds along the banks of the river fluttered a sea of moving color as everyone snatched up flags, coats, streamers—anything that could be waved—and stood flapping their improvised banners as Atwood smoothly sailed overhead." When they saw that he was flying with a passenger, "their amazement and admiration for his daring were redoubled."

He flew up the river, circled a monument three times, and in a "volplane" (a glide), circled once and landed in a field of daisies where he was confronted with an angry farmer and a crowd pressing close to the machine. But the mayor of New London, Bryan F. Mahan, made Atwood welcome, driving him about the city, hosting him at a clam bake for lunch and then accepting the offer of a flight.

Before Mayor Mahan took his seat, he handed his watch and chain to a friend to give to his wife in case there was an accident. The newspapers solemnly noted that the sixty-five-year-old mayor was the father of seven and the holder of several other important political posts. (The mayor was not alone in his fears. Before Richard Harding Davis, renowned as a daring journalist, flew with Frank Coffyn, he had his friend hold his watch, his ring, and his money.)

The mayor almost bailed out. "When Mr. Atwood made his ascent I stood up in the biplane and was just ready to jump," he confessed later, but they were quickly up and over the river. They circled at three hundred feet, and came across the starting line just after the varsity eight-man crews. "When Atwood hovered into view, the volume of sound increased until it seemed that the greeting to the crews had been but silence in comparison," said the *Post*. Circling overhead, Atwood followed the course of the race. "Every eye was fastened on Atwood, and only out of a corner of an eye did anyone notice the race."

Approaching the drawbridge, where the observation train was parked, Atwood dipped down nearly to the river, then swooped up "clearing the observation train by barely a safe margin and then dipping down again to the river surface, where his skids seemed to ripple the water, he was so low." As the Harvard crew crossed the finish line, Atwood's biplane rose up over them. (Harvard won by sixteen boat lengths.)

The mayor loved his flight. "I wasn't the least afraid after we had reached the river, for I can swim like a duck." He settled right in and had

Atwood circle a yacht where his friends were, so he could shower cigars down on them. Reclaiming his watch, he joked that he might just have to buy one of those aeroplanes for those trips to the state capital. "Atwood can have anything he wants in this city while I am mayor."

Atwood had set a record for the longest continuous cross-country flight in America, 135 miles. Everyone was happy but Yale—it was their worst defeat in twenty-eight years—and the governor of Connecticut, who said that Atwood could be arrested for violating a new state law, the first in the country requiring a license to fly over the state and the permission of landowners to pass over their land.

The next morning Harry Atwood was up at 4:30 A.M. He was not much of a sleeper. Six hours was a long rest, four usually stood him well. He called his boss, Starling Burgess, and woke him up. If the weather was fine, he would fly across Long Island Sound to the airfield at Mineola, as Burgess had suggested.

Alone, just after seven, he flew along the Connecticut coastline, about two miles inland, as illegal as that might be. Just past New Haven he saw a train, the "bankers' express," the railroad's fastest, making the run at sixty miles an hour. He raced, beating the train on the curves, lagging behind on the straightaways. Three times he circled the train, just one hundred feet up. Passengers hung out the open windows, waving hats and handkerchiefs, and cheering.

The Long Island Sound was about six miles wide where he'd have to cross, still a considerable distance to be at the mercy of your motor. He decided that he would fly on to New York City instead. "There are no pontoons on my biplane and I had no mind to run the risk of coming down halfway across to Long Island," Atwood said. "There was the chance that by the time someone came along to pick me up, I would be sitting on the bottom of the Sound waiting for them."

He was looking for Governor's Island out in the New York harbor, but he was running out of gas and was forced to set down in Astoria, Queens, just across the East River from Manhattan.

He landed in a lot behind the Astoria Gas Works, bouncing to a stop amid the litter of tin cans and old barrels. There was no one around. In minutes there were three thousand people crowding his machine. He enlisted the help of some boys to hold them back until the police, a Sergeant Orpheus and ten men, arrived. "Even then Atwood would not leave his machine, but, standing on guard, beguiled people to bring him what he wanted more than all else—gasoline and sandwiches," said the *New York Times*. Sergeant Orpheus declined his invitation to finish the trip with him. He was on duty.

As Atwood waited, he pulled some crackers out of his pocket and asked about directions to the island, surprised to learn there were only four bridges over the East River. He was dressed for business in the proper fashion of the Wright brothers, wearing a Norfolk dress jacket, tie, and a cap, which he turned backwards. "He was always immaculately dressed and never seemed to get his hands dirty, although he often worked on his engine," said fellow aviator, Elmo N. Pickerill.

With the machine refueled, some volunteers turned the propellers and Atwood headed down the East River for Governor's Island. Word spread wildly. The ferry boats that ran from Long Island City blew their whistles. "Atwood waved his hand, dropped to a level with the funnels of the river craft and glided along beside them until the passengers distinctly saw the aviator sitting erect in his seat among the shining wires, the motor pounding away . . . and the two propellers flashing," reported the *New York Tribune*.

"Many persons dance when they see an aeroplane in flight," said the *Tribune*. "Yesterday there were thousands of such on the river piers and roof tops; thousands of waving handkerchiefs."

Just after he had flown over Brooklyn Bridge, Atwood saw Singer Tower and the other skyscrapers in lower Manhattan near Wall Street. He turned and flew over them—something no one had done before and which all aviators agreed was a daredevil fool thing to do. The Wrights wouldn't let their pilots fly over cities, and neither would the French. Atwood was flying eight hundred feet up, leaving no room to glide to a safe landing should his motor quit. "Almost sure death," he said.

The curb brokers out on Broad Street had just begun their trading when Atwood appeared overhead. "There was a faint clack from the propellers that first attracted the attention of a messenger boy and then started him running up the street crying 'Airship.' Stocks were forgotten and all turned their faces upward in time to see the flyer slide into view over the banking house of J. P. Morgan & Co." said the *Tribune*.

"Such news flies faster than any aeroplane," the paper said. People ran into the streets, thousands of windows were opened, half a dozen people hanging out of each one. There was a rush for the rooftops. "Elevator men wondered why staid businessmen seemed so suddenly obsessed to swarm to the roofs," said the *New York Times*.

"To one watching from the roof of the Trinity Building it seemed as though the business of Manhattan had stopped abruptly . . . Everybody stopped whatever he was doing, and gazed into the air, open-mouthed. Sales of stock were held up and newsboys forgot to make change," said the *Times*. "We were all so excited it's a wonder some of us didn't miss our footing and fall," said a photographer for the *New York World*, who was on the roof of another building.

Atwood circled three-quarters of the way around Singer Tower, about fifty feet above the flagpole, before a gust of wind pushed him backward. He broke off his circle and flew back over the financial district at about one thousand feet; then, over Broadway, he turned downtown and headed toward Battery Park and the harbor. He circled a Staten Island ferry boat, circled an incoming steamship, the *Saxonia*, dipped in salute to an outgoing steamship, the *St. Paul*, and then, with the harbor alive with steam whistles, landed on Governor's Island, dropping in on prisoners cutting the grass.

He had been over Manhattan just five minutes. "It was some little time before the lower end of Manhattan could lose itself in work again," said the *Times*. People peered out across the harbor to see if he was coming back. They said they had not seen anything like it since Wilbur Wright flew up the Hudson in October 1909.

"An American does some real flying," said a *Times* editorial. "This is a vastly greater achievement than flying through the Niagara gorge or swooping down in blood-curdling plunges from the chill heights where nobody in his senses wants to go. Mr. Atwood gave the aeroplane the very best sort of an advertisement—one that will cause twenty or perhaps fifty times more people to buy and learn to use it than would the performance of all the circus feats that could be invented." The *Times* called "the attention of other aviators to the fact that by these exploits of real flying he has won more fame, more attention, and more newspaper space than all of them put together have obtained by doing foolish 'stunts.'"

Atwood was becoming a household word, the "Undisputed Air King" said the *Boston American* in a typical headline. He was in the headlines that summer more than the president. But then Atwood was a more dynamic story than the corpulent Taft. "Atwood Braves New York City Canyons," said the lead story in the evening edition of the *Boston Globe*. And right next to it: "Taft Hies to the Golf Links."   .

Other aviators did take note. "The feat is such an astounding one for a month-old aviator that most people are still wondering if it was really accomplished," said the aviation magazine *Aero*. Burgess was impressed with his flight instructor, calling the flight the "most remarkable exploit of the time" and "a tussle with violent air currents that had never been dared before." He would feature the flight in his advertising. (Only Connecticut's legislators were not impressed. They announced that Atwood might be arrested.)

Why had he chosen such a risky route, the reporters asked, when earlier he had prudently avoided crossing the sound? He was attracted by the challenge of strong winds, blowing then at about twenty-five miles an hour, he said. "This I wish to state emphatically. It was with no daredevil spirit or for the purpose of spectacular effect that I flew over New York City. I do not want the public to get the idea that I am a circus performer. On the contrary, I do not revel in dangerous flights—and none could be more so than over the skyscrapers," he said.

"The flight was made purely for scientific purposes. I wanted to test the effects of air currents over a city like New York with its hundreds of buildings. They play among the tall buildings as in a succession of steep hills. As you approach a skyscraper there is a strong upper current that tilts your machine, and as you pass the far side there is one that yanks you down. My machine could be kept under perfect control and there wasn't a moment when I was afraid that I was going to be pulled down into the street.

"Someone had to learn air currents over cities, and I thought it was time to do it. The currents in no case over the city in a high wind were as bad as I met over the mountains of New Hampshire. I did not encounter any air holes; I do not believe there are such things. There were, of course, sharp currents of air flowing downwards."

He admitted that he had been a little "air foolish." But, he said, "it is with aviation as it is with every other science—its truths can be learned only by experience." He saw his flights as experiments; each time he flew he wanted to learn something new. First-hand experience was what counted—as an inventor, this was a doctrine he would hold to his whole life. He didn't approach problems theoretically, as he had encountered them in his physics course at MIT. This was empirical, put-your-hand-on-the-stove science.

"I saw New York as you see it on the map, and I assure you that from aloft it looks ugly and wicked, a real inferno," he said. "I would not take the trip again for the crispest $10,000 bill ever turned off a government printing press." Before midnight, a New Yorker offered Atwood "a large sum of money" to fly him over the city. Atwood declined.

He took a cab to a hotel to rest and make a few phone calls. After three hours in the air, his head was ringing from the noise of the engine. "I have to have an hour of quiet after I come down or I almost lose control of myself," he said. "Street noises on unhappy eardrums are dreadful."

The first person he called was his mother.

"I'm alright mother, and I'm coming home tonight."

"How are you coming, by aeroplane?" she asked.

"No, by train."

"I was so worried over Harry on his flight from New London to New York, but he notified me immediately on landing, as he always does," his mother Florence told the *Boston American*. "But even though I was anxious, very anxious, I felt confident all the time that my boy would come out all right. Never has he attempted anything but what he has succeeded. He has been a good boy to me and his flying worries me. It seems as if he takes greater chances than the other aviators. The real significance of what that boy has done, and all in a short month! Just think of my Harry, who always seems a little boy to me, making one of the greatest flights in the world. I am glad he did this, but I am happier, much happier, that he is safe.

"I suppose I am selfish to wish he would give up flying, but then I am rather fascinated by it myself." She would like to fly with him but her doctor said her heart was weak and she should not hazard "air fright." "I would rather be up there with him all the time than stand on the ground and worry."

At the hotel, he was surprised to find a thousand-dollar check from the Burgess Company. He changed his clothes and quietly left town on the five o'clock train to Boston.

"Everyone who caught even the most fleeting glimpse of the biplane as it swept easily over the skyscrapers, realized that they had seen a memorable thing, but of all those who were busy talking it over during the rest of the day, Atwood himself seemed the least impressed with what he had done," reported the *Times*.

When his train stopped in New Haven, a crowd demanded that he come out to the platform and take a bow. The engineer and crew of the train he had raced earlier in the day were also there, and they shook hands with Atwood. Arriving in Boston, he was again greeted with cheers by a large crowd.

He had been the first to fly from Boston to New York. The country wanted more. The Washington, D.C., Chamber of Commerce had made a tentative offer of one thousand dollars for Atwood to continue his flight from

New York to Washington. The *New York Times* offered a trophy (and, of course, extensive coverage). Atwood conferred with Burgess. He had to go to Washington anyway to demonstrate a recently delivered Burgess-Wright biplane.

He planned to leave New York on July 4, make a stop in Atlantic City, and with good luck, he said, land near the Washington Monument by 6:00 P.M. the next day.

He would attend to one detail before flying about 250 miles to the capital: he would take the test for his pilot's license in New York. The exam, administered by non-fliers who judged the aviator from the ground, required one altitude test and two distance tests consisting of two sets of five figure eights, with each test followed by a landing within 164 feet of a designated spot.

Atwood did the first set of figure eights out over New York harbor and landed within nine feet of his starting point, close to the record of five feet, four inches. He took off and did the next set.

All the people on those ferries with the whistles blowing were clamoring for a look at him. Earlier in the day he had taken a passenger for a close look at the Statue of Liberty, circling within five feet of her torch. Instead of landing to complete his test, he climbed up to three thousand feet for a turn around the harbor. As he circled back over Brooklyn at two thousand feet, his engine quit. For more than five tense minutes, Atwood glided back four miles, "tortured," he said, "by the fear he would be dashed to death by treacherous air currents."

A group of army officers, who were stationed on Governor's Island, wondered at his daring this time over the rooftops of Brooklyn, gliding with the wind. "Of course, he knows his business, but shutting off the engine when the wind is at your back is not according to Wilbur," one said, referring to the Wright brother.

A bugler sounded the call to mess. No one moved, reported the *New York Tribune.* They watched the silent aeroplane approaching. Atwood eased down safely within a hundred feet of his take-off spot.

"I'm sorry I cannot grant you your license," said one of the judges, an army major. "You only made four figure eights on the last test."

"I thought I had made five of those things; that's why I jockeyed off as I did," Atwood said.

"Only four."

"Well," said Atwood, smiling, "don't you give a chap any credit for finding his way home when his engine stops on him over those buildings and he's compelled to glide with the wind?"

"I can't find anything in the rules of the International Aeronautic Federation covering this feature of the case," said the major.

"I'm sorry," said Atwood, looking out intently into the distance. How could he fail at this? He was the undisputed King of the Air. This wasn't college. It was a hot day, a tremendous heat had descended upon the whole country. It was 104 degrees in four cities and 100 degrees or higher in two dozen others—the beginning of "a July that tastes of sulphur and recalls the personal devil of early Methodism," said the *New York Tribune*. In Boston it hit 103 and 125,000 people rushed to Revere Beach. The *Boston Globe*'s evening edition featured a banner headline on the sports section: "Atwood's glides, spirals and other feats refreshing, aviator says, on a hot day." Without the license, he couldn't compete.

"I'm very sorry," said the major.

Atlantic City was where Atwood's luck ran out. He flew from New York in a punishing headwind that at times held his aeroplane stationary. The trip should have taken about two and half hours. It took him five hours to fly just 110 miles. All day the winds increased. He had flown as long, and used as much gas, as it would take to fly to Washington on a calm day. He had to land three times for gas and once because he had flown so long he was sure he was at Atlantic City. The stops added another hour to his journey. "I was thrown all over the lot," he said. At times ten miles an hour was the best he could make. "It was like bucking a stone wall," he said. He flew at between five hundred and fifteen hundred feet looking for calmer air. He needed to follow the beaches. He didn't have a map and had never visited the Jersey shore. "I had an idea that Atlantic City was the only one of them that had a boardwalk," he said.

He landed at Asbury Park by mistake. There was a boardwalk down there jammed with a fourth of July crowd and he had been in the air for an hour and a half fighting the wind. "I was never so certain of anything in my life as I was that the place below me was Atlantic City and down I came." He was more than one hundred miles short of his destination. His day was just starting. He pushed on.

The last twenty miles were the worst. "For minutes at a time it seemed as if the machine simply could not buck its way through in the face of such head winds. I just hung there like a ball in the air. An hour passed and I was still in the air with several miles of the twenty to be made." He must have flown fifty air miles to make just seventeen, he said. "To make matters worse my gasoline ran out again." He could tell by the murmur the engine made when he was running low. That was his best gauge. He needed to land. "I was almost catapulted from my seat by a sudden gust while 100 feet in the air. The plane all but overturned and when I effected a landing I struck with considerable force. The machine was undamaged, but this was my narrowest escape." He was just three miles short of Atlantic City.

When he arrived at last, landing on the beach, half the crowd was still waiting to see him, about fifty thousand people. On this record hot July 4, there were half a million people at the society resort. All the beaches were crowded. In the New York area, twenty people drowned, and another twenty-six died in the heat. On Broadway an actress in *Macbeth* was overcome by the heat and the show closed.

Once more Atwood was greeted by waving handkerchief and "deafening" cheers. Most of it was lost on him. After five hours of sitting alongside the engine, it was half an hour before he could hear distinctly again.

Later to please the crowds, he flew twice. Each time the wind was so strong that it held him stationary. People looked up, many seeing an aeroplane for the first time, and here was this machine that hovered in the air. What a curious invention. He couldn't fly on to Washington—not today. He would have to wait for the winds to die down.

In Atlantic City, Atwood met up with Charles Hamilton, one of America's pioneer exhibition flyers. Atwood had telegraphed Hamilton and suggested that he accompany him on his flight to Washington. They had met when Hamilton was trying to learn the Wright system of controls at the Burgess school.

As cautious as Atwood was, Hamilton was reckless. The daredevil "Demon of the Skies" had begun his career by jumping out of a school window with an umbrella as a parachute. He went on to be an exhibition dirigible pilot, glider pilot, parachute jumper, and finally an aviator. At carnivals and county fairs, he was famous for jumping with five parachutes, opening one, cutting it off, falling free, opening the next, and so on until he landed.

Hamilton soloed on his first aeroplane flight. Glenn Curtiss had refused to teach him. Hamilton hung around, asked a lot of questions, and once Curtiss left he stole a plane, took off and flew, a little wobbly, but successfully. On his next stolen flight, he got the hang of it, flying for twenty-six minutes. When Curtiss returned, he was angry but impressed. He gave Hamilton a few lessons, hired him as his second exhibition pilot, and sent him out west on the exhibition circuit. Hamilton competed in Los Angeles at the country's first aviation meet. Six months later he was a national hero. On June 13, 1910, Hamilton made the first round-trip flight between New York and Philadelphia. He won ten thousand dollars from the *New York Times* and the *Philadelphia Public Ledger* for completing the flight between sunrise and sunset.

On the exhibition circuit, he developed his signature "Hamilton Dive"—straight down from one thousand feet, pull out in front of the grandstands, and fly at full power just feet above the ground. He flew in blizzards, he flew at night, and he crashed.

He crashed often in gliders, dirigibles, parachutes, and aeroplanes— sixty-three crashes by one count. He had broken his collarbone twice, broken both shoulder blades, fractured his ribs two different times, dislocated his left arm and both legs, broken his kneecap, was nearly scalded to death by water from a broken radiator, and had been generally bruised, burned, and cut. He reportedly had two silver replacement ribs, a shinbone held together with metal, and a metal plate in his skull. "There is little left of the old Hamilton," he would say. At times he was in so much pain that he would have to be lifted into his aeroplane before an exhibition. He was a heavy drinker and a nervous chain smoker. (To light cigarettes while flying, he'd tie a lighted punk near his seat.) He had survived all this and was still a year younger than Atwood.

When he saw the first Burgess-Wright Model F fly, he bought it with money out of his sock. He stopped Burgess on a hotel veranda and asked if the aeroplane was for sale and for how much. Burgess told him it cost five thousand dollars and was taken aback when this disheveled man pulled off his shoe, pulled six thousand-dollar bills from his sock, put one back, and handed five to Burgess, who had never seen such large bills.

Hamilton refused lessons. He knew the Curtiss system and figured he could easily learn the Wright controls. He crashed just after taking off, within seventy-five feet of the ground, completely wrecking the aeroplane. Surveying his new purchase, he said: "The engine is still good, the radiator is undamaged, and the wind is in the tires. What more do you want?"

Once the plane was rebuilt, he decided (or his wife convinced him) to take lessons at Burgess's flying school. Burgess took him up a few times. One morning Burgess wasn't around, so Hamilton went up by himself. "With a sweep he went up 150 feet, then inside of seconds, he was down again," reported a correspondent for a Connecticut paper, the *New Britain Herald*. "When a friend ran out to the spot where Charlie landed, he found him sitting on the ground with part of the wrecked machine hanging around his neck. Charlie had a cigarette in his mouth. 'Got a match?' he asked."

After that crash, Burgess turned him over to Atwood. They flew together, racing trains and diving down on beach bathers. They had a swell time. When they met again in Atlantic City, July 4, 1911, Atwood and Hamilton announced that they would fly to the West Coast together in September. William Randolph Hearst was offering fifty thousand dollars for the first transcontinental flight. "The prize . . . is a corker," said Atwood. With two pilots they could spell each other, and they figured the trip would take three weeks. Hamilton was trying to make a comeback; he had been in a sanitarium the previous winter with tuberculosis. The Washington flight would be good practice.

On July 5, Washington was waiting with a great welcome for Atwood and Hamilton. The chamber of commerce laid out several thousand square feet of "dazzling white canvas" on the Ellipse behind the White House to mark the landing site. They prepared a luncheon in Atwood's honor. The capital's scientific clubs and societies were waiting to act as hosts. The *New York Times* was ready to award its trophy, "Conquest of the Air"—two classical winged-figures cavorting on top of a globe. One figure held a golden biplane aloft. The trophy was featured prominently in the *Times*'s stories and headlines and pictured twice in the paper. Everyone was "on tiptoe" awaiting Atwood. He would triumphantly complete the longest airplane journey in American history, a journey that had begun six days before on a lark with a trip to the boat races.

The chamber of commerce had Atwood's assurance that he would arrive around 2:30 P.M. on the fifth, weather permitting. The chamber's secretary had gone to Atlantic City to confirm the arrangements. But Atwood did not fly to Washington; he hung around Atlantic City making a few exhibition flights. The city had gone aviation mad. "Woman Flies in Aeroplane" was the largest headline on the front page of the *Atlantic City Evening Union* for July 5. The news: "Miss Edna M. Steck of New York, twenty years old and very pretty, made an eight minute flight" with Atwood. She "laughed at the collective gasp of the throng" as she climbed into her seat. Atwood dove down on the beach with her, causing her younger sister, Mrs. Walter Phelps Dodge, to tumble in the sand. "I wasn't the least frightened at any time," Miss Steck told her friends as they congratulated her. "Why it was delicious."

Atwood had said that he didn't like taking women as passengers. "They are sure to become hysterical at some stage and the first impulse of an hysterical woman is to stand up, which is not the proper thing to do in a flying machine flight." Nevertheless they seemed to be his most frequent passengers. "The only way they can be carried safely is by strapping them so that they cannot move their feet, and this does not accomplish the purpose sought, for sometimes they will get their arms around your neck and refuse to let go and then it is up to the operator to hunt a landing and at once."

In Washington around noon, a rumor spread among the thousands waiting that Atwood was holding out for money from the chamber of commerce. They had at one time offered him a thousand dollars to come, but then reneged and offered only a dinner in his honor. Atwood vigorously denied that he was delaying the flight. His only reward for the flight would be the *Times* trophy, he said, and the "small consideration" he had received for his Atlantic City exhibition flights. "Sportsmanship and a love of flying is all that prompted me to make these flights," he said. He reassured the chamber that he was coming.

Washington waited. The heat wave continued. Boston hit 104 degrees; five thousand people slept out on the common. Ice was scarce. Tempers were short. "Two men are driven insane by heat wave," said a headline reporting a man who stabbed his cousin and then cut his own throat.

The following day high winds grounded Atwood.

Three days after Atwood had landed, he was finally ready to leave Atlantic City with Hamilton as his passenger. As the aeroplane started its run down the beach, a large white bull terrier raced out of the crowd and charged headlong into the left propeller. The dog was sent spinning back into the crowd, dead. Atwood shut the engine and rolled to a stop. There was a six-inch-long crack in the wooden propeller, and one corner of the tip was loosely hanging on.

Atwood had no spare propeller and he was anxious to get underway. He and Hamilton wired the propeller back together, and fifteen minutes later tried to take off again. Atwood picked up speed down the beach for seventy-five yards, turned out over the ocean and climbed to two hundred feet. He turned back toward the shore, and the aeroplane fell into the ocean. "Atwood never lost his head," reported the *New York Times*. "He dropped so that the back of the plane struck first." Atwood and Hamilton immediately stood up, pulled wire cutters out of their pockets, and began snipping their way out. They were a one hundred feet offshore in ten feet of water. Lifeguards and three hundred swimmers raced out to them.

The waves were running high, knocking the aeroplane about, until it "had crumpled . . . up as though it had been made of cheesecloth," said the *New York Tribune*. The crowd dragged the plane ashore. The lower wing was destroyed and the engine was soaked. A crashed Wright machine is like a fallen bird. The living bird seems to weigh nothing, and is everywhere ready for flight, but the dead bird surprises one with its weight and slackness. For days the wreckage was exhibited on the boardwalk where thousands examined it.

They joked about their escape. "You can't be an aviator until you've had a spill," Atwood said of his first crash. "We got off lucky in that she didn't dive with us and dump us underneath. All we need to make us look presentable are some new or dry clothes. I didn't lose this," he said pulling a big roll of bills from his pocket. "So we're all right."

For Hamilton it had been a pretty soft landing. When the rescuers reached them, Hamilton told them he was only sorry that he had ruined a new pair of white flannel trousers. "I paid $6.50 for them on the Boardwalk, too. And I was crazy to wear them back to Waterbury [Connecticut], where they sure would cause a sensation."

The engine had quit, probably due to dirt in the gas, Atwood said later. Other observers thought the aeroplane was a little underpowered on the left side, where the dog had hit it.

The two aviators decided to send for Hamilton's aeroplane, a similar Burgess-Wright Model F, which was in Waterbury, Connecticut. Hamilton's mechanic hired a chauffeur and a large car, and drove all night towing the partially disassembled plane. They left at eight thirty in the evening and didn't arrive in Atlantic City until five the following evening. They were held up by roads so narrow on Staten Island that they had to cut some trees down, and they were delayed for hours by a washed-out bridge three miles north of Atlantic City. The *New York Times* was determined to put the best face on the delay of their trophy flight. This two-hundred-mile auto trip, the *Times* said in a front-page story, "established a new record for aeroplane transportation." When they drove into the city down Atlantic Avenue, they gathered a parade of thousands of cheering spectators.

The mechanics worked on the aeroplane through the night. Atwood and Hamilton woke early and arrived at four in the morning. For three hours they tried to get the motor to run steadily, but it kept quitting. Atwood had been in Atlantic City for three days already; he had originally planned a four-hour stop. Another pair of headline-making travelers were gaining on him: a donkey and an elephant were racing each other from Luna Park in Brooklyn to Washington, D.C. After a day of walking,

Judy, the elephant, and Jenny, the donkey, were already in New Jersey. The appearance of an elephant walking down the road in Perth Amboy had panicked some milk-wagon horses into overturning the cart and fleeing.

Atwood and Hamilton decided to risk taking off. Forty feet off the ground, the engine quit. They went back to the hangar for three more hours of tinkering. The cap of a cylinder had fallen in. They retrieved it with a stick and some bubble gum. Atwood was normally cautious, but he had many people waiting for him to complete the flight, and Hamilton's fearless nature may have influenced him.

They tried again. They rose two hundred feet, the engine quit, and they raced downward. Atwood turned to avoid a big creek. They hit hard. The front and tail of the aeroplane snapped off, both propellers smashed to pieces, both wings were damaged, and the motor was knocked about. Hamilton was thrown back alongside the motor when his seat broke. He saved himself by grabbing the piano wire that braced the wings.

A crowd rushed up the beach toward the crash, reaching Atwood as he limped away, saying "I am not hurt; I am disgusted."

In Washington, the Atwood watch had become a staple of daily life, one the *Washington Post* recorded in verse:

Atwood Will Not Fly Today

'Twas the Fourth and all the glory of the District held its sway
In a safe and sane observance of the nation's natal day
"Harry Atwood's going to fly here" was the phrase that drew the throng
And the speeches went neglected and the speakers were forlorn
For the mighty Harry Atwood was "a tootin' of his horn."
"Harry Atwood's going to fly here" was the Shout along the way—
But, alas! came disappointment—"Atwood will not fly today."

Two more stanzas followed each disappointing delay—"Still another crash impended, and he dropped into the sea"—and the ode concluded:

And the birdman was preparing to make aerial records hum,
But a sprocket, or a motor, or some other trivial thing
Had prevented the intrepid one from taking to the wing,
Just the same old daily story on the Ninth came o'er the wires:
"Leaves at two," "at three," "at four," and the operator tires,
Still there's hope with each day's dawning, and today's the day, they say,
But we fear that they will flash it: "Atwood will not fly today."

Atwood hired fifteen men, boat builders and gas engine specialists, to work all day rebuilding the plane. They used the undamaged parts from Atwood's wrecked machine. He offered an incentive if the work was finished by evening. In all he spent one thousand dollars. They worked until midnight.

They were off at last, leaving at 5:00 A.M., only a dozen people to see them go, and the rest of the city as quiet as a cemetery. "Even the aviators were fearful that the ill-luck that had pursued them would stick," said the *New York Times.* They had slept only three hours. They were anxious to "show the critics—and there have been some of them—that we weren't four-flushers," fakers not flyers, said Atwood.

They followed the tracks of the West Jersey & Seashore Railway. The sun wasn't up, but the humidity was great. After eighty miles they had to land for gas, gliding down by the Delaware Insane Asylum. "When we landed the inmates rushed out, waving their arms wildly and cheering us," said Atwood. "I suppose we were the first aviators they had ever seen."

Word spread to Washington: Atwood was coming. He was seen leaving Baltimore. Washington's Engineer Commissioner himself had received a phone call. The city's board of commissioners hurried to greet Atwood. The chamber of commerce ordered up its long-delayed luncheon. The city scrambled. "Expectation of aviator Atwood's arrival . . . turned the Senate topsy-turvy," reported the *Washington Times.*

People were climbing to the roofs and gathering in the streets to watch the sky. "Several times interest waned, but each time something that resembled an aeroplane appeared on the horizon and sky scanning started again," said the *Times.* A slight black dot appeared in front of a gray cloud with a silver lining (or so it was described). He was here at last. The crowds "craned their necks skyward and shouted the name of Atwood."

"When the machine was sighted, a roll call was in progress in the Senate. But, led even by such sticklers for form as Senator Lodge, Senators Penrose and Root, the solons ignored duty and fled like schoolboys," said the *Times.* The Senate had not even officially adjourned. "Sen. Gallagher came out with a huge pair of binoculars. Sen. Bacon became popular because he had been up in an aeroplane once and he told his colleagues all the secrets of man's mastery of the air."

The aeroplane circled the Capitol dome and headed up the Mall toward the Washington Monument, where Atwood was expected to land. A mad race was on. "Vice President Sherman, calling a crowd of senators as he went, set off hot foot for his automobile." Other "automobiles, filled with men and women high in official and civil life, paid no attention whatsoever to speed laws and rushed pell-mell to Potomac Park. In a few minutes after the alarm had been sounded, 4,000 persons had gathered on the Monument grounds."

The biplane stopped short of the monument, turned above the Smithsonian, and flew back to the Capitol and then off to the north. The city was, all at once, thrilled, baffled, disappointed, and insulted. They had been waiting forever for Atwood, and here he was just above them, and then so quickly he left.

"The luncheon was waiting, the Chamber of Commerce wore a smile, which grew broader as the biplane grew nearer, but which faded to a ghost when the machine went around the capitol and started back home," said the *Times*. "'At least he could be a gentleman, and keep his engagement,' said the ladies. 'The mean thing! Why, he just flew right in, turned around, and flew right out again.'"

But it wasn't Atwood. Hap Arnold, who had made sport of Atwood back in flying school, had tweaked him again. Lt. Arnold and Lt. Roy Kirtland were standing by to escort Atwood into the city with the Signal Corps' Wright Model B. Tired of waiting, they took off determined to give Washington what it craved. "There was not a soul from Hyattsville to Washington who had not been duped by these two army aviators," said the *Times*. Their superior, Brig. Gen. James Allen, had led the race to the landing site. Even Starling Burgess, waiting for Atwood out at College Park, Maryland, had been fooled. The "Atwood Hoax" was uncovered in the next day's newspaper, and Arnold glued the story into his scrapbook, and kept it with his papers his whole life.

Atwood and Hamilton had not even made it as far as Baltimore. They had run into more trouble. Like a wind-up toy running down, their aeroplane had flown lower and lower until, just skimming trees and rooftops, the great heat forced them down eight miles from Baltimore. The air, Atwood explained, "simply has no buoyancy on a day as humid as this . . . and the carburetor of the machine couldn't generate the gas necessary to give us power.

"We had the engine running at what was nearly top speed, but still we couldn't force the biplane up further. And even at the low altitude at which we were sailing it was hot, suffocatingly so," Atwood said. "Skimming along above the tracks of the Pennsylvania Railroad we had to fight to keep above the telegraph wires and poles.

"It became almost insufferable," he said. "We had been in the air for some time at a stretch and were pretty well stiffened up," as well as tired and hungry.

Atwood battled to clear barns and trees. They were dropping lower; 150 feet over Havre de Grace, Maryland, 65 feet over the Bush River. They could see people smiling up at them. They flew over seventy-five miles not more than 50 feet up. "Once or twice in passing over woods we very nearly touched the tops of the trees . . . Hamilton had more confidence in the engine than I did, for I thought that going so close to the trees was positively dangerous.

"At one point I had to circle a little stretch of woods because I couldn't get over the tree tops," said Atwood. "At another point, I was caught between telegraph poles and slowly sinking to the tracks, when an express train came along with a rush, forced the air up under me and lifted me above the dead level to safety. Otherwise I might have been struck by the train that, in fact, saved me."

At an altitude of eighteen feet they passed a house. "We were low enough to the ground for people to put stepladders on their roofs and touch us," Atwood said. They could see the smoke and haze of Baltimore ahead—they knew they couldn't clear the city. They "narrowly missed getting mixed up with telegraph wires" and dropped in at Stemmer Run, Maryland.

Surprised residents rushed forward: "What's the matter?" "Too much heat, that's all," said Atwood. He had just flown a record 148 miles, 525 miles for the journey so far and was just 42 miles short of Washington, a city that was tiring of waiting.

"Tonight," said the *Times*, "many thousands who climbed up to their roofs and other thousands who went down to the polo grounds in Potomac Park and waited there for hours to see the conquest of the air that had been promised them every day for a week, went to sleep muttering between their gasps, half stifled in the superheat of their homes: 'Oh, Atwood, he is a myth! He is like the tomorrow of Alice In Wonderland—never here but coming.'"

Forty miles to Washington. An hour's flight. A short putt to sink the shot and take home the trophy. Up early once more, Atwood and Hamilton took off at 4:30 A.M. to avoid the heat. Over Fort McHenry they received a seven-gun salute and waved handkerchiefs in return. They flew easily to the government airfield at College Park and landed thinking the journey was complete. Atwood thought College Park was inside Washington's city limits. Burgess had arranged to meet him there. College Park was in Maryland—Atwood was eight miles short again.

Burgess had not finished demonstrating the army's new biplane, so it was readied for Atwood to complete the journey Burgess later called "the longest shot my young company had yet played." The army officers, including his old classmates Arnold and Milling, gathered around Atwood to congratulate him on his flight. In the new Burgess-Wright Model F, he climbed to forty feet and started into his first turn when the engine quit and the plane crashed. The wings were wrecked, the skids were damaged. Atwood had only a few scratches. Burgess shipped the wreck back to the factory. He had crashed this same aeroplane just three days before. It had been a bad week for flying: this was the third crash in four days at the army field and Atwood's third crash in five days.

There were only three other aeroplanes on the field—the only three aeroplanes anywhere near the nation's capital. Atwood couldn't use them. The army owned two and Hamilton owned the other. He and Atwood had landed in that plane just hours before, but Hamilton was going home. He was fatigued by his tuberculosis. In good health he was thin and wiry, only 120 pounds or so; now he looked gaunt, and his clothes hung loosely upon him. He was shipping his aeroplane back to Connecticut.

"I guess it is all off," Atwood said sadly, "and nobody regrets it half as much as I, for I had my heart set on making the complete trip." The *Times* declared the trophy won and the journey done. This was such a disappointing ending. Atwood wanted to fly into the city—they had been waiting for so long. He ordered a new plane shipped from the factory in Massachusetts. But he grew tired of waiting. After a couple of days he bought Hamilton's disassembled machine for $3,725 one afternoon and was off.

"Over the airfield he gave a remarkable exhibition of volplaning, diving, banking and making figure eights," reported the *Times*. He circled the field and then dove to within thirty feet of the ground. People shouted: He's down! The doctor called for a stretcher, and "then without the least apparent effort" he climbed back four hundred feet above them. The trains of the Baltimore & Ohio slowed as they passed, so the passengers could watch. He then took his pilot's test again. He cut ten figure eights and was awarded Federation Aeronautique Internationale license number 33. The crowd cheered.

"Atwood seemed as pleased as a boy on a holiday," said the *Times*. The army aeroplane flown by Milling escorted Atwood to the edge of the field and in ten minutes Atwood was finally over Washington.

He circled the Capitol, congressmen rushing out to see him, he flew over the Library of Congress, the Capitol grounds, and Union Station, where a locomotive whistled in salute; then he shot down Pennsylvania Avenue toward the Washington Monument. Atwood circled, climbing to a thousand feet. "For a minute the aeroplane seemed to be perfectly still, and then like a flash of lightning it shot down directly for the top of the monument. The spectators shivered, and on all sides could be heard saying that Atwood would surely be killed." They rushed to the monument, but Atwood soared over those who expected to find him crushed. He "circled the park, while the crowd cheered him again and again," said the *Times*. He climbed to five hundred feet and spiraled down around the monument, nearly touching the earth as he finished.

Atwood flew "like an eagle . . . swooping suddenly as if bent upon some earthly prey"; he circled the Washington Monument "like a moth fluttering around a candle"; he soared "like a gull"; he sailed "with the easy grace of some great creature of the skies," said witnesses of his flight, trying understand this new bird. But this eagle-moth-gull-creature kept fooling them—it would dive down so close to the ground that medical personnel ran for the ambulance. It glided and flew in circles, like a bird in distress. At one moment it was graceful and the next awkward, its movements hard to anticipate. The spectators were watching something they could only struggle to name. They tried a roster of birds, a few insects, some grand appellations—the "new monarch of the skies"—and at last called what they were seeing "modern."

"Surely the aeroplane has arrived. It is no longer an experiment, a toy, or an easy road to suicide," said one magazine, *The Outlook*. "The only question that confronts us is, what are the limits of the aeroplane's development and usefulness? He would be a rash prophet who drew those limits too close."

Others were not as impressed. It had taken Atwood ten days to reach Washington from New York, not one day as intended, said the *Washington Evening Star*. And the *Scientific American* noted that twice the distance was covered in a circuit of England air race, which took only thirty-one and one half hours. (They didn't mention that only one plane finished the race in that time; the only two other planes to finish took two weeks.)

President Taft missed the show. He was on the golf links in Maryland. The next day Atwood took the show to the President's door: he flew back into the city from College Park—a short, simple flight, but nothing had been simple since he left New York. He flew in a driving rain that at times nearly blinded him, in a twenty-mile-an-hour wind that made flying treacherous and rocked his aeroplane like a seesaw as he landed by the Potomac River. He wouldn't normally fly on a day like this. He was drenched. "I intended to look very presentable, but I guess I look more like a drowned rat than anything else," he told the two young women who greeted him. At least the heat had let up.

His hosts drove him off to a hotel to change for the chamber of commerce's luncheon. There was still some talk of raising a purse for his flight, but it came to nothing. They offered Atwood three cheers and lunch. He had flown four times further than anyone in America and escaped three crashes for that lunch. Afterward he called on the president.

He readied his aeroplane and stood by awaiting a signal from the top of the War Department building: Taft had risen from the lunch table. Atwood took off, circled the Washington Monument twice, and flew toward the White House. Halfway there, he shut his engine to glide in, but the aeroplane, caught by the wind, dove sharply toward the trees at the edge of the South Lawn. The crowd gathered outside the White House fence gasped. A few weeks before, the French Minister of War had been killed at an air show; Taft had asked the aero club to assure that the plane could land safely. Atwood restarted his engine, righted the biplane, and rose over the trees on the South Lawn just as Taft came out to the South Portico and watched with a smile. Atwood cut his engine and glided down on the lawn, missing the large fountain at the center, and set down so lightly that Gen. Allen of the Signal Corps said, "He would hardly have broken an egg if he'd hit it." The aeroplane came to a stop just thirty feet from the president.

Also on the portico were the acting secretary of war, the army aviators Arnold, Milling, and Kirtland, other dignitaries, and Atwood's mother, her eyes full of tears as she embraced her son. She told the president that it was the proudest day of her life.

In a brief ceremony, Harry Atwood was presented to Taft as a graduate of MIT. On behalf of the Aero Club of Washington, Taft gave Atwood a gold medal commemorating his flight: "I hope it will only be one of a great many that will come to you in the future, and they will come with as little injury and as little apparent danger as you exhibited in flying down here to the White House grounds."

Taft had declined the offer of a flight, saying he might disturb the balance of the machine. On other occasions he declared himself ready for a flight "whenever an aeroplane was produced that would lift his avoirdu-pois," as the *Scientific American* phrased it.

Atwood's mother wanted to fly with her son from the White House, but he declined—it was a tight spot. He taxied straight toward the fountain, and it looked for a moment as if he wouldn't clear it, but he hopped the fountain by a good twenty feet and rose up with the White House behind him, a moment frozen in time by the photographers, a moment of prom-ise when the century, the aeroplane, and its pilot, were young.

The next morning before leaving Washington, Atwood's mother asked to go to Potomac Park to see the aeroplane once more, the Burgess-Wright that Atwood had purchased from Hamilton, the one they had both crashed in Atlantic City, the one that Hamilton had bought with money out of his sock.

Washington had caught biplane fever. On the weekend after Atwood's flight, the army aviation school had a record number of visitors. Atwood said he would return and fly again. But seven days later, a windstorm threw the aeroplane three hundred feet up in the air and smashed it down against a bandstand. Even the engine was broken in two. It was a total loss. Atwood was in New York, planning an even greater flight.

⁀ The Biplane Dance

August 14, 1911. The happiest day of his young life. "I had more fun today than ever before," he wrote in the *New York Times*. He was off on a new long-distance flight, an attempt to reach New York from St. Louis, the symbolic center of the country. If he succeeded it would be a world record, twice as long as his Washington flight. But that journey had been an impulse of the early summer. Now, it was only a few weeks to Labor Day, and Harry Atwood was an experienced aviator. In his ten-week career he had flown nearly sixteen hundred miles in an era when most aviators didn't stray far from the aerodrome. What's more, after ten weeks he was still alive. This flight was planned. Two mechanics and a railroad car of spare parts would follow him across the country. There were two spare aeroplanes waiting, and there was a ten-thousand-dollar prize.

He hired a manager to oversee the operation, and line up appearances to underwrite the costly flight. He flew from St. Louis in triumph and along the way was greeted with a welcome usually reserved for liberating armies. In the air he had mastered his realm and flew with ease. "Over the Illinois prairies I lay back at full length and let her glide easily with the wind," he said. He was following the railroad tracks. "I had a time table with me and knew every station . . . When nearing each town I would descend as low as safety would allow and circle around the station once in order to be sure of its name." Alerted by the railroad telegraph up the line—"Atwood gone over—speed terrific"—everyone was out on the tracks to cheer.

"Just above Alton there was a fork in the railroad tracks and I was at a loss which one to take," Atwood recalled. "I saw a signal tower and there was a man in there who certainly was a quick thinking railroad man. I dipped the machine until I passed just ten feet above the tower and only about two feet above the telegraph wires. I pointed at one track and then at the other and the man ran down from the tower and pointed to the one I should take. There was not a word exchanged."

In the towns, "I could see the white exhaust from the whistles of the trains and the factories announcing my approach." Over one city, Joliet, "they fired off a gun there and I thought one of my cylinders had blown out until I looked down and saw the puff of smoke." Over another town, Dwight, he dropped to three hundred feet and stunned the town into silence. Not until he had flown past could they recover themselves to cheer.

"I would wave my hand sideways, aviator fashion, so they could see it from below," a wave he would use throughout his life, and that his daughters would copy. "At one farm a man was standing outside his house and heard the puffing of my engine. He stood there for a few moments with his hands in his pockets looking in every direction. Finally he became so nervous that he jumped this way and that. Then he happened to look up, saw me, and brought out his wife.

"At another farm a man was plowing with a three-horse team in a cornfield. The horses shot down the field as if they were mad, tearing up corn as they went . . . I don't believe he ever did see me, and is probably wondering still what was the matter with his team. After that I was careful not to pass close to a farm where there were any horses at work.

"As I went high over the farms and then swooped low whenever I saw a village or town below, it was joyous to see how the people turned out and attempted to shout messages of encouragement. At every crossroad there were vast crowds and in every town there seemed to be thousands waiting to see me pass . . . I'll never forget those shouting crowds of people."

He flew on through two thunderstorms, one with large drops "that stung like fury." He had only his cap to protect him. He flew without goggles, helmet, or gloves. He did carry a lunch bag and a small brown leather valise lashed to the aeroplane, containing a change of clothes, tooth brush, a topographical map, wrenches, pliers, and lubricating oil.

He stopped to rest and take on gas twice. By day's end, after five hours and forty-three minutes of flying, he had a new American record for a one-day flight: 286 miles. Atwood had set the old record flying from Atlantic City to Baltimore.

He arrived in triumph. He had originally hoped to reach Chicago after two days, but he made it in a day, flying into a city that had biplane fever. Some three million people crowded in and around Grant Park during the nine days of Chicago's International Aviation Meet. They hung out of windows (not a hotel room was vacant) and climbed signs and light poles to see more than thirty aviators compete in the largest air meet ever. Among the flyers was Lincoln Beachey, who flew down Michigan Avenue touching the tops of cars with his wheels. At one time there were even eight aeroplanes in the sky at once. "Whether We Suffer from 'Aero-mania' or Rave with 'Aviationitis', It's All the Same—the Air Bug's Got Us and We're Proud of It," said a headline in the *Chicago Sunday Tribune*.

Atwood's progress was telegraphed to the meet. He was sighted when he was ten miles away. "A voice shouted, 'That's Atwood from St. Louis.' Immediately the vast assembly was in an uproar," said the *New York Times*. "'Atwood, Atwood,' a thousand shouted in concert with such a volume of sound that the flying men over the field heard and shifted their machines so they could get better views of the coming aviator," said the *Chicago Daily Tribune*.

The cheering increased when he reached the field. The other aviators flying the course fell in behind him. Atwood started to land, but "the crowd sent another volley of cheers after him," so he pulled up and cir-cled the field once more before landing near the judges stand. As he stepped out of his seat, "he was immediately surrounded by a great, cheer-ing crowd, and lifted to the shoulders of several men and borne from the field followed by thousands of cheering men, women and children."

"I never saw such enthusiasm," Atwood said, once he was placed on the ground again in front of the official's stand. Everyone wanted to hear about the flight. "If I can only have the same good fortune on the balance of my trip to New York . . . I am going to open the eyes of the world," he said. He was handed fifty congratulatory telegrams.

At the meet there had been five accidents that day—from stalled en-gines, a broken support wire, and a snapped propeller—but here Atwood had flown a record distance and made it look easy. "Dressed in a natty Norfolk suit, he seemed as clean and cool as if he had just alighted from a Pullman car," said the *Times*. His only complaint was his aching ears. "I was pretty tired after the trip, but it was just like a picnic to me. I would rather be up in the air than anywhere else."

It had been a remarkable day—"Atwood's whole voyage from St. Louis was one long continued cheer from waiting crowds," said the *Chi-cago Daily Tribune*. But the next day he left after a roaring dispute in which there was "much vehemence of language and gesticulation." Once the flying was over and the cheering faded, Harry Atwood was often in an argument over a business deal.

At first he had been barred from the Chicago aviation meet after well-publicized arguments with the meet's organizers. Atwood wanted to fly his way—arrive on his cross-country tour and do figure eights over the city and circle tall buildings. The meet officials said it was too dangerous; they wanted Atwood to fly by their rules. The other aviators rallied to his side and began raising money for Atwood to rent another field to perform independently. "I can make circles around most of these fellows that are here, and they know it. They agree with me that I ought to be allowed to show what I can do," he said.

That dispute was settled and Atwood was welcomed as an air hero. The meet's organizers raced each other to greet him and hoist him to their shoulders. He delayed leaving on the next day until 3:30 P.M. so it could be a feature of the meet's program. For his appearance and delayed start Atwood and his manager said he was promised one thousand dollars. The meet policy was to limit payments to all aviators to five hundred dollars, the rest coming from prize money.

"The trouble started when somebody with a badge, but unidentified, told Atwood that he must leave the grounds by 3:30 o'clock, or he would not be allowed to start at all. Atwood responded with heat that he would start when he pleased or someone would get hurt," reported the *Boston Herald*.

"This subject was scarcely quieted when the air pilot was tendered a check for $500 as a gift because he landed here. 'I landed here yesterday to please the crowd mostly, but I was promised $1000 for doing it,'" the birdman cried, 'and I want it.'"

"Loud language over this point continued as the aeroplane was brought to the starting line. The check for $500 was thrust into his hand and rejected, because still uncertified. The propellers were whirring and half a dozen men were required to restrain the machine while Chairman Mudd did a quick job of certification."

Atwood circled the field once, not four times as had been planned, and flew away, with small American flags trailing out behind his wings. A squadron of aeroplanes that was to have escorted him stayed on the ground. The crowd, unaware of the argument, waved their hats and cheered as Atwood sailed off, and then turned its attention to the next attraction.

In his short career, there had been several arguments concerning Atwood's business arrangements. At his first aviation meet, in June near Boston, he had upset the meet's organizers by flying the relay of reporters during the meet. At the meet's end, when he had won the ten-thousand-dollar top prize, the organizers refused to pay. Long after Atwood had left Washington, he kept after the chamber of commerce in open letters to newspapers saying he was promised one thousand dollars. And on this journey from St. Louis he was often at odds with his manager, A. Leo Stevens, over the flight arrangements.

He further antagonized the Chicago promoters with a telegram he sent after two aviators were killed at the meet. Many aviators criticized the management for continuing the events without pause after the deaths. Atwood called the promoters "fierce and uncivilized" and sent his telegram to the afternoon newspapers. The promoters called him "most unsportsman-like" and said that Atwood and his manager had caused them "all kinds of trouble."

He flew in stages across Indiana and Ohio. Farmers from all around came out to the railroad stations. When Atwood circled down low to read the stations' names, they called up to him, asking him to land. They had brought him lunch and bouquets of flowers. A headline in the *Toledo Blade* caught that summer's thrill: "Earth-Beings Breathless As Flyer Wings Away To The East." For Ashtabula, Ohio, a town close to the Pennsylvania border, Atwood's flight was the most excitement since the British navy was off the harbor in the War of 1812. Residents grabbed ladders and climbed the roofs of houses, barns, and factories. They could see Atwood working the levers of his biplane. In Wauseon, Ohio, the factory whistle blew and the "population literally flew up; Charley Prichard was upon the apex of the Opera House front before the last note of the whistle died away." All along his route, the telegraph operators were busy answering requests about Atwood's location; two minutes without a word brought a new inquiry. Everyone wanted to see an aeroplane. In Auburn, New York, the convicts at the state prison offered Atwood five hundred dollars to land in the prison yard. Prison authorities wouldn't allow it.

Venice, Ohio, stole Atwood from the sky. The "airship crazy" town gathered on the baseball field and waved him in with an American flag, fooling him into thinking it was his Sandusky landing site, which was three miles away. Atwood, it was reported, appreciated the joke. He was driven into Sandusky to check the landing site, and to get a shave, shampoo, and shine at a barbershop. Venice was so pleased to make the news, the citizens gave him their highest honor, naming its "crack" baseball team, "The Atwoods." The renamed team lost its next game, 16–3.

When he landed in a small country town, everything stopped. When he made a twilight landing in Fort Plain, New York, the town treated it like a patriotic holiday, hastily assembling its brass band and drum corps, crowding into main street, placing Atwood on a box to hear a welcoming address, and keeping him up until two in the morning. The news went out over the telephone party line when he landed in Pettisville, Ohio:

"'Say-y-y, do you know that there is a flying machine here in town?' said a feminine voice over the party line.

"'You don't say!' replied another feminine voice. "Where?'

"'Down in Charley Galman's pasture lot.'

"Bang!

"Another resident was on the way," reported the *Toledo Blade*. "The operator had to stick to his post. So did the postmaster, the general storekeeper, possibly the doctor and a few faithful housewives who had bread in the oven. The others were down in Charley Galman's pasture lot.

"Valerius Webber was pointed out as the man who saw H. Atwood coming. 'He was coming down fast and, just made a circle, coming down graceful, like a bird,' said Mr. Webber. He was called upon to repeat the story, with amplification, numerous times.

"'It's got a chain gear, ain't it?' observed one of the amateur mechanicians who wanted to see for themselves how the thing was run. Then someone put up the ropes."

"The kodak brigade was there" snapping pictures, and someone set up a pop stand and was soon sold out. "Then Galman's pump got a punishing."

Atwood talked with everyone for a "quite a spell" before he went to a neighboring town for lunch and a haircut. A man invited Atwood to a reunion: "'We thought that it would be a real nice to have you stop and eat chicken with us.' Quite a few said that Mr. Atwood was a fine fellow."

Atwood returned and prepared to take off. The special officer cleared the way. The aeroplane rose quickly, the spectators cheered, and "then they all went home to do the milking."

Atwood was at peace in the sky. "I am sure that when aviation becomes common, it will add a viewpoint to life," he said. "Seen from my machine, houses look as small as dog kennels, towns appear to be clusters of toy houses, and the rivers look like brooks. Over the town the temperature is slightly warmer than over the open country. It is curious that above the din of a city one may sometimes hear such distinct sounds as the barking of dogs."

"The low level of the country, which is dotted with fields and houses, is conducive to the best kind of flying. I never found myself so interested. I just hated to land," said "the first aeroplane tourist of America," as the *Cleveland Plain Dealer* called him.

"It's been just a lazy run all the way. Anybody could do it. If the experiment in aviation would be confined to straight-ahead sailing I am sure the problem would be more quickly and sanely solved. The people who look up from the ground in amazement at seeing me at a dizzy height would be surprised at the simplicity of it. I sometimes fix my planes at the right angle and sail along without touching them for ten minutes a stretch, and then lean back in my seat to figure out my location from the timetable or eat my luncheon."

The flight did have the routine life-threatening hazards. Welcoming committees, with the best intentions, continued to select landing sites that were too small. Landing was out of the question in Bloomington, Illinois, where "it looked as if they had picked out a backyard for me to land in and that was crowded with people as thick as flies." The same was true of the state fairgrounds in Springfield, Illinois, and the courthouse lawn in Sandusky, Ohio, a small square occupied by five thousand people and bounded by telephone wires. In Elkhart, Indiana, it took him two attempts to fly free from an enclosed half-mile race track, grazing the trees so closely that his manager, Stevens, along for the ride, was knocked about and cut by the branches that hit the plane. Stevens declined further rides.

In Cleveland, they thought Atwood was endangering the public with reckless flying when he attempted to land the correct way, against the wind. They had set up a small strip on the beach facing the wrong way and Atwood had to dive down over the crowd to land. "On the east end of the pier there were about 5000 people, and to the consternation of everyone, Atwood banked out around and came in from the east, flying directly at the pier and at the people," recalled reporter Max Cook. Atwood "started waving one arm wildly. The police started shoving the people, and the plane missed the heads of the people by a hair's breadth and just barely missed a pole that had a boat rental sign on it, at the pier. He came down and finally landed just inches from the water's edge."

The officials and other privileged spectators who stood in a roped-in enclosure on the beach may have gotten the biggest scare. "A half dozen threw themselves flat on the ground, a dozen more scattered in panic, and a stout man was crawling under an upturned boat as the plane skimmed overhead, some ten feet above the sand," said the *Plain Dealer*. The next day a newspaper editorial scolded Atwood for foolish flying.

After the landing, a constable stepped forward and seized Atwood's aeroplane. The Standard Oil Company attached his plane for $300, which they said Atwood owed for gas and oil back at the airfield in Massachusetts. This was just a misunderstanding, Atwood claimed; the gas and oil had been given to him. He had an expansive idea of credit, and a habit of leaving bills unpaid. He posted a $350 bond to release the plane.

He was also pursued by a Mrs. A. B. Williams of New York—a relative said the *St. Louis Post-Dispatch*, a sister-in-law said another paper, the only woman in the official party that saw Atwood start his journey. Other newspapers reported her as Miss Williams, his fiancée, or hinted at a romance. She followed him across the country. Now and then it was noted that the handsome young aviator was married, though separated, and had a three-year-old daughter, Bethany. That didn't put off any of his admirers.

"Since making the announcement that I would fly from St. Louis to New York, I have had 1,120 letters from Chicago and vicinity. Some of the people, mostly women, wanted to accompany me; others wanted my photograph; still other women wished to be married to me," Atwood told a Chicago paper.

In Cleveland, as elsewhere, he was mobbed after he landed. "Women and girls crowded around him in a way which recalled the most popular days of Theodore and Alice Roosevelt," said the *Plain Dealer*. "Three girls tried to kiss him, and it took two park policemen, one on either side of the aviator, to get him free of his excited admirers."

One aviator's wife, Adelaide Ovington, grew tired of her husband Earle's "adorers." "The birdmen of those early days came in for a lot of hero worship," she said. "They would get as many notes as a matinee idol and much the same sort . . . One skyblue note, I remember, was particularly to the point: 'I am a young girl nineteen years old, single, and fair to look at, brave, and will go the limit.'"

Back home, Mrs. Atwood hated Harry's flying and hated the press. Was she worried about her husband? a reporter asked. "My friends know how I feel about that, but the people here probably don't care how I feel. So what is the use of my telling you how I feel?"

By Cleveland, Atwood had reached the halfway point, and the trip was beginning to wear on him: the noise of the engine, the danger of the landings, and the hunger of the crowds.

"Atwood is having trouble getting sufficient sleep," said Stevens. "He hears the drumming of his motor all night, generally." He slept less as the flight progressed. Crossing New York State, on the last six days of the flight, he reportedly slept only four hours in all. He would fly on one hour's rest.

He was anxious to get to New York. "Oh, these little hopping flights are getting on my nerves," he said after flying 123 miles, with two stops. "I want to make 300 or 400 miles a day, and I could easily do it if it were not that my engagement calls for stops. The distance between Chicago and New York ought easily be covered in three days."

To relax he would play the piano in the evenings. People thought he was the picture of ease, flying out of the sky and then entertaining everyone with song. But he was trying to calm his nerves. When he could, he began to choose country quiet over the ovation and noise of the city beyond. Ten miles outside of a planned stop in Erie, Pennsylvania, he set down in a cornfield, with only a farmer and a cow nearby. The cow jumped the fence in fright. Atwood spent the night on the farm.

He was still enjoying his time in the air, but he was being knocked about by whirlwinds off the Great Lakes. Flying out of Cleveland, the wind "almost disabled my machine," he said. "Part of the way I had to go ahead at an angle that almost threw me out of my seat," and "at one place I made a sheer drop of 400 feet."

Even so the "flight was one of the prettiest of the lot. The sky was spattered with clouds . . . Over the lake I could see the white fringe on the waves as it washed along the shore, and to the south I could see the vineyards for miles."

Flying to Buffalo his hands were numb from the cold crosswind off the lake, but he had other problems. The city was hidden by smoke from the steel mills. He flew around the city looking for the racetrack at which he was to land, at one point circling low over a confectionery shop, shouting down for directions. The shop owner "seemed to have been struck dumb . . . Stockstill he stood, his mouth wide open and his eyes riveted to the mechanical bird," said a Buffalo paper.

The city's smoke drifted east, and Atwood ran into it when he left the next day. "Not far out of Buffalo I found the air, even at a great altitude, filled with fine grains of sand. I steered in all directions, high and low, to avoid it, but it was not until I reached Batavia that I found the air clear." The dust was so bad that he flew with one hand, trying to ease his eyes with the other. He skipped Rochester: "the smoke there appeared from a distance to be likely to confuse me."

Even under good conditions it was difficult to pick out the right landing field. He had been tricked by crowds waving him in at Venice and

again at Cleveland. And in upstate New York, in what turned out to be
Nelliston, he set down at twilight. A boy, Harry Nellis, came running up to
him.

"Where am I?" asked Atwood.

"You're in Ed Nellis's cow pasture, mister," said the boy, an answer that
went down in town history.

The railroad tracks were his guide. He flew without a compass. In upstate New York, he detoured to Auburn, leaving the tracks for the first
time, and was lost in the clouds and overtaken by darkness. "I had gone
ten miles, perhaps, when, away from the railroad tracks, I was completely
at a loss to know where Auburn was . . . The more I went, the more con-
fused I became. I was a lost sailor of the sky, wandering among the
clouds." He climbed up high to scout out landmarks. His gas was running
low, and if he landed he could be miles from a refill. "I dropped low toward some farmhouse, thinking I might get in talking distance of someone and ask him the direction, but no farmers appeared and I had to rise
again to keep from hitting some barns."

On his expected route, thousands waited in parks and on roofs in Syracuse and Utica. "All the telegraph wires were burdened with the query:
'Where's Atwood?'" said the *New York Times*. In Auburn, at the city paper,
the telephone "bells jingled continuously . . . 'Heard anything from the
flying machine?' It was worse than a county election."

He found Auburn at last, and the crowds he had risked so much for almost tore his machine apart. They "stood awed and orderly while the
landing was being made. Then someone started to run toward the machine. It was like an epidemic. The poor, curious, thoughtless crowd
swept across the grass," said the *Auburn Daily Advertiser*. "From a distance
the movement looked exactly like the swirl of torn paper and dried
leaves, in a gutter, before an autumn breeze . . . 'Can't somebody stop
this?' he cried."

A detail of soldiers from Company M was helpless, as was the extensive
"special police." "Apparently everybody was a special policeman for the
occasion for nearly everybody bore a tag to that effect. Even a few dogs
were seen with the legend, 'Atwood Special Police,' fluttering from their
collars," said the *Advertiser*.

"Atwood was visibly worried and kept calling to the crowd to keep back.
He stood at the levers working them backward and forward which kept the
rudders moving and this had a tendency to keep those at the rear of the
machine away somewhat." They broke three ribs on the plane. When at
last order was established, Atwood got into the air again, determined to

reach Utica, about seventy miles away, by way of Syracuse. But darkness caught up with him after just fifteen miles. Landing in the last light, he found himself all alone. All the farmers were eating dinner or doing chores. In Auburn, the convicts at the state prison were "bitterly disappointed." They never saw Atwood.

He was through with crowds, with what he called the "circus features." "Tomorrow I will disregard all scheduled landing places," he said, upsetting his manager. He not only skipped the contracted exhibitions, he avoided cities. He passed Utica without stopping for a five-hundred-dollar prize, flew three miles south of Schenectady, and turned south again to avoid Albany. He was just "two bird hops away" from New York, he said, and he would not be delayed by the promoters any more. At the stop near Albany, his aeroplane was prepared for the final leg down the Hudson River. Aluminum pontoons were attached under the wing, and the mechanics, Frank Lawson and John Lamet, worked late into the night to rebuild his worn engine, the scene lit by five beacon-like acetylene lamps. The mechanics were exhausted and sick.

Atwood's crew benefited from the greed of an angry farmer. He charged each car fifty cents to enter his private road, and demanded one hundred dollars from Atwood to pay for damages to his apple orchard. Crowds were deterred.

He loved the flight down the Hudson most of all. He was back among mountains, where he felt at home. "Those mountains! Man never felt more a sort of kinship with the birds—that he can do the things that birds do—than I did when I was climbing 1,013 feet to get a landing site on the crest of Baxter Mountain there near Cold Spring, across the river from West Point." As he rose in tight ascending circles, he said he could almost look back upon himself, the way you see a long train rounding a curve. "That was the one and only time during the entire flight that I felt like what they call a 'bird-man.' The sensation as I climbed up the side of that crag was the greatest I ever had. I just simply slowed up until I got to the top and then I landed on a ledge."

As he flew past Rhinecliff, New York, he broke the world record for a cross-country flight. He flew under the bridge at Poughkeepsie and circled around the parade grounds of West Point where he was invited to land; but finding it crowded with soldiers, he decided instead to land across the river, circling Baxter mountain. After refilling the gas tank, he was off to finish the flight, the triumphal arrival in New York.

Within half an hour he was in trouble. He was losing power. Something had broken in the engine; it was weakening, and he could tell this was worse than other breaks. He dropped down over a river pier and asked for the nearest open field. He did not trust the pontoons. "Right around the mountain," said a man.

He came down in a tight spot in a hayfield, narrowly missing a hayrick. He had landed on a mountain ledge, in a marsh, in fairgrounds so small he had brushed the trees taking off, but this he said was "the worst box I've been in since leaving St. Louis." He was trapped in a pocket only 150 feet square, hemmed in by tall trees, apple trees, and Red Hook Mountain. Without a southeast wind, he said, he might have to take apart his plane and move it to a better field. It started to rain, adding to his troubles; the soft ground would make taking off even more difficult.

He was just twenty-five miles from New York City, about forty minutes in the air to the end of an arduous journey. In New York, the piers were so jammed with crowds awaiting his arrival that river-side traffic had trouble getting through. The *New York World*, the sister paper of the *St. Louis Post-Dispatch*, had arranged for a dirigible to fly out over the Hudson to greet the aviator with a banner welcoming him to the city. It was nearly dark before people gave up and went home disappointed. The New York press poured into the village of Nyack where Atwood was stuck. Two extra telegraph operators had to be added to handle their dispatches.

This was the first major repair of the entire trip, and as luck would have it, the first time Atwood had been this far from his two mechanics. The bearings in the connecting rod of the engine had burned out and the connecting rod had broken. A local machinist worked nearly all night on a new casting.

Atwood was flying the same aeroplane he had used to go from Boston to Atlantic City, but now both wings were covered with names and initials in ink and pencil from people along the route who had snuck a signature when no one was looking. "At Elkhart a man went around selling lead pencils for people to write their names on my machine with," Atwood said, "while at every stop there was somebody who was waiting to tell me how to finish my flight the most proper and scientific way.

"The signature fiends are bad enough but the souvenir fiends are absolutely dangerous. Why, if I wasn't on the watch those people would walk off with the whole aeroplane chopped into small pieces. I have had some of the most amusing and aggravating experiences with the country people along the route, I can tell you . . . At pretty nearly every place I landed some fellow asked me to carry a letter to his girl up in Boston. Of course, I agreed to do so."

In Nyack, the town kept vigil, standing through downpours to watch the plane and the mechanics at work. Atwood stood on his plane surrounded by a crowd behind a rope. From the crowd's viewpoint, this was wonderful, but the tired Atwood may have felt like a caged amusement. He leaned away from the crowd.

But they were eager to help. "Kind friends there, to the number of twenty-five, lifted my machine over two fences into a field that made a better starting point," Atwood said. He didn't mention that a widow's pear tree, right in front of the plane, was cut down at midnight by two citizens. She was furious.

Once the aeroplane was set down, he tried the engine. It wouldn't start at first, then it backfired and the plane caught fire. "I thought the flight was at an end then sure," Atwood said, "but my friends again responded and buried the gasoline tank in enough sand to extinguish the flames before any damage was done.

"Then they cut down the trees in front of me and made a clear space between the trees just big enough for me to fly through. I really think that I touched the branches of the trees on both sides as I went into the air."

It was a rainy, foggy day, and the promoters telegraphed asking him to wait until the next day, a Saturday, when there would be good attendance at the fairgrounds they had booked for the end of the flight. But Atwood was on his way. "I don't know why they should imagine that I would delay a whole day in reaching New York when I had started from St. Louis to make a record," he said. "My record as a cross-country aviator, and what prestige I may enjoy as an aviator was more to me than a few extra show dollars for somebody else," he said. "I am not a showman."

In the harbor came his most anxious moment. It was foggy and he could not see the island well. "I was just a bit too nervous then, for I realized that in a minute or two more the flight would be mine, and I did not want anything to happen at the last moment."

"Well I'm glad it's ended," he said as he got out of his aeroplane, and spoke of the next long-distance challenge, a coast-to-coast flight. But the weary Atwood had second thoughts. "I may give up aviation. It is too risky. Man after man has made new records in aviation of late, only to drop suddenly to death. I have been much more careful than many birdmen, but I feel that if I stay in the clouds too long I shall some day meet my fate also. It is practically inevitable that, sooner or later, an aviator, no matter how careful he may be, will end his flights with a sudden plunge to destruction."

In that one moment, Atwood provided newspapers with a choice of two headlines: "Pacific to Atlantic May Tempt Atwood Next," or, "Atwood May Give Up Flying."

Harry Atwood had flown 1,265 miles in twelve days in his "wonderful space-annihilating flight." The old world record holder had taken thirty days to cover 100 fewer miles. Atwood's actual flying time was twenty-eight hours and thirty-one minutes.

"All Welcome the Conquering Air Hero" said one advertisement. Around New York, Atwood couldn't attend a show or have dinner without being pointed out and receiving an ovation. When he was dining at Churchills with his friend Hamilton, a page calling Atwood to the phone revealed his identity. "Immediately there was excitement throughout the big dining room and amid handclapping and cheers the orchestra struck up 'Come, Josephine, in My Flying Machine,'" reported the *St. Louis Post-Dispatch*. "Enthusiastic men and women crowded about the aviator's table congratulating Atwood and shaking his hand," while "several of the more enthusiastic women . . . moved forward with plain intent to impress their approval on his lips."

Victor J. Evans, a Washington patent attorney who had offered the ten-thousand-dollar prize for the flight, was surprised by Atwood's success. "I didn't think it was possible, but I am pleased to learn that I was mistaken," Evans said. He had put the money up because he believed that Washington's chamber of commerce had treated Atwood poorly.

His achievement excited the *Scientific American*. "Atwood's performance unquestionably proves that the flying machine has a future for swift transportation." It was "a record full of promise."

"Atwood was able to fly every day and each day he made headway," the magazine noted, and that moved it to say that "in making his long-distance tour Harry Atwood has shown the aeroplane, when favored with good weather, to be fully as dependable as the automobile" (an overstatement, the *New York Times* pointed out).

In four months, Atwood had gone from being a college dropout with a small automobile garage to one of the world's leading aviators. He earned fifty thousand dollars in the last half of 1911 and was given a touring car. His manager had big plans for him, saying he had lined up appearances at meets, fairs, and other events worth ninety thousand dollars. But Atwood had other things in mind. "There is nothing for me in small flights now, and I am opposed to flying purely for exhibition purposes." He was considering vaudeville; he had been offered a lucrative twenty-five-week lecture engagement. Even though he acknowledged it would be considered "unsportsman-like for me to go before the public and talk about what I have done," he would be able to finance a trip across the continent without outside backing.

His flight was finished, but the promoters were still trying to lure him to fly across the harbor to Sheepshead Bay and give an exhibition. Atwood wanted to go home. At midnight, he relented and accepted an increased offer of five thousand dollars.

The next morning his mechanics called him and told him that his aeroplane was soaked from a heavy rain, the engine was still weak, the harbor was foggy, and the field at the Sheepshead Bay racetrack was thick with mud. Atwood called the flight off, told a few reporters, and boarded a train for Boston. He didn't tell his manager or the promoters. Several thousand who showed up on each day wanted their money back.

Stevens couldn't believe that Atwood would walk out on five thousand dollars. "He will never get such a magnificent offer again. But what does he do? He leaves town by train and left me to meet" the promoters. "Believe me, it was embarrassing. I'm the blue-eyed child with the golden locks in this deal, all right."

A. Leo Stevens was an experienced balloonist with a reputation for keeping calm in emergencies. Once a farmer had shot at his balloon. "Stevens did not even duck, but kept his right hand on the rip cord, ready for the worst.

"But just say aeroplane or Atwood [and] Stevens goes for altitude at a more abrupt angle, stays up longer and comes down less refreshed these days than Atwood," said the *New York World*. "He tries to talk as rapidly as his feelings prompt" about "Atwood's contempt for the feelings of his manager."

Stevens had labored to arrange for Atwood's appearance in various towns and cities which were ready to pay, only to have Atwood choose another route. "These peculiarities of temperament gave Stevens insomnia." He had slept only fifteen hours in the previous twenty-one days.

In New York, Stevens had to stake out a hotel lobby to find his aviator. He sat for four hours in the lobby of the Hotel Manhattan, where Atwood said he would meet him. He tipped a bellboy to keep him awake. He finally found Atwood at a different hotel, and saw him for five minutes. Atwood dressed and went out on the town for dinner and a show, while Stevens chased after the contract. "Atwood has been found a most difficult subject for the business managers of aeronautics," observed the *St. Louis Post-Dispatch*. "He is a college man with sportsman-like instincts and the game appeals to him more strongly than the money." He had refused advertising money, including an offer of one thousand dollars to fly an aluminum typewriter with him.

Even with the prize money, Atwood had made little from his cross-country flight. He had paid four thousand dollars to cancel his last twelve stops. That left him six thousand dollars to pay expenses of some nine hundred dollars a day, he said, which included the two mechanics and the railway car of parts. The promoters had received the lion's share of his prize money, Atwood claimed, and they had "bungled his affairs woefully." "As soon as they take aviation out of the hands of promoters the better it will be," he said.

Back in Boston, he was received with a "wild greeting" and "crowned King of the Air" at the Harvard-Boston aero meet. He had been a spectator at the previous meet, less than a year before. He flew a few miles from a nearby golf course to the meet. While the band played "Hail to the Chief," cars horns honked, sirens wailed, and spectators cheered and called in a "deafening din," he was presented with two trophies: one a bronze figure of the Goddess of Flight, and the other a silver loving cup inscribed with the names of the six reporters he had taken up in his aeroplane back in June. Then, against his objections, they lifted Atwood from the aeroplane and carried around the field "to the delight of the crowd and his very apparent embarrassment," said the *New York Times*. His parents were there watching. "I'm mighty glad to get my boy back again," his mother said. When he had arrived at the train station, she had sprung into his arms. And so once more that summer Harry Atwood received the cheers of the crowd.

The country had caught biplane fever. Reporters were stationed at airfields, some papers had regular "News of Aviation" sections, and there were aeroplanes buzzing around in many of the comic strips—it didn't take much elaboration to make hijinks out of trying to get off the ground. The *New York Times* speculated on coming of the "aeroplaning novel." There was a new drink in Boston: an "Atwood cocktail. It puts you up in the air."

Attending a performance of "Over Night" at the Shubert theater, Harry Atwood and his parents were spotted in their box. At the end of the first act, one of the actors stepped to the footlights, and pointing to Atwood's box, called for three cheers for the air hero. "Everyone turned and then the whole house came to its feet and cheered and cheered. Atwood bowed and smiled."

The summer of 1911 was over; the great heat had passed. At a South Boston playground, five hundred children, dressed in white, concluded the summer recreation program with a performance of two dances: one, a traditional maypole dance, and the other, a "biplane dance."

⌒ The Uncrossed Ocean

This is Harry Atwood in the first blush of his fame: "Mr. Atwood impresses one with his honesty, his sincerity, and his enthusiasm the minute he is introduced. He gives everyone a hearty shake of the hand and looks one squarely in the eye," reported the Portland, Maine, *Sunday Telegram.* "His talk resounds with the ring of truth and to meet him and talk with him is to believe in him."

He is a clean-living fellow, others said. Strictly on the square in all he does. "Though he has been an aviator less than a year, he already has the almost indefinable characteristics which have been said to mark the birdman, one of them being a modesty which leads the aviator to talk about anything, rather than what he has himself accomplished," said the Concord, New Hampshire, *Monitor.*

When he arrived in St. Louis to begin his flight to New York, he did not swagger into town the headline hero ready to meet the public. He hid in the train and had his manager lie, saying Atwood would be along on a later train. He dodged reception committees whenever possible. The *St. Louis Post-Dispatch* thought him "democratic but retiring."

But he could not hide anymore. Harry Atwood's life had become a newspaper life, a front-page headline life, everything gallant and brave. He was, in those years before World War I, a reporter's dream story: Atwood sets a new world record, Atwood says ocean flight is possible soon, Atwood to address chamber of commerce, Atwood gives a flying lesson to a young actress, Atwood followed by another admiring woman. Even the smallest incident was noted: Aviator in trolley collision; Famous flyer given speeding ticket on New York's Fifth Avenue—page one, the *New York Times*. (Fined five dollars for speeding twenty-eight miles an hour. "'Oh, shucks!' exclaimed Atwood . . .")

Reading the stories, one wonders to what degree the newspapers created Atwood by schooling him in the value of a good story. After a year or so in the headlines, the modest, shy, boyish aviator begins to speak with more drama. He promises great things. He tells reporters that he "expects to" have an announcement soon about some development now secret.

The reporters were under his spell. They never asked the hard questions, never qualified what he said. If he announced that he would soon fly across the continent, or across South America, or across the Atlantic, they reported it. Aviation was incredible, it was all so new. Who could really tell what was possible and what was not? So why not print it all? The modest aviator became one of those public figures, always on the move, making plans. Atwood wanted to be an inventor, and this public self may have been his first invention.

In the months following his record-breaking flights, Atwood made many announcements. He was pursuing the two top prizes in aviation: to fly from coast to coast, and to cross the Atlantic. "You can be assured that I will not rest content on my laurels. I will not be satisfied even after I have crossed the continent from New York City to San Francisco in the air. And I surely expect to do it," he told the *Illustrated Buffalo Express*. "I would rather ride through the air than eat."

To qualify for William Randolph Hearst's fifty-thousand-dollar-prize, the transcontinental flight had to be completed by October 10, 1911. Eight aviators, including Atwood, had announced that they would attempt the flight, an expensive expedition, requiring a staff of mechanics, a railroad car of parts to follow the aviator across the country, and perhaps a spare aeroplane. Orville Wright thought it would cost at least twenty-five thousand dollars. After walking out on his manager in New York City, Atwood faced many difficulties attracting backers. He would not fly to someone else's schedule, not risk his life to entertain a carnival crowd. He had less than a month to find the money and put together a team, and that assumed a flawless three-week flight.

Atwood had cut himself free from all promoters. He parted with Burgess when his contract ran out, leaving with a thousand-dollar bonus. Charles Hamilton, his Atlantic City flying partner, would not be joining him as announced. Hamilton had returned to the sanitarium that fall. He would recover to fly and crash a few more times in the next two years. In

January 1914, the survivor of sixty-three crashes died in bed from a lung hemorrhage. He was twenty-eight. (And neither would Atwood fly across the country with his mother, as some had reported.)

Even though he was the best qualified flyer in the country, Atwood couldn't raise the money for the flight. What promoter would want anything to do with him?

Four aviators actually started the journey, and only one finished, long after the Hearst deadline. Cal Rodgers, a Wright brothers school classmate, flew coast to coast in twelve crashes, an aerial boxing match: forty-nine days to fly 4,231 miles. He lost thirteen and one half days to repairs, and eleven to weather. Only the vertical rudder and the oil drip pan survived the entire trip. His plane was almost completely rebuilt every fourteen days: he used up eight propellers, six sets of wings, three seats, two radiators, two engines, four propeller chains, and so on. (This was still better than the first transcontinental auto trip which had taken sixty-five days in 1903.)

Rodgers broke Atwood's distance record on October 10 in Marshall, Missouri. If any flight from this short era is remembered, it is Rodgers's. A reproduction of his aeroplane, the *Vin Fiz*, named for his grape drink sponsor, is in the Smithsonian's National Air & Space Museum.

While Rodgers was crossing Arizona, Atwood announced that in three weeks he would begin an even greater flight. He would fly across South America for one hundred thousand dollars, crossing from Brazil to Chile. "I may cross the Andes Mountains, but that will depend upon what conditions are prevailing," he told the *New York Times*. The short article didn't say who was offering the money. Nothing ever came of it.

The problem with aviation today is that too many promises are made that are impossible to fulfill, wrote Albert S. LeVino in *Harper's Weekly*. Le-Vino was the manager of Wright-trained pilot Frank Coffyn. "Undoubtedly the reader, as he opened his morning newspaper, has read from time to time the announcement that 'John Jones, the famous aviator, will today fly over the city' or 'will start on a record-breaking cross-country journey' . . . Thereafter nothing more has been heard of John Jones's promised flight." This is crying wolf, LeVino said.

"It has long been the marvel of many who know the care with which newspapers are edited that space is so readily forthcoming for almost any kind of statement so long as it has the magic word 'aviation' in it," he said. "There seems to be a three-hundred-and-sixty-five-day-long silly season against which not even the sanest city editor appears immune."

In later years this would be known as selling blue sky, vending nothing

but empty air, promising much, hoping to convince enough people to finance a dream into reality.

Atwood had other announcements. He was determined to be the first
aviator to cross the Atlantic. All his activities were directed to that goal.
He proposed a flying school. "I should be at the head of the school, but
would only give what personal instruction was necessary. I do not like to
teach myself, and while the school was in session I should probably take
long cross-country flights." The school would be part of larger plans. He
found backers.

The General Aviation Company announced itself to potential investors in February 1912 as "New England's latest and greatest aviation enterprise." Harry Atwood signed for three years. The company bought an
old racetrack, renaming it Atwood Park, and a dock for hydro-aeroplanes
at the shore. They took over a defunct company's aeroplane manufacturing plant in Boston where students would learn aeroplane building and
mechanics; and it claimed $250,000 in capital, offered in preferred and
common stock.

The company's newspaper and prospectus, the *Aviation News*, was an
exercise in blue sky promotion—promising blue sky and then filling it
with aeroplanes. Later in the season the company expected to have
branch schools in Bretton Woods, New Hampshire, Newport, Rhode Island, and possibly Puerto Rico. It expected to conduct research with the
"company's own engineers," to build Curtiss- and Wright-type aeroplanes,
to establish the *Aviation News* as a "full-fledged public journal of aviation,"
and even to do exhibition flying—"no other form of entertainment will
ever appeal to the masses of the people more than aviation." All that
would only be the opening act. "The General Aviation Company proposes
to be a pioneer in hydro-aeroplane work, as it expects to have one of its instructors or students make the first attempt to cross the Atlantic . . ."

Atwood was that instructor. He was also the company engineer, or as
the newspaper prospectus said, "a number of the company's organization
have served their time technically in the big electrical factories." A number that was likely one. He was also the editor of the newspaper and the
chief instructor with no intention of teaching.

It was, after all, an aviation school—"Students flying every day, weather
permitting," read the advertisement. "The company expects to provide
instruction for at least 250 aviation pupils during the spring, summer and
fall," which would make it by far the largest school in the country. If all
those students succeeded, it would triple the number of licensed aviators
in the United States.

Atwood Park, the aerodrome, was an old racetrack in Saugus, Massachusetts, with a fifty-room hotel, which had been shut down years before when the town put an end to the gambling and prostitution. "The field is within a 5 cent trolley fare of Boston and Lynn," noted the prospectus, and was at the "western edge of the famous Lynn Marsh, containing 10 square miles of level land."

Once the school opened, more than thirty students languished, waiting to fly, said Melvin W. Hodgdon, who was a student at the school in May 1912. About half waited for Wright training, given by either Arch Freeman or Atwood on the one Wright aeroplane available, the plane Atwood had flown from St. Louis to New York. "With only one plane for two instructors, bad weather, strong winds, mechanical problems, and failure of the instructors to show up, it was thus a fortunate pupil who received more than two lessons a week," said Hodgdon. Since four hundred minutes was assumed the required flying time to complete the course, it meant three or four months to graduate."

H. Roy Waite had managed to take two lessons with Atwood. On each of the five minute flights, Atwood did not say one word, in the air or on the ground. Waite went to learn elsewhere. The prospects were worse for the Curtiss students, who were stuck running up and down the field in a "ground hog," an aeroplane that never left the ground. With the instructor sitting on the wing to prevent a student from hopping the plane into the air, "the plane roared down the field at thirty-odd miles an hour," said Hodgdon. "The run lasted about 15 seconds but it took usually ten or fifteen minutes to position the plane for the return 'flight.' Lessons were only given when there was no wind and the Wright plane was not using the runway. Few students got more than three or four runs a week."

The school also advertised instruction in a Bleriot monoplane. The Bleriot was rumored, but never delivered—"Sr. Guiseppe Colucci was in Europe purchasing" one, the students were told.

Atwood Park did have one modest triumph: the first air mail in New England. Atwood flew a postmaster a few miles to Lynn carrying eight hundred letters and postcards. The postmaster missed the mark and dropped the mail in a ditch. Arch Freeman made the next attempt with the company's "Skyline Mail Service." This time the mail fell in the ocean. It was later retrieved. No other deliveries are on record.

But the real business of the General Aviation Company was raising enough money for Atwood to fly the ocean. In January, with dramatic flair, the company announced that it was secretly building an aeroplane for a flight starting in August. "The machine is being constructed in secret, the various parts in different factories, and the details of its construction have not been divulged," said the *New York Times*. According to the same article, Atwood's manager elaborated:

"'Actual tests have been made. A man has actually gone through the experience of applying himself to active work for more than two days on a stretch. By this I mean that he has had no respite, no time for sleep, no opportunity for taking his attention from his work. The test has been made with a task certainly as difficult as that of staying at the helm of the machine for forty-eight hours or more. Atwood will go into training to make himself fit to stand a similar strain.

"'Atwood will subsist largely on malted milk tablets, and will use thermos bottles for hot or cold drinks while in the air. The aviator, wearing heavy, fur-lined canvas clothing, will be housed in a covered body of a preparation of celluloid, so that he will be protected from the force of the weather.'" The small cabin would be heated with a radiator. There was no mention of any navigational instruments.

The General Aviation Company hoped to convince the secretary of the navy to assign six cruisers, arrayed across the ocean, to accompany Atwood. He would fly from Newfoundland to Ireland, reportedly 2,450 miles; by one account, he would land on the ocean to rest and have two meals, and by others, he would need the ships for several gas stops. He was inventing an inflatable rubber pontoon.

"'As for the machine, I will say that it is to be altogether different, in many ways, from those that are now known,'" his manager said. "'In short it is to be equipped with an apparatus, or with a device, hitherto unknown, which is expected to make the handling of the aeroplane on a trans-Atlantic trip a more simple matter than it would be in any machine which is in use today.'" Other aviators hearing this might guess that they were making claims to a working automatic stabilizer or autopilot. The first such devices were actually perfected years later, first by Orville Wright in 1913, and then in the breakthrough design of Elmer Sperry the following year. Or his manager might have been talking of an invention Atwood would patent three years later, a paired set of propellers, both forward and rearward of the wings so that "their pulling and pushing actions respectively will cooperate" and "the balance of the machine will be automatically maintained by their normal operation."

Atwood's managers hinted at much and told nothing—a dance of the veils for possible investors. They were building a single engine hydro-aeroplane, with another engine in reserve, ready to be switched on. "'Atwood's machine is expected to make a speed of fifty miles an hour on the

average.'" The wind was optimistically estimated to add another sixty or
seventy miles an hour. Apparently, no one expected a headwind. "'Atwood's machine will carry enough gasoline to last throughout the entire
trip and allow some extra for contingencies,'" his manager claimed. To
any aviator this scheme—to carry all that gas—unveiled the impracticality
of the entire plan. Lifting the fuel and then flying with a powerful, reliable engine, were the limitations that kept aviators from trying the ocean.

The proposed flight was just a come-on, said LeVino. "It is on such
publicity that many aviation stock companies are formed . . . Rich as is the
future of the flying machine, the aeroplane industry can no more support these get-rich-quick parasites than can any other business."

Frank Coffyn, in *Harper's Weekly*, scoffed at the plan, while not naming
Atwood. "He says he's going to take two hundred gallons of gasoline with
him. There's a weight of 1,400 pounds to start with in fuel alone, not
making any mention of lubricant, food, etc. And Breguet, who managed
last October to lift a total weight of about 1,400 pounds beside his machine, stayed aloft only five minutes! Possible to cross the Atlantic in an
aeroplane very soon?" Anything's possible, said Coffyn, "but only Heaven
knows when it will be accomplished!"

When Atwood made his cross-country flights he flew with no more
than twelve gallons and his aeroplane weighed about fourteen hundred
pounds.

On the first day of the new year in 1912, Harry Atwood was sinking in the
bay off Lynn, Massachusetts. Two weeks earlier he had flown 130 miles
over the water, which the magazine *Aero* said was a new world's hydro-
aeroplane duration record—two hours, forty minutes—and just eight
miles short of the longest distance anyone had flown over the water. He
had used every drop of gas in his tank to fly from Lynn to Narragansett,
Rhode Island. He "was chilled through by the biting rush of the wind"
and the first thing he did after landing was to light a cigar. On Christmas
Day he had entertained twenty-five thousand people in Rhode Island
with exhibition flights; by then he had his name in large letters on the
lower wing—he couldn't break free of exhibitions. But on the first day of
the year in which he planned to fly to Europe, he was clinging on to his
sinking aeroplane.

"He got up only a few feet when his motor stopped suddenly, and
the wind whirled the aeroplane around and carried it out over the bay,"
said the *New York Times*. "Atwood made frantic efforts to get his engine

working again, and finally it popped a few times." But then it stopped and he struck the water. One of his pontoons was taking on water.

"No boats were in sight, and as the machine began sinking on the side of the defective pontoon, Atwood made haste to disentangle himself from the aeroplane." He removed one of his two suits of clothes and climbed out on the wing toward the good pontoon. "Atwood's weight, however, carried that pontoon also under, and he was at the point of trying to swim through freezing waves" when he was rescued by two fishermen who raced out to him in a power boat. He was helpless from the cold when the fishermen reached the plane. He was taken to a nearby home "suffering from exposure and immersion." The plane sank and was later recovered.

He had been trying to fly north, about eighty miles, to Portland, Maine. The Portland Board of Trade had offered a large prize, and thousands had been watching the sky for him. This was a route he might fly at the start of his ocean crossing.

Talk of a secret aeroplane that could carry three-quarters of a ton of gasoline was good publicity. And perhaps his company *was* working on such designs, but by spring Atwood didn't have that aeroplane. No one in America did. If he was going to fly the ocean in August, he needed a big aeroplane soon. He visited Orville Wright a couple of times, but Atwood couldn't interest him in the project. "They invented the airplane, but don't know what to do with it," Atwood said, voicing a common complaint about the Wright brothers.

In April Atwood announced another secret plan. This one was in the safe of his former employer, Starling Burgess. The plan called for the largest biplane yet built in America. The span of the upper wing was two-thirds longer than Atwood's Burgess-Wright Model F. Atwood had designed pontoons for the plane and it would have a new feature, "a pneumatic life-boat fitted with five air-tight compartments . . . placed on the lower supporting plane beside the aviator," said *Aero*. The aeroplane would carry a ton of gasoline, more than 250 gallons, and use a single seventy-horsepower Renault motor. Atwood would fly from Boston to St. John, New Brunswick, and from there follow the steamer lanes eighteen hundred miles to the Irish coast.

The plan was presented with the usual blue sky optimism. "The estimated air speed of the biplane is 50 miles an hour. The currents of east-flowing air at certain levels, Atwood believes, will add a like speed to his flight, making his actual time in air less than 24 hours," said *Aero*.

"Atwood states that the greater part of the $15,000 necessary to finance the trip has been pledged. The contract . . . calls for the completion of the biplane within 50 days from the date of the actual order." Everything existed in the ether; the money was not in hand but pledged, the contract awaited an actual order. And the flight plan itself had one flaw: Atwood couldn't carry enough gas to get him all the way across. At best he could cover fifteen hundred of the eighteen hundred miles. Atwood still hoped to enlist the United States Navy to bridge the gap.

On April 10, he met with President Taft at the White House. He presented his case to Taft, the secretary of the navy, the rear admiral, and Taft's secretary of state, Philander C. Knox, who believed that aviation could bring about international unity. Atwood wanted the president to assign a scout cruiser or a torpedo boat to accompany him across the Atlantic. After flying one thousand miles, he would land on the ocean and refill his tanks from the ship.

Taft refused him. The navy was not going to be an ocean-going filling station, he said. There was nothing in it for the navy. If Atwood dies, they have assisted a civilian to his death. If he succeeds, the glory is his alone.

Atwood had thought a great deal about what an ocean flight would be like. In a story he wrote for the *Saturday Evening Post*, he talks little about the logistics or the possible routes, but dwells on the physical hardship that the aviator would have to endure:

"He may be obliged to alight on the water during a frightful storm when the waves are running high. He may be obliged to abandon his aerial progress at any time and permanently . . . until assistance can be reached. He may encounter widespread fogs or calm, mirrorlike seas— one almost as annoying as the other—and in any case he will have to sail through one long lonely night . . .

"He will undoubtedly experience great difficulties in retaining his normal physical and mental equilibrium throughout many hours of relentless, nerve-racking and continuous vigilance—without for an instant escaping the deafening roar of a mighty engine. And for at least twenty-five hours he must sit in one position listening to the roar of that powerful engine, straining his eyes through daylight and darkness to keep in touch with all indications of trouble, enduring prolonged exposure to the elements and fighting off an ever-increasing drowsiness.

"The length of the vigilance, together with the incessant and hypnotic roar of the engine, must sooner or later produce a physical and mental fatigue that will be well-nigh over-powering unless he has some means of fortifying himself against it.

"Each and every aspirant to the undertaking of flying across the ocean, I presume, feels that he is peculiarly and individually qualified to go through the ordeal. . . . It is doubted, however, whether any of them fully appreciates the constant and grinding strain the mentality of the first transocean airman must endure—unless he has means to fight it off—throughout the long hours of the journey."

The ocean awaited Atwood as a prolonged cross-country flight without mercy. There would be no escape, no landing in a quiet pasture to rest his ears, no safety if the least little thing should break. A snapped control cable could set him down alone on the sea, a sea which could be calm or in "turmoil," and he would be far from where any fishermen might race out to rescue him. The entire article has a funereal tone, far removed from the skylarking aviator who flew down to see the boat races in New London. The ocean, as Atwood imagined it, would magnify all the strain of his record flights and could break him.

Around the time he wrote this article, he had been flying with Grover Loening, the aeroplane designer employed by the Wright Company. Loening, with his long aviation experience, later singled out a flight with Atwood as "my closest approach to a fatal accident":

"The Wright flying boat we were testing at Toledo on the lake had been ordered by the Navy, and we were measuring full-speed runs about one hundred feet above the water on a very bumpy day," Loening recalled. "The tail was held by outriggers, and although it did vibrate somewhat, according to all the then-existent Wright company data it was strong enough. However, the plane had been out in the water and on the beach for some days, and the fittings may have been rusty or had a flaw in them. For, without any warning, after a particularly severe bump the entire stabilizer and elevator unit ripped away from the outrigger supports and the plane plunged to the water.

"We hit nose-on at an angle of about forty-five degrees, and the entire front, seven or eight feet of the hull, including our seats, to which we were still strapped, plowed bow first into the water and then stopped and literally bounced back out again—with lots of water in the hull, but with the boat structure and bottom intact, and Atwood and I still in our seats, soaking wet, a bit dazed, but uninjured.

"The plane was still afloat, and we could see that the tail had dangled on the control cables, acting, no doubt, as an air brake to help parachute our dive, so that the actual shock of hitting had been materially reduced. If this accident had happened on land, there would have been no question of the fatal results. The coolness and competence Atwood displayed on this occasion were further proof of his ability."

This may have been Loening's closest call, but it would be a minor entry if Atwood's more serious scrapes were listed:

Four crashes: two in Atlantic City, followed by one in the Burgess plane he was demonstrating for the military, and the crash with Loening.

Four dangerous engine failures: over Brooklyn during his license test; over downtown Baltimore during an exhibition, when he was able to re-start his engine and head for the harbor in case it stopped again; over Lynn Bay on New Year's day; and on his next attempt to fly to Portland, Maine. ("Despite his close inspection of the face of death, the aviator seemed not in the least unnerved," reported an impressed Biddeford, Maine, *Daily Journal*. Gliding down to a safe landing in the woods of Maine, Atwood estimated "his chances of meeting death when his motor stopped being three out of five.")

Several forced landings due to high winds, including his first New Hampshire flight; and also on his second flight into Maine, part of the "hoodoo" that kept him from reaching Portland.

Other forced landings due to mechanical emergencies, including his landing in a tight spot in Nyack, New York, and a time when he lost oil in Pittsfield, New Hampshire, due to a loose bolt and dropped so suddenly some feared he had crashed.

Three times that he almost sank with his ship: the first Atlantic City crash; the January plunge into Lynn Bay; and at an August 1912 exhibition in the Portland, Maine, harbor when North Pole explorer Rear Admiral Robert E. Peary was part of the rescue party. To keep the lower wing above the waves, Atwood hopped from pontoon to pontoon trying to steady the aeroplane.

Two other water mishaps when he had been lost on Lake Erie, once out of gas, another time hiding out from a storm.

One mid-air collision, with Eugene Ely at an air meet in Canton, Ohio, in September 1911. Ely, circling at one hundred feet, was caught by a gust of wind and lost control, crashing. Atwood was hit as he was taking off. Both aviators had only minor injuries; Ely had a black eye and some cuts.

There were numerous other close calls, aborted take-offs, landings on small fields dodging crowds, avoiding people on beaches (Cleveland, Atlantic City), flying near tree level on that hot day outside Baltimore, turbulent windy rides, and other incidents that went unrecorded.

The danger of flying at a time when aviation could be defined as "a mere succession of unforeseen incidents" was starting to wear on Atwood. The close calls were piling up. He had said he could be killed if he contin-ued to fly; it was too risky. He wanted to walk away from flying, walk away before he was killed trying to avoid a crowd as he landed or took off, or before he was betrayed by his machine. But he was famous for flying. And he needed the money. If he could capture a big record, he could fund the research he dreamed of doing.

A few of his fellow aviators thought that Atwood didn't like to fly. "Of all the fliers connected with the Burgess Company . . . Atwood liked flying the least," Helen Bolster, company secretary, told Bartlett Gould, a historian of early aviation. "She had the feeling that he had a repressed, perhaps subconscious but none the less real dread of flying, and forced himself to fly as a matter of ambition, pride, or similar drive," said Gould. H. Roy Waite, who had taken lessons with Atwood and later bought his Burgess-Wright biplane, agreed with this assessment. If they are correct, said Gould, "then Atwood must have been possessed of a courage of a rare and high type." But they may have misread his nervous nature, his tension before flights, his exactitude in the air, his need for quiet once on the ground, and his distaste for competition and exhibition flying.

Most aviators in Atwood's time had short careers. They stopped flying after a couple of years. Of all those who flew in 1911, Earle Ovington claimed to be the only one still flying nine years later (and he had taken a break). Some "officers find that it gets on their nerves and they become practically worthless as aviators," Hap Arnold told the chairman of a congressional committee studying military aviation. "And he must quit or he will kill himself." Arnold was speaking of himself. In the year and a half since he left the Wrights' school, Arnold had set records, but flying had taken a toll on him. A near-crash left him too nervous to fly. "I cannot even look at a machine in the air without feeling that some accident is going to happen to it." (Arnold conquered his dread and flew again four years later.)

For many flyers, after a number of close calls and after seeing friends killed, a light went on: I may die—I could be killed. This light usually went on when a flyer reached his late twenties or so, right around the time of marriage. "You didn't plan to continue flying after you were married—unless you were an optimist," Arnold said.

Harry Atwood was approaching thirty. He was still flying exhibitions, raising money for his ocean flight, but by the summer of 1912, he was towing his aeroplane from one engagement to the next. He towed it from the White Mountains to Sherbrooke, Quebec, to the lakes in New Hampshire to Bangor, and Portland, Maine. When asked about his record flights of just one year ago, last summer's hero told a Portland, Maine, newspaper: "There were a good many mornings when I was not particularly enthusiastic about starting out but it had to be done and so I would get into my machine and continue on."

The crowds that turned out to see him were sometimes disappointed, as the *News and Critic* in Laconia, New Hampshire, reported. Atwood had made four flights one Sunday and finished up around four in the afternoon, when most people were still making their way to the resort at The Weirs, which had hired him. No one knew he was done. "The large crowd was kept waiting fully three hours until all the ice cream and peanuts had been consumed and at a late hour it dawned upon them that they had bought a lemon. Sorry that they did not see you fly Harry, but advise them next time to take a bucket lunch and stay all day. The waiting and rubbering to see the 'plane' thing go was indeed tiresome."

Maybe the truth about Atwood's flying was a double truth: maybe he did dread it—as he dreaded fire and, perhaps, deep water—but maybe he also was drawn to flying, and, once up and away from the crowds and promoters, he could bring his taut, nervous energy to a restful focus. At a July 4, 1912, exhibition in the White Mountains, he flew several thousand feet over the summit of Mt. Monadnock (3,165 feet). It was a story that he told for fifty years, and it was transformed in the telling to a higher peak and the altitude record for 1911 (which was actually 12,825 feet). He had flown up there chasing an eagle, he said. The details of the story may have become elastic, but it was probably an accurate report of how he felt—like the eagle, like the aviator who had flown the highest that year.

The whole grand enterprise of the General Aviation Company folded on June 2, 1912, just five months after its boldly announced beginning. Atwood and Freeman flew away in the Wright biplane. "Many local people lost money on this, having taken stock," a Lynn newspaper later reported. Not one student had finished his training.

The General Aviation Corporation was a blue sky enterprise that set a pattern for so many of Atwood's later businesses: chartered for one purpose—a flying school—it provided income for a much larger undertaking—crossing the ocean. Some investors may have believed in the good of having an aviation school in their town; some may have believed in the Atlantic flight. The appeal could be tailored to the listener and wherever he placed his confidence. Great things were promised, stock was sold, people lost money, and Atwood headed west to start a new business.

Atwood went to Ohio, where several ventures kept him flying on the Great Lakes. He still wanted to fly the ocean. In 1913, Lord Northcliffe in England offered a ten-thousand-pound prize for an ocean flight. Atwood was conferring with Orville Wright again. Chances of making the flight were much better than they had been just two years earlier when Atwood had first met with him. Orville believed the flight could be made from Newfoundland in twenty-five hours. But the longest anyone had stayed aloft in an aeroplane was eleven hours. The old problem remained: whether to build an aeroplane that could lift a ton of gas or a seaplane able to refill from passing ships. "As for me, I should want a good life boat along," said Atwood.

Glenn Curtiss, America's leading seaplane builder, was the closest to building an ocean-worthy plane. After a summer of tests and nearly thirty design changes, Curtiss had achieved the magic number, lifting twenty-two hundred pounds of sandbags in a test. The biplane's top wing spanned seventy-four feet, the largest yet built in the country, and as large as the plane Burgess planned to build for Atwood. A Royal Navy pilot would fly, and the United States Navy would deploy ships along the course to aid in navigation and, if needed, rescue.

In August 1914 the Curtiss plane was ready. Then war came to Europe. All flights were off. The co-pilot, a trained engine mechanic George E. A. Hallet, remembering his youthful optimism fifty years later, doubts they would have made it. There was a whole range of problems no one had even realized were problems: carburetor icing, ice build-up on the wings, vibrations from the engines shaking apart the fuel and water connections over a prolonged twenty-six-hour flight. As Hallet recalled, he had special overalls made with eighteen-inch-deep pockets, and stuffed them with "plenty of tire tape and safety wire and LePage's glue, which was good for fuel line joints." He planned to crawl out on the lower wing and replace spark plugs—in flight, with the engine running. A plug was often good for only an hour or two. "Wearing a lineman's belt and having rings fastened in suitable places around the engines, I could hook on and have use of both hands . . . Of course I had to take some nasty shocks in disconnecting the spark plug wire and replacing it." It was an era in which aviators proposed to conquer the ocean with deep pockets filled with tape, glue, wire, and other quick-fix remedies.

After the war, the United States Navy made the first flight across the Atlantic in 1919. Three Curtiss flying boats set out from Long Island to Newfoundland to the Azores to Lisbon to Plymouth, England. The navy stationed ships every fifty miles along the route. One plane made it to England twenty-three days later.

"Every morning brings its new hero," a doctor, already jaded with aviation in 1910, had dismissively written in the *Scientific American*.

Harry Atwood never crossed the ocean—not even as a passenger.

⌒ Father, Hero, Liar

When the United States entered World War I in 1917, Harry Atwood did not serve. Experienced aviators were scarce, but the navy did not want the thirty-one-year-old. He took the standard physical examination, which, he said, included having a gun fired off, without warning, just behind the ear to see if he was the nervous type. "Any time you fire a gun off behind my ear I'll jump right through the roof," Atwood said. They had it all wrong—you needed quick reflexes to fly, he said. But they didn't see it his way until it was too late to become a pilot.

Quite a story, and one that differs from all other accounts of World War I induction tests, with the possible exception of some British examinations that tested would-be pilots with sudden noises—but no guns. No matter. When he told this story in the 1930s, it was enthusiastically reported.

"Father could sure sling it," says Katrina, laughing until she has to cough. "Yeah, he believed his stories by the time he told them."

Spoken like a daughter who was born as her father was leaving town under suspicion.

⌢ The Art of Navigating the Air

Every morning brings its new hero. On the morning Harry Atwood was still a hero, he made his declaration of independence.

"By October 1 positively I expect to have given up all exhibition flying. I expect to buy a farm somewhere and settle down with half a dozen machines to perfect the art of flying—not the science, mind you; not the design of the machines, nor the power of the engines—simply the art of navigating the air," he told the *Boston Post* in August 1911.

"This may seem queer to many of my friends, but here's the reasons. Aeroplaning is in the first of three stages through which all modern inventions seem to pass. The three are, first, an exhibition stage; second, a pleasure stage, and, third, a commercial stage.

"Now, as I have stated, the aeroplane, even at the present time, in spite of all the improvements that have been made of recent years is only in the first stage of development. The second is fast approaching, and it is this stage which I am anticipating. For in the second stage flying must be made safe enough to permit a person to feel that they are undergoing only slightly more risk running an aeroplane for pleasure than they would be running an automobile."

An ideal view. He would repair to his own aviator's Monticello and become an artist of flight. But he couldn't give up exhibitions—he needed the money—and he didn't settle down. His pursuit of flight led him to four cities and towns in the next four years, the travels of a blue sky salesman in the early era of flight.

For Sandusky, Ohio, Harry Atwood was a prize catch, a boost to the city, the early-twentieth-century equivalent of the scramble to win the railroad or the state university. He came promising an aeroplane industry, and, initially, he did not ask for one cent of investment.

He was in the local news daily in the spring and summer of 1913 and spoke like a city father, another midwestern civic booster. "I hope to develop an industry that will mean much to the advancement of our city. I say 'our,' because I now consider myself a resident of Sandusky," he said. When a nearby town was flooded that spring, he joined a rescue party, risking his life when his boat nearly overturned and his party was stranded overnight.

Atwood had designed and was building a flying boat aeroplane. He planned to run a summer passenger carrying business with his planes. The *Sandusky Register* took a booster's pride in the aeroplane, which, they said, "bids fair to revolutionize the flying game," and, if successful, "will make this city famous the world over as the home of the first craft of this kind." No description or photo was ever provided in the many stories. The first flying boat had a waiting customer in Providence, Rhode Island. "This fact shows that the boat is almost an assured success or else [the customer] would not have invested so much money in it," said the *Register*.

Another Sandusky paper, the *Star Journal*, also praised "what experts declare to be the greatest 'air-water' machine ever constructed," but at least offered a photo and a description. It was a typical flying boat of the era, much like Glenn Curtiss's designs. The biplane had a forty-foot wingspan and rested in the water on a boat-shaped hull. With an eighty-horsepower Curtiss engine, the sixteen-hundred-pound plane was capable of flying sixty miles an hour.

Even with a waiting customer, Atwood was in a dispute almost immediately. In a test flight, a gear in the drive shaft came loose, sending the left propeller tearing into the wing. He faulted the local company that had made the drive shaft, returned it, and refused to pay. They replied that they had designed it to his specifications, and they took Atwood to court. He maintained a statesman-like poise, saying, "I have imbibed the booster spirit and as a 'booster,' I shall refuse to say anything that might tend in any way to injure a Sandusky concern."

The Roberts Motor Company had the sheriff seize the plane, just as Atwood was going to fly it for the customer, who was in town from Rhode Island. Atwood was "downhearted." His customer returned home. The sheriff's deputies left the plane out, uncovered, in a heavy rain, rusting the guy wires and ruining the engine's electrical equipment, Atwood said. "The machine has been seriously damaged and I would not risk making the flight." The *Star Journal* added, "there has been an intimation that a suit for damage will result."

"I do not see how I can remain in Sandusky," Atwood said. "If a man who is doing nothing worse than attend to his own business and invest his own money in it cannot do these things without the danger of being tripped up every time he tries to accomplish something, it is about time for him to leave the community."

That got the attention of the city's business groups. They were "considerably agitated" about losing the proposed aeroplane factory. "Atwood is the best advertisement Sandusky ever had," said one businessman. "For months—indeed, ever since Atwood announced his intention of remaining in Sandusky—when strangers have come to town the first thing they have spoken of was the fact that Atwood was here, and inquired about the progress of his flying boat." The businessman's faith was borne out only a day after his statement, when the *New York World* ran a story about Atwood's Sandusky activities. The Sandusky Business Men's Association settled the dispute.

The next week, they were rewarded with a record flight, two hundred miles over Lake Erie. For six hours the world worried while Atwood was lost. He was turned around in a thick haze until he saw smoke from a steamer and followed that. He had flown in his flying boat, the *Aermaide*, which he now owned. (The delivery was so delayed, the customer cancelled his order.)

The *Register* celebrated. For the hours he was lost, Sandusky's name went out to the world. "Nearly every large newspaper in the country was keeping the wires hot with inquiries . . . Atwood is an international figure and anything concerning him is regarded as good news anywhere." The newspaper proposed that the local ad club debate the advertising value of that flight. "What would it have cost Sandusky, in dollars and cents, to have secured like publicity if such publicity could have been purchased at all?

"What was that little trip across the lake worth to the city?

"Let's welcome Atwood," said the *Register*. "It would not be out of place for every factory whistle to be blown when Atwood enters the bay. Bells might also be rung."

Rival cities were trying to lure him away. A Sandusky citizen started a subscription to raise money for a testimonial. The ad club appointed a committee to aid Atwood in his business, asking him what he needed. He

Atwood at age 27, at the controls of the Wright Model B. (*National Air and Space Museum, Smithsonian Institution.*)

Classmates playing pranks on Atwood at the Wrights' flying school: They convinced him to whitewash a line several hundred feet long. Left to right: Howard Gill, Capt. Paul Beck, Lt. Thomas "Dashing" Milling, Phil Parmalee, and Art Welsh. (*Bart Gould Collection.*)

Another prank: teaching Atwood to develop a sense of balance. Cal Rodgers, seated, keeps score. (*Special Collections and Archives, Wright State University.*)

THE FLYING LESSON

Atwood instructing a pupil

Burgess Company and Curtis

Flying School

Squantum

BURGESS AEROPLANES ARE USED BY

U. S. WAR DEPARTMENT   HARRY N. ATWOOD

C. GRAHAME-WHITE   CHAS. K. HAMILTON

MR. AND MRS. MARTIN   CLIFFORD B. HARMON

Atwood's first job out of aviation school, chief instructor at Starling Burgess's new flying school. (*Bart Gould Collection.*)

Atwood taking off from the south lawn of the White House after landing and meeting President Taft, July 14, 1911. (*National Air and Space Museum, Smithsonian Institution.*)

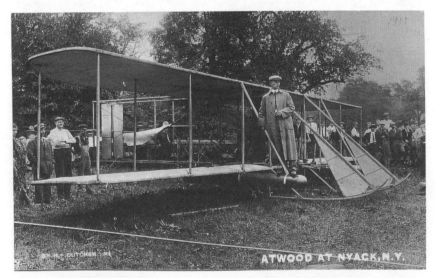

Forced landing at Nyack, N.Y., near the end of Atwood's record-breaking St. Louis to New York City flight, 1911. (*Courtesy of Frank Trask.*)

A hero's welcome at the Harvard-Boston Aero Meet, 1911. (*Courtesy of Katrina Atwood Copeland.*)

Crowned "King of the Air," Atwood was presented with a bronze figure of the Goddess of Flight, and a silver loving cup inscribed with the names of the six reporters who had survived his relay flight. (*Courtesy of Edward Young.*)

The most prominent aviators of the day, a 1911 postcard. (*Courtesy of Frank Trask.*)

Harry Atwood and his mother, Florence. (*Courtesy of Katrina Atwood Copeland.*)

Two views of the much-modified Curtiss F-type Flying Boat, which was rejected by the Navy, circa 1919. (*Peter M. Bowers Collection.*)

needed a dock and a hangar. They immediately got him dock space and began building a hangar. At a testimonial meeting in Atwood's honor, he was "presented with a purse of gold."

"I want to express my thanks to the people of Sandusky for the practical moral support they have given me," said Atwood. "Whatever I may do hereafter will be done with the idea of advancing the interests of Sandusky, as a city." But the competition was heating up. "I don't want to leave Sandusky if I possibly can help it," he was saying just a few weeks later, sounding like a baseball team owner on the eve of decamping.

He needed more from the city. He planned an aviation school, a passenger service, and an aeroplane factory. Stock would be sold. Atwood would give up exhibition flying (again). He asked the Business Men's Association to supply the land and the building for the factory. "The manufacture of flying machines is an industry that is still in its infancy," said his supporter, the *Register*. "Those who have followed the game say that it is sure to assume proportions that will place it on even footing with the automobile. This may be several years yet, but the time is coming and here is a chance for Sandusky to get in on the ground floor."

A week later, Sandusky lost its prize; it had been outbid. The Toledo Railways and Light Company had offered Atwood buildings for his flying boat factory and room to start the "largest school of aviation" in the country.

He had been in Sandusky only six months. Atwood flew to Toledo, facing a strong headwind. "The people stood and watched the birdman disappear around the Marblehead lighthouse and everyone felt sorry that he was leaving," said the *Register*. "There was probably not one in that scattered gathering of people who did not silently wish Atwood success in his new field of endeavor, in as much as it could not be arranged to keep him here."

"Atwood encounters unfavorable winds," said the headline, accidently prophetic.

Toledo had won itself a hero-entrepreneur, and Atwood had won for himself a nearly ideal set-up. He had, after all, dictated his requirements. Toledo's prize quickly tarnished—the grand plans of autumn gave way to a small scandal by winter.

Atwood was again flying exhibitions. He tested aeroplanes for the Wright Company. The factory and school never developed. He was also experimenting on an aerial torpedo for the government, he said. The unmanned aeroplane would be guided by a clock to release its bomb. There is no record, beyond this brief mention, of Atwood's design.

Later during World War I, other inventors came close to perfecting the aerial torpedo. Elmer Sperry, having invented an automatic gyrostabilizer in 1914, combined that with a steering gyro and began work on an aerial torpedo in 1916. The following year the navy awarded Sperry a two-hundred-thousand-dollar development contract. By the armistice, Sperry was still working out the defects in the small pilotless biplane bombs.

In January Atwood announced that he would marry again, this time to Ruth L. Satterthwaite from Reading, Pennsylvania. The press called it "a genuine romance of the air." They had met in Maine two years earlier, in 1912, when Atwood had gone to Maine for the wedding of a fraternity brother. She was attending finishing school in Boston and was said to be "the author of considerable literary work and interested in music." She joined him later that month at a nearby resort and they flew for more than an hour.

A year later, Atwood was on the train to his exhibition flights at The Weirs, New Hampshire, and met her again. They flew together for half an hour. Two years later, as Atwood told it, the same flight had lengthened to two hours and twenty minutes (much as it had in the story of his first flight when Orville Wright had gone to town).

"The nervy young woman's" flight was big news back in her hometown of Reading—the first woman to fly in New Hampshire, said the press, and maybe the youngest to fly in the country. She had asked repeatedly to fly with Atwood. Spectators "thought that she would hesitate when the time came," but "she had the courage to do what thousands of men would not think of attempting." She planned to fly again the next day.

Her parents did not approve. Her mother wired her, advising her to fly no more. Catharine and Alfred H. Satterthwaite were hard-working Quakers with good standing in Reading. Catharine's father, the Honorable Joel B. Wanner, was a Civil War veteran who had been mayor twice. Alfred was one of F. W. Woolworth's earliest partners, one of the "dime store pioneers." As a partner, Alfred had invested in and ran the Reading Woolworth, and he had prospered along with the company. He was a Mason and a Rotarian. The Satterthwaites' work and days would fit easily into their family history; generations of "worthy endeavor." It would be all of a piece.

Harry Atwood was as transient as a vaudevillian. He had been married before. Flying was a daredevil's profession, to which he added inventing, one unsure thing on top of another. This was not the man you had in mind when you sent your daughter to the right society parties.

The day after her flight, Ruth and Harry Atwood were in a serious car accident. They were thrown from the car as it overturned, and, said Atwood, "alighted unhurt," in time to see his "machine turn several somersaults as it continued down the embankment." Ruth "was so unnerved by her auto accident she has not again ventured in Atwood's hydroplane," reported her hometown paper. Atwood's mother flew with him instead.

Ruth's parents, a family story goes, told Atwood that if he would not see her or write to her for one year and still wanted to marry her, they would give their consent. He showed up exactly a year to the day later.

After reading about Atwood's engagement, Cecile E. Harris of Toledo decided she had her own romance to tell. Harris, age twenty, and the newspapers said "unusually pretty," claimed that Atwood, "earnestly professing his love," had proposed to her in the third week of September 1913. She thought it over for a night and agreed to a November wedding—though she couldn't remember the exact date. They "were together practically all the time during the mornings, afternoons and evenings." She was a "check girl" at a hotel where Atwood lived for a time. She sued Atwood for breach of promise, asking fifty thousand dollars for suffering "great humiliation" and "great distress of body and mind, severe nervous shocks and failure in health."

With the breach of promise case pending, Harry and Ruth were married on a weekday, March 2, 1914, in a short courthouse ceremony in Reading. Ruth was twenty-one; Harry was thirty. Only the Satterthwaite family was in attendance. They were delayed half an hour while a judge questioned Atwood's 1913 divorce certificate issued in Reno, Nevada, which lacked the official notary seal.

Atwood announced that they would take a round-the-world aeroplane trip, and then they registered under assumed names in a New York hotel and hid from reporters.

The courtroom was packed for *Harris v. Atwood*. One hundred people stood where they could along the back and sides of the room.

Atwood said he had only treated her as a "friend in need" and had loaned Harris and her mother ten dollars one time, twenty-five dollars another. He knew what it was like to be short of cash, he said. He had put his arm around her waist, but never kissed her. His lawyers called a witness, Harris's boss at the checking concession, who said that Harris was "deceitful," didn't turn in all the money she gathered, and that, anyway, she had no special claim since "most every night" Atwood took home a bunch of girls from the hotel.

Harris's lawyers said that Atwood made one hundred thousand dollars yearly, and that he "did live and maintain himself luxuriously and in total disregard of expenditures."

Atwood's lawyers replied that he made nowhere near that much, and in fact owed seventeen thousand dollars.

Harris's lawyers subpoenaed the new Mrs. Atwood, but she did not testify. She produced a doctor's certificate saying she was too ill to leave her home in Reading.

The jury, after deliberating forty-five minutes, ordered Atwood to pay Harris five thousand dollars in damages.

A few months later, Atwood left town with his new wife and their baby, Katrina. Harris's lawyers said they were still trying to collect the five-thousand-dollar judgment.

He did not go back to Sandusky. When he had visited just a few months before, the constable had attached his flying boat soon after he landed. He owed twenty dollars on a year-old towing bill. This was not fair, Atwood protested. He was on his way to pay that bill, but now he might fight it. "I like Sandusky and I want to say that I am not through with the city by any means. I regret that anything like this has happened. The account would have been taken care of tomorrow. My boat was seized before I had an opportunity to come to the city." His parting words.

The headline hero disappeared in silence. For the next two years there were no record flights, exhibitions, or announcements of new companies. Harry Atwood had gone with his wife and infant to rent a house adjoining the Satterthwaite's in Reading. Backed by a local capitalist, he worked in secret on a new aeroplane motor and a large new flying boat. He emerged with a much-praised motor, an innovative aeroplane, and a sober business plan that did not set out to do all things in aviation at once. Most important, the motor was tested and the plane was built. These weren't paper dreams.

Europe was at war and spending on aircraft. Once there was no money in the United States for aviation except for exhibitions; now foreign money was reviving a tiny industry. Atwood had what everyone wanted: a reliable motor. Airplane motors sold for between six thousand dollars and fifteen thousand dollars and could be made for one thousand dollars.

The Atwood 12-180 was a V-shaped 12-cylinder, water-cooled engine capable of 190 horsepower. Atwood carefully stated that it was not experimental: "There are no new and novel principles introduced into the construction of the apparatus which would make the design in anyway radical or questionable." He had designed the engine to meet government criteria.

He was looking for backers to produce the engine. He sent out fifty-two letters to the boards of trade in different cities saying he would establish his factory in their city if they would match his investment. Twenty cities expressed interest.

Reading was the first to reply and inspect the engine. "It was found, however, that the German sentiment in Reading might not be favorable to the production at this time, of an engine that might be used in the European war," reported a Williamsport, Pennsylvania, newspaper. Reading was not far out of step with a country that was striving to be neutral in "thought as well as action," as President Woodrow Wilson had said in August 1914.

Williamsport was the next to answer. The town had companies that built engines for Detroit auto makers. They inspected the Atwood 12-180, were impressed, and invited Atwood to present his plan. "Enthusiastic, stating firmly that he is not a promoter and has no intention of urging the board into any action it did not want to take . . . and explaining again that he is willing to back his idea with half the needed money, Mr. Atwood pleased everyone and his frankness was strongly in his favor," reported the *Williamsport Gazette and Bulletin*.

This was not an "experimental proposition," Atwood emphasized, "but a tried and tested machine which is bound to sell." His business plan was sensible: At first they would produce only one model of the engine in a small factory, jobbing out much of the work to the skilled machine shops in town. They would also build aeroplanes, but only on order. "He said emphatically . . . that the factory is not going to be a flying school . . . No exhibitions will be given in town or out of town."

"If he sold only 10 [engines] the first year he would consider it good business," reported the *Gazette and Bulletin*. But, smart salesman that he was, he did see bigger things ahead. As many as five hundred engines could be produced the first year. And once the war was over, there would a huge demand for aeroplanes. In ten years the aeroplane would surpass the motor car industry, Atwood believed. "The plant which gets the business now will have a monopoly later," he promised.

Local investors pledged fifty-five thousand dollars in cash, matching Atwood's investment of twenty-five thousand dollars and the value of his patents, engines, and aeroplanes, which would be used for testing the engines on the calm waters of the river above the dam. Atwood proudly noted that only local money was invested, none from outside promoters or speculators. He would not sell his patents, or license them, unless he was in charge of production. Even then he sheltered his patents in a separate company. (The city directory listed two companies; the stockholders' aeronautic company and the Atwood Manufacturing Company.) He was wary of outside control, wary of a banker's dictating changes in his design. This was the demon that he (and all inventors) faced: how to maintain control of an invention, and still attract the money needed for production. Solve that problem, and with good timing, you could be a household name. For Atwood this was a more vexing problem than anything he had ever encountered while flying.

The Atwood Aeronautic Company, Inc., opened at the end of May 1916. Atwood shipped in his two aeroplanes, including the large one he had built in Reading, said to be larger than the flying boat *America*, which Glenn Curtiss had built for a proposed Atlantic flight. Atwood's plane could seat five people in a metal boat-shaped hull and "was driven and controlled almost exactly the same as an automobile."

Right off the company received a large order for engines from an unnamed country, possibly Britain or France, for ten engines a month for six months. The first lot was due in three weeks. The small factory staff of twelve men would be doubled and would have to work day and night to get the job done. Each engine would be tested by the foreign government's inspector before being accepted.

The investors gathered to hear the good news. The engine had been selected over Curtiss, Wright, and other engines—on drawings and explanation alone. They heard the technical report of an engine specialist who praised the engine. The same government had contracted for an additional 50 engines, and was eager to have all 100 engines in six months, if possible, Atwood told them. They would have ordered 150 engines, if the factory had the capacity. He was even turning away work; he declined a contract for a 250-horsepower engine, still under development. Locally, three "sportsmen" had ordered planes. And they were in the running for a contract to build six aeroplanes for a South American country.

With that, the subscribers paid their pledges: "Without exception every man either ratified his subscription or increased it . . . This put everyone into good humor," said the newspaper. "The company will start out with the most rosy of futures and bids fair to be one of the biggest things that has ever come to Williamsport."

Success. Harry Atwood's timing was perfect. Europe was hungry for aeroplane engines and aeroplanes. After years of failed ventures and hard work, the aviator was achieving his dream, becoming an inventor. This was just the start. There were larger engines being developed, and he had so many other ideas, "some of them unusual," said the newspaper.

A year later the Atwood Aeronautic Company was out of business. Just as the United States government was gearing up to buy unprecedented numbers of engines, Atwood was leaving town. He owned his patent and the drawings, dies, jigs, tools, and patterns for the Atwood 12-180.

A small item in the newspaper, from December 10, 1916, provides a clue to the failure: "Harry N. Atwood, of the Atwood Aeronautic Company, announces that, with the arrival of N. E. Hopkins, production engineer, the output of the plant will be speeded up and from now on ten fully inspected motors will be produced each month." Near the end of the first contract, they still had not produced the required ten motors a month. The order for fifty additional motors was likely cancelled.

Atwood's company may have been poorly managed, or he may not have been able to find enough workers. There was already a shortage of skilled workers in Williamsport when he arrived. He had told his investors that he had a list of forty experienced men willing to come to town.

Sandusky, Toledo, Williamsport—a pattern was emerging. Atwood went back to school.

In April 1917, the United States declared war on Germany, entering the "European War." A military draft was declared and there was a shortage of all war materials. The United States armed forces had only 381 aeroplanes when the United States entered the first air war of the modern age (and of that total only 55 were thought to be serviceable). Aviation had lagged in the United States, clowning at country fairs, while European governments had funded extensive developments. Three days after the United States declared war, one of Atwood's fraternity brothers, who was the director of the du Pont Powder Company, started an aviation school as a "patriotic donation." Tuition was free; upon graduating students were required to enroll in the air corps of the army or the navy. Atwood may have talked the du Ponts into the entire scheme.

He was hired at the princely sum of $650 a month, triple what the chief instructor was paid, to "devote his entire time, skill, labor and attention" to the Delaware Aeronautical Company. The school was set up on the Raskob Estate in Claymont, Delaware, with six aeroplanes, including the workhorse of the era, two Curtiss "Jenny" JN-4s. The school was well supported with a staff of fourteen, including a shop supervisor, three mechanics, a carpenter, chef, cook, and two waiters. There were three hangars and four other buildings, two leveled runways—the first in Delaware—amid a field of cowpeas.

Twenty-nine "stalwart, clean-cut" Ivy League college men were chosen from a waiting list of three hundred. They lived spartanly, no smoking or drinking, and rose at four in the morning for the first of four flights. In sixty days they should leave as trained pilots for government service. That was the plan.

The students were taught by General Manager Atwood and his chief instructor, the "fighting airman" 'Tommy' Birt, glowingly described as "an eager, smiling Englishman, former member of the Royal Flying Corps who distinguished himself by reckless exploits on the battle line in France and by daring flights across the English Channel," said the *Delmarvia Star*. "He piloted the gunners through the clouds on the French front—where, he does not care to say—but in some of the thickest of the battles. He was hit and his machine smashed when some 500 feet in the air and he was brought to earth, wounded, but by luck escaped death. After six months in the hospital, he went to fight again, but was assigned" to the Royal Canadian Flying Corp "to train the the airmen that England so badly needed."

The students could learn a lot from an aviator like that—if only they had one. In the official records and historical studies of the Royal Flying Corp and the Royal Canadian Flying Corp, there is no listing of the "fighting airman," and neither did Birt have an aviator's certificate from the Royal Aero Club.

Flying instruction began in June and the school's neighbors became quick judges of flying form. "When she swings off and wobbles like that, one of the students is running her," a resident explained to a reporter. "When she goes straight through the air like a knife, Atwood or 'Tommy' Birt has his hands on the wheel."

But Atwood was never interested in teaching, and wasn't much for the details of heading an organization. He was frequently traveling on Aero Club of America business, government business, and in Detroit overseeing the production of two aeroplanes for the school. He saw a much bigger role for this school in the cowpeas. "My trip to Washington revealed that the United States Government is contemplating a colossal equipment of aircraft, and men to operate same, and the opinion is now prevalent throughout Government circles that this present war will be terminated only by domination of the air," Atwood reported in June to the directors of the school, Pierre S. du Pont, Irenee du Pont, and

John J. Raskob, who were also, respectively, president, director, and treasurer of the du Pont Powder Co.

A bill was being hurried through Congress for the largest single-purpose expenditure in United States history: $640 million for military aviation ($30 for each household in the country). An aviation industry would be born instantly. Before 1917, the largest aeroplane order in the country had been 22 planes. In eight years, the four largest manufacturers had produced only 59 planes. From April 1917 until the armistice on November 11, 1918, 13,894 planes and 41,953 engines were produced. Seeing this coming, how could Atwood be satisfied with a cowpea flying school?

Events at school soon required his closer attention. A month and a half after the school began, on July 20, a student was killed. When Allan O. Smith was taking out one of the flying boats, Atwood and Birt told him not to leave the water, but the temptation was too great. He had 370 minutes of flying time, about half that required to solo. This was to be his last day at the school. Smith took off, and Atwood dispatched students to ready the rescue boats on the river. At one thousand feet, as Smith started back toward the airfield, he hit some turbulence and a tricky crosswind. The plane wobbled, the engine coughed, and he dove down, hitting the river at about one hundred miles an hour. The plane sunk in about twenty to forty feet of water. A passing steamboat arrived immediately, but by then only part of the upper wing was visible above the water. No one could budge the plane, or pull Smith's body out of the wreck.

The du Ponts had known Smith; the twenty-six-year-old had been the head gardener at the Raskob Estate. They fired several employees at the school and reprimanded Atwood.

Accidents continued at the school, costs were high, and the du Ponts were disappointed with how little flying time the students were logging. By summer's end, only three students of the twenty-nine had soloed. Another four were reportedly ready to solo.

The school was costing nearly double what the du Ponts had expected. Atwood had many answers—more equipment was needed than first thought, engine prices had jumped 75 percent due to their scarcity, and "the accidents, including the burning of the automobile, two bad wrecks of JN-4 machines, loss of one flying boat, have all tended to show excessive operating cost." When you considered all that, Atwood said, "the cost had been but very little greater." In all the du Ponts had committed $131,252.19 to the school to produce three novice pilots.

Atwood conceded the school could be run better. "I believe that within the next few weeks you will be as satisfied with the school's running as I have been dissatisfied in the past and you will understand better than ever the service which you are rendering to the Government by supporting the organization," he told the directors in early August. If the board members investigated other schools, they would realize "what comparative good results are being obtained."

His remedy for the school's problems was not to hire more instructors or boost flying time, but to propose a new venture. The school could "render invaluable and timely assistance to the Government by performing a certain amount of research work," he reported to the directors. "This school is in an excellent position to discover the needs of the aeronautic profession and to offer suggestions for improvement by means of graphic designs, models or possibly perfected apparatus."

The school should spend "an amount not exceeding $10,000 per year on research work." He was not suggesting "commercial development or exploitation of any apparatus, for such work would be very costly and would detract from the initial purpose of the school." In fact, the research would be "particularly applicable to the enlightenment of students during their course of instruction." They would identify and solve various aerial hazards in what would amount to a school of invention. With a successful invention, "the Delaware Aeronautical Company might some day be transformed from a patriotic burden to an income-producing organization."

He was already preparing applications for four patents on his own inventions to be taken out in the company's name. Two may have resulted from the Smith crash: "The usage of air-inflated rubber balls enclosed in the empty chambers and pockets of aircraft fuselages and hulls to prevent the sinking of aircraft damaged by falls into the water, and to minimize the danger of splinters piercing the body of the aviator at the time of the crash." And: "An aero-dynamic indicator to denote the limits of air-stability of any aircraft so that the danger of side-slipping, stalling, and nose-diving may be minimized." A third was for a "wing mechanism" to act as a brake to stop a plane in a few feet in an emergency landing (possibly like the split flaps Orville Wright patented in the 1920s). The last invention was an intriguing description of a jet engine: "A thermo-dynamic engine involving the principle of the direct transforming of heat energy of gases into gas velocity without the usage of mechanical operating mechanisms." None of these patents—if they were applied for—were granted.

He also proposed that the school use a textbook, which he had "more than halfway towards completion" and could be ready for the spring 1918 flying season. For the winter months, he suggested that they establish a flying school on the west coast of Florida, which would not require expensive hangars or outbuildings.

Atwood had thrown everything he could into his report to the directors. He promised to run the school better, promised a leading research role in the coming arms buildup, and earlier had even offered to put the Atwood 12-180 back into production as a donation to the school. He closed by asking for a personal interview with the board.

Three weeks later the school was running short of funds. Atwood promised that his weekly report "will also probably show that we have tripled our flying time over the past week." In the past, one of the du Ponts would simply write a check for ten thousand dollars to keep the school going.

Now, after just six months, the du Ponts were through with their patriotic burden. "I am unwilling to extend further financial aid to the aviation school," wrote Irenee du Pont on September 19, 1917. "I have lost confidence in the ability of the present management to accomplish the results we hoped for in the education of students in the art of flying." Arrange to sell one of the aeroplanes immediately, he instructed, and "give Atwood the notice necessary to sever his employment by the company under his contract."

Harry Atwood was leaving town again. He had failed more than a few times, but then the young aviation industry was a frontier. Things were wide open, all sorts of inventors, businessmen, and daring aviators came and went, perishing by bad timing, led to the slaughter by their own optimism. Frontiers are always on the move, and the adventurous can pack up and follow. On the frontier, credentials and committees don't matter, only what you can grab today. There was a huge aviation buildup. Suddenly everyone was in the business; 175,000 people were employed in an industry that could scarcely support a handful of workers the year before. Atwood would not be left out.

It was like flying, in a way. There's turbulence sometimes, or what the early aviators called "holes in the air." When Atwood was first flying, these holes in the sky, that feeling of falling from a level flight into a churning upheaval, "caused no end of difficulty and apprehension," he said. "Some persons predicted that they would prove an insuperable difficulty and would check further development of the air machine. I don't like to seem boastful, but every time I went in the air for a while I enjoyed meeting an 'airhole,' and gradually I became convinced that, the machine being strong enough, any aviator should be able to bring himself through. The 'airholes' are never wide, and the mere momentum of the machine will carry one 'across,' if I may express it that way.

"The aviator must be ready, however, for the next bank of air, or the bank of air on the other side." That was the art of navigating the air, an art Harry Atwood continued on the ground.

⌒ Grabtown

Two memories from the edge of all memories, from childhood. The adults seen from afar by their child spies. Details, not the big picture or the business transaction. The world first seen in all its strangeness.

Sallie Ives Robenolt was a little girl when Harry Atwood came to town, to Smithfield, North Carolina, a small place of tobacco, cotton, and the Bible. There was also a sawmill and a factory to make wood veneer, and that's why Atwood arrived. He was building a seaplane for the navy. Smithfield was 120 miles, over rough roads, from the ocean. There wasn't even a large lake.

In September the town was busy with all the tobacco men buying and selling the harvest. There were always parties then. Robenolt remembers a big picnic party and her father and all the men gathered around Harry. They were laughing at a story Harry was telling. Harry was smoking a cigar.

Ben Grimes grew up a few blocks from the factory. It was an abandoned and weedy place. The doors were wide open. And there was this seaplane, just the fuselage. The wings were missing. "I used to sit in the cockpit of this would-be plane. I was crazy for flying—I'd read about the World War I flying aces. That was my dream world. My mother would find me over there." He was eight or nine years old, a barefoot boy, flying this wingless seaplane into aerial combat. Later he joined the navy to fly, and ended up in a submarine.

Only when he grew up did he ask himself: What was a seaplane doing in Smithfield? Improbable. Like a children's story.

The admiring crowd, the abandoned airplane—in sum, they were Atwood's life.

Harry Atwood's navy seaplane was late and overweight. In June 1918 the navy contracted with his new company to purchase four experimental Curtiss F-type flying boats to study "the feasibility of using the veneer process as developed by the Carolina Aircraft Corporation." The company "had no facilities except the use of a small foundry pattern shop of the Raleigh Iron Works," and the navy said it had enough planes under contract, yet Atwood had impressed a visiting navy board and grabbed his share of the frenzied wartime build up. Around Raleigh, investors and the chamber of commerce lined up behind big promises: a plant employing two thousand people immediately to produce twenty-five planes a day. The company lobbied the army for a large contract, claiming it could build five hundred planes for half of what the government was paying and guarantee delivery in 180 days.

"Within the next month or so, a glance from the window may reveal a made-in-Raleigh aeroplane circling over the city, flirting with the church spires and terrorizing the old Confederate sentinel on top of the monument in capital square," said the *Raleigh Times*, whose publisher was excited by Atwood's promises.

Three miles from the center of Smithfield was a small crossroads hamlet, Grabtown (Ava Gardner's birthplace). The boys in Smithfield said there's so many pretty girls, let's go grab one. In much the same way, potential contractors were chasing War Department money.

That fall the company left Raleigh and moved to better quarters in a Smithfield veneer factory (where Atwood also had a business interest) and told the navy the plane would be ready for testing by October 15. But there were delays. The first plane was about 90 percent complete when the war ended three weeks later.

Just days after the armistice, the entire aviation industry was pulled apart. Orders were cancelled for thirteen thousand planes and twenty thousand engines. By 1920 there was no money at all for new airplanes. The navy cancelled three of the four flying boats.

When the board of inspectors gathered to see the first test flight in January 1919, the plane wouldn't fly. Ensign J. D. Buckstaff, who had been in charge of inspecting the plane each week, wrote a long, angry report: the plywood-veneer flying boat weighed too much, and Atwood had changed the proven Curtiss design without his permission. The navy and Atwood had differing ideas of what the word "experimental" meant in the contract. The navy wanted an aeroplane built to their specifications, the reliable Curtiss seaplane in a new material. Atwood wanted to build his seaplane with their money, the plane he thought they needed. He never followed rules—it was the missed figure eight again.

"I have repeatedly invited the attention of Harry Nelson Atwood to these serious violations with no avail," Buckstaff wrote in February. "Atwood contended that the work was purely experimental and that if finally rejected, the responsibility would rest with him. He has often stated that he would rather the Navy reject the plane as he could then use it for advertising purposes in connection with his veneer production."

A month later, Buckstaff was fed up with Atwood: "This inspector certainly cannot recommend the acceptance of this craft by the Navy as it is not built with standard Navy practices as called for in their contract."

Atwood was quick to reply. He wired the navy that the plane had flown after the inspectors had left, "in twenty-five mile hour wind with live load seven hundred and eighty pounds with good control." And two weeks later it had flown several times with three and four passengers. Sure, the plane was 470 pounds too heavy, weighing about one-quarter more than the Curtiss F flying-boat. But, Atwood argued, because of his superior veneer it would not soak up water, while the Curtiss would absorb 150 to 200 pounds of water. The Curtiss hull was built of two thin layers of wood with a fabric sandwiched between. The early flying-boats were plagued by waterlogged hulls, which is the reason the navy was interested in Atwood's design.

He had been experimenting with veneers since Reading and was so proud of this veneer that he offered to instruct the navy in his technique. The many design changes had been made to accommodate the increased performance of a veneer plane: it was ten miles an hour faster with wooden veneer wings replacing cloth-covered wings and required a smaller tail area. The increased size of the veneer struts made the usual "skid fins" on the wing unnecessary. All these changes had been approved by the inspector, who was "most enthusiastic regarding our developments . . . and proclaimed the merits of our new work throughout our communities," said Atwood. He had modified the Curtiss F flying-boat beyond recognition. Atwood's flying-boat was one of a kind.

"It is not improbable that we have made many mistakes," he said. "If we cannot rectify any of them, we will gladly take our loss, but we do want opportunity to make good even though it may cost more than to fail." He eventually agreed to make many changes to conform to the contract.

The work dragged on, the Carolina Aircraft Corporation was dissolved, and the navy assigned a new inspector. The plane was tested again (without a navy pilot). "After a series of preliminary trials the Contractor found that due to the excess of weight on his machine he could not meet the performance test in climbing or straight away flying," the inspector reported. In one trial, the plane flew at "an altitude of 25 feet" for about one mile. Atwood conceded that the plane was a bit heavy and asked for a larger engine.

The new inspector thought the flying boat was "very well constructed" and deserved another chance. "After observing the maneuvering of the machine on the water and in the air at low altitude this office believes that if the machine was equipped with a Hispano-Suiza 150 H. P. motor that the whole project would be a success." This motor was on hand at the testing site and could be quickly installed. The navy disagreed. The tests went forward with the 100-horsepower engine required by the contract and Atwood flew the seaplane to its predictable death: the plane couldn't lift the required load and the navy rejected it. This was Harry Atwood's last recorded flight.

Years later he said that the plane "flew marvelously" and that "we really thought we had something" until he had left it out in the rain, the glue loosened, and the whole plane fell apart. The glue—not Harry Atwood—had failed.

The navy had ordered four flying boats to be built for $16,000 (without engines and instruments). The company had spent $20,993.70 to build the one plane the navy rejected.

The Smithfield Veneer Products Company, with Atwood as vice-president, continued on for a few years after that. Atwood was experimenting with other composite wood products. He had been granted five patents and filed for another six. He had some new ideas that just needed a few investors.

A few days after Thanksgiving, in 1922, the Smithfield factory burned to the ground. It happened at noon, after the workers had gone to lunch. Town gossip judged it a convenient insurance fire, no doubt Atwood's idea. A flashy figure in a Bible belt town, he was a natural topic of gossip. He was sometimes seen racing by in his Cadillac touring car. (Once he gave a young Presbyterian preacher quite a ride—eighty miles an hour over the dirt roads all the way to Raleigh.) And some of his comments really left an impression. Sallie Robenolt remembers his joking, "'I like to marry them young and tell them nothing.' I can see mother's face . . ." she says, her voice trailing away.

"We understand there is very little insurance, if any, on the plant," reported the *Smithfield Herald* and that was more likely the truth. One resident and stockholder, Nathan M. Lawrence, lost everything he had in that fire. He took his family to a small town up north where Harry Atwood was reinventing the wheel.

II

We move over the land and the air with the freedom of timeless gods . . . long chained, like Prometheus, to the earth, we have freed ourselves at last, and now can look the skylark in the face.
—WILL DURANT (1926)

It Had to Be You

From the first, when I met Katrina, she interviewed me: who I was, what I had written, how—the whole story—I had gotten Tess, the border collie who was with me. She even made a few notes. She was in charge, an alert intellect, a vigorous voice, smiling. She was a consummate storyteller, attuned to whether a story was drifting or if she was losing your interest. She spoke with extensive dialogue: "He'd say . . . oh, well maybe I'm making that up now, but something like that." I don't think I asked a single question for more than an hour.

She talked about "life with father," the adventures, the lectures, the piano playing, all of it. She also played the piano. As a girl, she had worked and worked to learn it. Eight hours and she'd still be trying to memorize a piece, she said. Her father played by ear; play it once or twice and he could pick it up. She sat to down to play, and I recognized the tune: "It Had to Be You."

But as the second hour came around, she turned feisty, annoyed, sad. Her voice lost power. She did have emphysema and smoked short unfiltered Camels. But more than that, her recollections had led her to some difficult history. She grew hesitant; behind each answer was an inner debate. The last story she told me was how he had sent her and her sisters away one day in the middle of the school year.

Reinventing the Wheel

Harry Atwood drove past Bill Stone's house four or five times a day. He drove his Cadillac over the curb there. The wheels flexed as they hit the curb, absorbing the shock. Atwood had a potential investor with him. He would ride into the curb again to show how smooth a ride his patented Rubwood wheels provided. It was an impressive demonstration. Bill Stone invested; the first stock he ever owned. Stone was thirteen years old. He owned two shares, at fifty dollars each. He took off from school for the stockholder meetings. Others in town were there, fellow investors: the town treasurer, a bank executive, the village pharmacist, two postal clerks, a retired hatter, and the village baker, who had invested his life's savings.

Monson, Massachusetts, like Smithfield, was a small town of three thousand. Monson was fifteen miles from Springfield, a prosperous mill city, and right in step with the stock market speculation that swept America in the 1920s. While relatively few people actually owned stocks, "playing the market" was the talk of the nation. Monson invested in Harry Atwood. If he succeeded, so would they. The Monson National Bank put a big Rubwood wheel out front.

Atwood had brought his Rubwood invention north with him from Smithfield. When he was working on the navy seaplane he was looking for a better way to waterproof wood veneer. He began experiments combining rubber and wood. The "experts . . . declared emphatically that there was no known way of making wood adhere to rubber in any satisfactory or practical manner," said the *Monson Register* in June 1924. In fact, the "rubber industries were spending millions of dollars yearly in order to keep splinters of wood out of rubber; and that therefore, they did not see how they could become interested in spending millions of dollars to put it back in the rubber."

Many combinations were tried, but the moisture in the wood, even after it was kiln dried, made it separate from the rubber. "Suddenly, after long discouragement," Atwood combined unseasoned green wood and raw rubber "in steam vats under pressure." "It was an experiment of exasperation." The result was a "composite . . . mixture of wood and rubber which was inseparable," said the *Register*, in a story that quoted no source, but was the Rubwood gospel according to Atwood. "This experiment was against all precedent known to the rubber trade. In fact, it was impossible to find any rubber expert who would believe that such a procedure was possible."

Rubwood possessed the "properties of metal, wood and rubber. Rubwood is flexible and yet is stronger than the wood which is used in it. Rubwood is rigid and yet possesses a flexibility approaching rubber. Rubwood bends like a steel spring and flies back into shape . . . It does not possess internal flaws and defects." Rubwood could be made from any kind of wood, of almost any size, including waste wood and scrub wood having no market value. Mostly "regenerated" or recycled rubber could be used.

Atwood patented sixteen wheel designs, each with a different profile and construction. He also patented a pulley and six composite laminated structures, including a submarine hull.

He had tried for years to interest large companies, said the *Register*, until some Monson men invested. This "was not a scheme of stock peddling. It was the possibilities of the industry's success that drew the stock buyers." The company would expand slowly, said the *Register*, maintaining local control by not borrowing outside money. "Local confidence seems strong and it appears to be only a question of adherence by Monson people to make this industry one of its best."

A small factory was set up, running on hydroelectric power from the Chicopee Brook. Orders came in quickly for kiddie car wheels, shoe heels (patent 1,640,686, "saves the feet," said the inventor), piano castor wheels which didn't mar floors, indoor roller skate wheels, baby carriage heels, jack spool heads for textile mills, and "unbreakable toilet seats" which the Dupont company used in its powder mills, where no metal could be near the floor due to the danger of sparks. The larger car wheels themselves were still under development, the company's slogan—"Rubwood Wheels for Automobiles"—not withstanding.

A year later, Allan S. Locke, a Wall Street lawyer, investigated Atwood's company on behalf of prospective investors. "I find that various branches of industry doing business with the Rubwood company rate the product as one of the best on the market and are almost universally soliciting business with the company on an exclusive basis." Most customers were "AAA-1" companies and the largest in their fields. In the previous sixty days there had been over one hundred thousand dollars in orders, he reported in August 1925. In the next year, he conservatively estimated that the company would gross five hundred thousand dollars. The kiddie car company wanted a thousand wheels a day, and there were hundreds of thousands of dollars of orders for spool heads. Once the company was fully operational it had enormous potential. The price of rubber was high, making the product attractive. With the British restricting rubber exports from their colonies, the price had quadrupled in four years.

"I have never inspected a more simple or more reliable process of manufacture," Locke said. "Their product is consistent and reliable and losses and rejections are absolutely normal." He added that "the company is wisely withholding manufacturing larger objects" until further refinements.

The Rubwood Wheel Company needed to expand, but it was hindered by its ability to raise money, said Locke. The company was undercapitalized. Atwood, as company president and majority stockholder, had refused offers to buy the patents, exclusive sales rights, or a controlling stock interest. He didn't want to lose control of his patents. He knew how quickly the inventor was forgotten and how easily license agreements were evaded.

The patent license was the company's most valuable asset, said Locke. "The patents have been classified by several responsible law firms as constituting a monopoly."

Atwood planned to expand with local money. The company outfitted practically every Ford in town with Rubwood wheels. With each set of wheels, it was as if Atwood had deputized another stock salesman. Visitors, potential investors all, would be driven around—there were practically no paved roads in town. Atwood's favorite demonstration, after hitting the curb, was to ride over the trolley track ties on Main Street, "just as smooth as velvet," as one observer recalled.

The baker, Herman Heinrich Markus, was one of the leading stock promoters. He gave one prospective investor "a ride to golf grounds over a rough road to demonstrate how perfect the wheels were," he said. "All my business was to boost the company, go from one party to another and see if I could get people interested in that. I know that if they see the product and the factory and see everything about the company they are willing to put their money in."

Harry Atwood had returned to the mountains of New England. He loved New England and he loved the mountains. He bought a large white house up on East Hill and moved the servants—a chauffeur, a maid, and a cook—from Smithfield. He added a local handyman.

They were helping him run the household and look after his three children; his second wife, Ruth, had died two years earlier.

He paid his help well. "Father, who had been poor, had not been used to money," Katrina said. "When he brought Vera Smith up from the South as cook and general everything, he gave her twenty-five dollars a week. If you'd gotten three dollars a week that would have been a heck of a good salary in those days."

He was extravagant with his daughters' Sunday school money, as well, giving them twenty-five cents when all the other children put a nickel or a dime into the collection plate. This was part of her father's showmanship, Katrina said. "We put a quarter in and got so many oohs and ahhs," she said. So they wised up and, after the chauffeur dropped them off, bought ice cream before church, and put less in the plate. "Then we were accepted by our friends."

Their neighbors were dairy farmers who lived modestly, in accord with the unspoken New England virtues of reticence and frugality. The Atwoods lived expensively. He owned the first shortwave radio in town and had a remarkable three radio sets in one room alone. At a time when regular radio broadcasts were just beginning, and when a radio could cost more than a new Model T touring car, he had wired the house so there were speakers in each room. He often had radio parties. A crowd would gather to hear the Irish tenor John McCormack. Atwood had always loved music and in Monson he owned his finest piano, a Steinway grand.

He also indulged his love of fine automobiles. He bought two new Cadillacs a year and owned seven cars in all, including a Stanley Steamer, which he bought because it intrigued him. The cars had Rubwood wheels, as did the girls' scooters. Little sample wheels were all over the house as ashtrays.

To house the cars he had a concrete tunnel built right under the house, large enough to park ten cars. "He was cement happy," said Bernice Vaill, who lived next door and, with her sister Phila, played with the Atwood girls. He built a concrete porch around three sides of the house, with a fountain in the middle. On rainy days, the neighborhood children rode their bicycles there until Vera snuck them cookies, or if she was tired of the noise, shooed them away. He moved through the house cementing things that caught his interest. He had his handyman pour concrete down between the walls. "The walls bulged out all over the place," said Bill Stone. "He had a hell of a mess on his hands to straighten out there."

The entire house was open to experiment. Katrina didn't know what to expect when she came home from school. "He was always changing bedrooms. I had three or four. No stability. I would come home and find he'd decided to cement in there. He was a cement artist. He only saw a house in terms of how much cement he could pour into it and fireproof it."

Concrete was a high-technology wonder, an invention that was seeing exciting applications back when Atwood was making his record flights. The *Scientific American* devoted its March 18, 1911, issue to concrete, writing: "It has long been the habit of the historian when speaking of the constructional or mechanical side of human progress to name its various eras after the predominant materials of construction. Hence, in their succession, we have had the eras of stone, bronze, iron, and steel. To-day we find ourselves well launched in what may justly be called the era of cement." The "most monumental of all modern engineering works," the Panama Canal, was under construction—five million cubic yards of rock, sand, and cement. The canal was featured in the issue, along with an article extolling the one-piece concrete house, which said that the problems of dampness and dreary color had been overcome. Thomas Edison himself was an enthusiastic promoter of concrete houses and furniture. In Monson, as elsewhere, cement had put the granite quarry out of business.

When, in 1913, *Scientific American* asked its readers to list the ten greatest inventions of the era, the readers chose reinforced concrete as number six, ahead of the phonograph, incandescent electric lamp, steam turbine, radium, submarine, and others. (Wireless telegraphy was almost unanimously first, followed at some distance by the aeroplane, X-ray machine, automobile, and motion pictures.) Concrete, like the aeroplane, was still a heroic invention.

Atwood had plans for an entire cement housing development. He had amassed fourteen hundred acres near his East Hill home, making him the largest landholder in town. He laid out "pleasure grounds for the townspeople" and planned twenty-five houses of concrete and steel, each with six or seven rooms and "every modern convenience." The Rubwood powerhouse would provide electricity, and water would come from a nearby spring. Monson had a history of the local mill owners' providing parks and monuments, and Atwood matched them. In his fourteen-acre public park he eventually built two concrete pools, one sixty feet long and the other a wading pool, and a concrete grandstand overlooking a baseball field for the Monson Aces.

Behind his own house he built a concrete swimming pool, the first one in the area. It was fed by a spring up the hill. He opened it to all the children in town. "During the hot days the pool was just alive with laughing, happy children who were loud in their appreciation of Mr. Atwood's kindness," reported the *Monson Register*. "We all learned to swim there," said Ken Carpenter, who went to school with the Atwood girls. Jesse Smart Clark learned from her friend Gene, who promised Jesse one of her dolls. "Oh, and I wanted that doll so bad," Clark said. But she got out as she reached the deep end. Gene pushed her back in and she had to swim. Gene gave her the doll.

Out behind the pool in a little house under an elm tree lived the Atwoods' pet bear, Topsey. Atwood had gotten Topsey as a cub up in New Hampshire. The bear drank Cokes and ate barrels of candy. When Topsey got older and his play got rougher, he was moved to the barn, which he shared with a horse that had heaves and a cow with a wire in her stomach. They were watched over by the Atwoods' gardener, an old man twisted with arthritis who had just shown up one day. He had no relatives. Atwood had a room built for him by the barn and paid him ten dollars a week. He tended a rose garden and just loved his roses. The gardener died there, leaving behind in a trunk all his possessions: a dress suit and a gold pocket watch.

Topsey died in a barn fire. Atwood tried to race into the flames to save the bear, but neighbors and fire fighters held him back.

The children in town loved Harry Atwood. "He was just like a father to all of us," said Stone, who took two trips to the White Mountains in New Hampshire with Atwood and the boys' club at the Congregational Church, the Regular Fellows. Atwood loaded them into two Cadillacs, one of which the chauffeur drove. "He always said, when he got tired or nervous, he'd go to the mountains. It was always relaxing for him to go to the mountains," said Stone. He often took his girls hiking in the White Mountains, perhaps too often for Katrina, who said, "Mount Washington is the biggest blister I ever walked up."

"He was good to his children, his girls. He was a wonderful father," said Bernice Vaill. "Did everything to get them acquainted with other children in the neighborhood. Invited the other kids in the neighborhood up.

Picked up kids in a Cadillac and a LaSalle. Took kids to Sunday school. Towed toboggans around the hill."

"Was quite a steep hill down one side of his house and he made a toboggan run there with a jump in it," said her sister Phila. "Tow us back up the hill in that Cadillac. The Rubwood wheels would travel in the slippery snow."

"Father was inventive in everything," said Katrina, "inventive in the games we played. He could improve on anything. Fox and hounds [hide and seek]—that was terrific. Mostly he was the fox—up to the time he lit beside a snake that was all coiled. He didn't like snakes. That would end that." When she was little, he told her that if she inked up a potato and rubbed it on the mirror, she could go through the looking glass just like Alice. Sometimes they put on family plays. He played the piano, while his daughters danced and sang.

Katrina has "loving, great, gorgeous memories" of those times in Monson with "Poppa Harry," the kites the pioneering aviator would build with them, and the way he challenged their imagination. "I remember talk after talk: 'Wouldn't you girls like to be the first ones to go on a flight to the moon?' He constantly talked of flight into space. He felt that it was possible in his lifetime."

He was left to raise his three daughters after his wife, Ruth, died at age twenty-seven. Their children were ages five, four, and one. She died in October 1920, before he came to Monson. Her hometown newspaper said that she "had been in impaired health for some time" and was admitted to the hospital in Reading for an operation. "Fifteen days later . . . she suffered hemorrhages" and died. Some in the family said it was a miscarriage. Her parents wouldn't talk about it.

Two years earlier the Satterthwaites had lost a son, Alfred, age twenty-eight, to the devastating Spanish influenza epidemic of 1918, which killed more than twenty million people. Alfred had sold life insurance, but had had none himself. He left a widow, Helen, and two children.

Harry and Helen were infatuated with each other. Thinking they could raise the five children together, they married, fought and argued for ninety days, and divorced. Helen later said that Harry was mean and crazy. But in some ways she was a good match. An author of detective stories, she could keep up with his schemes. When she left him, as her daughter, Marcia Sternbergh, said, she made sure she left with the deed to the land and house, which was in her name. "He put her on the train and said good-bye to her and she walked all the way through the train, hopped out, and got into her flivver, which she had left somewhere . . .

rushed down to the lawyer's office, and got the deed in her own little hands." He got the deed back from her a year later, and in return she likely received a nice settlement. "That was one she sure liked to tell."

There was a lesson in this, he told his daughters. "Don't forget, girls. If you want some advice—watch it on marriage. Every affair I ever had I married. That's why I have the black mark in so many marriages. I think I would prefer you to have an affair." This is what Katrina remembers and she lets you judge if he said this in jest. Several years later he did marry again, for the fourth time, to a local telephone operator and Irish immigrant, Mary Dalton, whom the girls adored.

The family gathered each Friday night for such talk, at what they called the Atwood Family Fools. "We were allowed to discuss anything. If he'd been unfair to us, we'd say that. It cleared the air and he learned more about us," said Katrina. "After a time, he said, 'now we're going to call it the Atwood Family Functioning.'"

One night he let them try liquor, in a manner that fit the experimental style of someone who had flown over Manhattan to test the winds. This was during Prohibition and he had just received a delivery of bootleg liquor. "So he brought in bottle after bottle. We were all urged to have anything we wanted. As soon as we finished something, we were urged to have more. We all tied on a little one because we had never had it before. His point was: I want to know how you would react when you go out later on in life.

"Not much happened with me. Sure, I got progressively potted, I guess. But I turned philosophical. I was nodding my head, agreeing: 'Yes, Yes sir. Now I have a thought.' That took care of me."

Ruth "was smiling like a Cheshire Cat. She had a hell of a good time for herself. The last we saw her she was running around the house to sober up. She tied on a beaut." Katrina doesn't recall if her youngest sister, Gene, was part of the experiment. "Now there was no harm pulled. Also he introduced us to cigarettes. And I wouldn't try them. Now I'm hooked."

He proceeded experimentally with the girls, trying out different methods to discipline children who could be as willful as their father. At times he just let them run free, paying no attention to them, and at other times he was strict, making them choose their own willow stick for a whipping. "If I didn't bring in a good stiff willow stick, I had to go out and get one that was."

At the family meeting the girls objected to this punishment. "He said, all right, the next punishment you get, or any one you choose, you may tell me to take it back and nothing will happen to you. We said okay. Now sometimes he didn't live up to things. But he happened to." Her two sisters used theirs quickly—"well, we were of course all doing things. And I saved up mine. Because I thought, well, heck, wait till something good happens.

"And then I did a very bad thing. He *loved* animals. I think he might have preferred them to humans half the time. So I had thrown the cat in the swimming pool to see if he could swim. Because I wanted to know. Because everybody said a cat couldn't swim and I couldn't believe it. So I threw the cat in." (He swam easily.)

As he got ready to punish her, she claimed her exemption. "I've never seen him angrier," she said, but he honored it. Confronted with his own experimental approach, he told her, "You don't have to experience everything yourself. Read it in a book."

He tried another tactic. If the girls behaved, he would give them a remarkable ten-dollar weekly allowance (about half the average wage of a factory worker). He put up cards, and each time they were bad, he took away a card: five dollars, one dollar, fifty cents, or twenty-five cents. "The first week we were so good; the cards stayed up there. All of us got ten dollars. The second week a few cards came down. The third week we were back to our usual—we had no place to spend the money."

Harry Atwood was starved for cash. The Rubwood Wheel Company needed to expand to fill back orders and Atwood himself, with all the cement, pools, autos, and land deals, was running through a lot of money.

On a sales trip to sell Rubwood to a library furniture company, Atwood met an employee who took an interest in the product. He came to visit the Rubwood factory and was so smitten that he stayed to praise Rubwood in front of a stockholders' meeting. Before he left, he loaned the company money and told Atwood that it would it be no problem to get investors. The employee contacted his brother-in-law, George Thayer, a New York City real estate investor, and George's twenty-six-year-old son, Wilfred Jr. Wilfred was excited by what he saw at the Rubwood factory. He wrote his father to tell him that the investment was so good that it should be kept in the family.

George Thayer was interested, but still cautious. The Thayers visited the factory twice and then met with Atwood to review the company's patents and audits. George was "anxious to make a place for his son" in the company. The Thayers offered to buy ten thousand dollars of stock. Atwood was disappointed. He talked them into twenty thousand dollars. Wilfred was given a position—unspecified, unsalaried—with the company.

By the end of 1924, Rubwood was still cash poor. Atwood told his stockholders that the company was issuing more stock, doubling the capitalization to five hundred thousand dollars. Each share of common stock sold would be matched in a special arrangement with stock from the holding company, Rubwood Inc., which actually owned the patents. The holding company received a 5-percent royalty on all sales. Only three people besides Atwood owned that stock. Everyone else had invested in the manufacturing company, and didn't own anything of the most valuable asset, the patents. Atwood promised the shareholders they would receive some benefit from the holding company. He was not specific.

Many people in many different places, at large meetings or in private, heard Atwood's promise, but no one could say exactly what he had promised. He told the Thayers he couldn't put his promise into print until they sold more stock. They invested another twenty-five thousand dollars, and agreed to sell eighty-five thousand dollars of stock. Atwood at last gave them a temporary note saying that they were entitled to the dividends from 250 shares of the holding company, but not to ownership of the stock or voting rights. The Thayers believed they were entitled to the stock outright.

This was just what Atwood feared, what he called "a conspiracy to jeopardize my holdings." The Thayers' lawyer drew up a new agreement for Atwood to sign, which gave the Thayers a participating mortgage in all of Rubwood's assets.

"I am not going to sign that thing," said Atwood. "Here you have me giving away my stock in this corporation, in these inventions that I have spent a great part of my life inventing and you are taking away from me control of my patents. I will never agree to do that." They stopped selling the stock and took Atwood to court.

The Massachusetts Superior Court heard seven days of testimony in an attempt to define just what Atwood had promised the Rubwood stockholders. Herman Markus, the baker who had worked for nineteen years in Monson, remembered the excitement when Atwood first announced the new stock benefits at a December 9 stockholder meeting: "There was a small room and everybody talking, and a hall between and another office, and we all had so much confidence in Mr. Atwood and everybody felt glorious and so fine. I think half of the discussion is forgotten, that is all."

At the end of the month, Markus, like the Thayers and others (including Atwood) took more stock. "Yes: I signed myself for ten thousand dollars, but of course, I am working nights and days; I work pretty long hours, and I told Mr. Atwood I don't know as I be able to sell that stock unless I take it myself, and I didn't have any more money to put in but I would be glad to put it in if I had it." He did buy the stock.

Milton C. Howe, a local hatter, was also at that December 9 meeting. "What impressed me at that meeting was that we were likely to get some benefits from this arrangement which didn't exist before."

The Thayers' lawyer asked him, "Did you ever obtain from Mr. Atwood any written statement of your rights?"

"Not that I know of."

"Did you ever ask him for any written statement?"

"No sir."

"You just assumed that you had some rights, did you Mr. Howe?"

"Yes, sir, that is all."

The stockholders had left Atwood a lot of room to be inventive.

The Thayers' lawyer pressed Atwood. What had he promised the stockholders? Dividends? Royalties? "If he held one share of Rubwood Inc. stock, how much benefit would he get under your agreement made that day?"

"I stated an intent at that meeting, not a specific performance," said Atwood.

"You didn't give them any definite rights then and didn't intend to?"

"I stated a specific performance and a certain agreement . . . and I stopped there."

He intended to give dividend benefits, Atwood said under more questioning. Always had. The Thayers' lawyer took Atwood on a lengthy walk through the mathematics of his promise, which apparently worked out to only a one five-thousandth portion of the dividends from 1,350 shares of holding company stock.

Was this right? the attorney asked. Is this math correct?

As Atwood sat there, Judge Louis S. Cox spoke up for him. "He is trying to work this out. He isn't as good at this as you are." He was, after all, just an inventor who couldn't be expected to know stock management, even if he was company president. Time and again Atwood claimed that he had no memory for figures. He had no memory of stock transfers, of land in his name that really belonged to the company. He was evasive and sometimes managed to turn the questions back on his examiners.

The Thayers, as the judge saw it, were shrewd big-city money who knew the marketplace. He just didn't believe George Thayer when he said that he had not known the nature of the holding company or of the existence of preferred stock.

What was the correct proportion of dividends?

Atwood couldn't say.

"Is there any proportion they are entitled to?"

"I think they have got more than they are entitled to," said Atwood.

He tried once more to walk Atwood through a simplified version of his promise: Let's say one hundred dividends are paid on 1,350 shares of holding company stock. If they have 500 of the 5,000 shares of the common stock last issued, what return do they get from the holding company stock under Atwood's promise?

The judge jumped in: "If you can answer that you can get a job as a policeman here in Boston, or possibly a fireman, if you would rather have that. Now . . . that is arithmetic."

Things were looking good for Atwood. He couldn't say exactly what he had promised, but that wasn't held against him. The Thayers' lawyer looked like a nitpicker for trying to define what was due them.

Judge Cox was not convinced that Atwood was out to defraud the Thayers and other stockholders. "It strikes me that a man who seeks to cover up a deed does not tell the village druggist and the village baker and the village shoemaker and the cashier of the bank and everybody else around the place that he has done it," he said.

Atwood had won the judge's confidence, even though his vague promise was based on misrepresentations. He didn't own the stock that he said he owned, the stock on which he had promised dividends. He claimed 1,350 shares of the holding company. Actually, this was tied up in a voting trust with two other stockholders. The benefits he finally assigned the Thayers and others may have been spoken for elsewhere. And while the Thayers were trying to win the holding company stock, Atwood sold an option on it all. Nor did the holding company actually own all the patents. Nearly one-third had been sold to an investor. And, further, there weren't as many patents as Atwood had testified—150 to 160, with patents "I might say coming in almost weekly." Rubwood owned 15 patents at the time of the trial. Another seven were granted in the next two years. This was just a peek at the Atwood school of management.

At the end of the testimony, both lawyers approached the bench. "It may be a little unusual, but I am going to say something to both of you before I hear you," said Judge Cox. He was "not impressed" by Thayer's testimony.

"It is difficult for me to believe that a man like Mr. Thayer Sr., who apparently inherited something from his father and spent a portion of his life, if not all of it, in taking care if it, and who never dealt in anything except New York real estate mortgages and stocks and bonds, would go up to the Newport House in New Hampshire and be talked into a purchase of $20,000 worth of stock—just like that. It may have been that way but they have the burden [of proof].

"On the other hand it is certain in my mind that Mr. Atwood at different times and at different places and to different people made promises with respect to this Rubwood Inc. stock which he had . . . there isn't any doubt in my mind that he emphasized the promise on the evening of Dec. 30th when he called the Thayers in and said go out into the highways and byways and get some money, a very natural thing for him to do. Just what he promised is of course a question."

Atwood had made many promises and yet he had promised nothing. He had floated his promises around the stockholders' meetings like some fragrance, a hint of something beautiful far off. The best Judge Cox could tell was that Harry Atwood had promised to make a promise.

He was a skilled blue sky salesman selling the fragrance of possibility, a master of intent and expectations, a spellbinding talker with piercing blue eyes. As the aviation school prospectus had said some fifteen years earlier: the company expects to fly the Atlantic, expects to establish other schools, and so on. And as he had told reporters: he expected to have an announcement soon about a secret airplane. He was stating an intent, not an actual performance. Big things were always *about* to happen. He was exciting to be around. As the baker had said, "We all had so much confidence in Mr. Atwood and everybody felt so glorious and fine." Everybody rode the bubble of Rubwood stock skyward.

Judge Cox ruled in Atwood's favor. He had never promised the Thayers any stock from the holding company. The Thayers appealed the decision to the Massachusetts Supreme Judicial Court and lost. Harry Atwood never paid his lawyers.

Rubwood was in demand. Bert Anderson, Monson's pharmacist and a stockholder, met Atwood on the steps of his pharmacy. There's an offer to buy the company, Atwood said. He could sell out and get the stockholders several times their money.

"Let's sell," Anderson said without hesitation.

Atwood brought the good news to one of his larger investors, William P. Jordan, who held stock worth $27,500. He would need $15,000 to get the machinery in order for the sale, he said. They would get the best price possible for the company that way. Jordan loaned him the money. The money disappeared. When it came time to close the deal and accept more than $300,000 for the Rubwood Wheel manufacturing company, Atwood refused to sign.

Other money was missing. One owner of a company that had a large contract with Rubwood said that Atwood would collect money and not give it to Rubwood. In a sale to another company, he allegedly kept fifteen thousand dollars for himself. Some ten thousand dollars in the Rubwood account in the Monson National Bank is reported to have "mysteriously disappeared." When George Thayer arrived to redeem a promissory note for five thousand dollars which had come due, a bank executive, the cashier Harry Kendall, had to tell him there was "insufficient funds." Kendall was also treasurer of Rubwood Inc., an investor, and a friend of Atwood. He was superintendent of the church Sunday school, which the Atwood daughters attended with his children.

There were many questionable transactions. Jordan said he been tricked into signing a form releasing Atwood from any liability. Markus said that he had bought ten thousand dollars worth of stock for seventy-five thousand dollars, but Atwood had never delivered the stock certificates. The company treasurer had watched Atwood tear up a letter that would have delivered stock to an investor.

At one director's meeting, the board voted Atwood a sixty-thousand-dollar mortgage for money he had advanced the company. His legal counsel, Allan S. Locke, called the mortgage "an outrage against the stockholders." Earlier, Locke had investigated Rubwood for some investors and delivered a glowing report. Atwood had retained him as general counsel and called him frequently—not that he followed his advice.

Locke also wanted to know why the land Atwood had bought as a trustee for the corporation was in his name, including some of the fourteen hundred acres he had bought for his planned cement housing development. Atwood, as usual, was evasive. At the trial he had been asked about some of his land deals: "This land that you purchased for this company, the title of it, it stands in your name today, does it not?"

"No sir, not all of it."

"Some of it?"

"To tell you the truth, I don't know just how the title stands. I was buying it and I don't know it has been transferred. Yet."

"Don't you know perfectly well it hasn't been transferred?"

"To who?"

"To the corporation."

"Yes sir. It has not been transferred to the corporation as yet."

He ignored his own legal counsel. "I tried several times to get him to transfer these titles, but he became less and less interested in so doing as time went on," said Locke. He also wanted to know why Atwood hadn't cancelled an earlier mortgage, as he had promised. "I was able to do nothing as to having recommendations for proper management of the corporation carried out." After seven months, Locke was through, and besides, Atwood had only paid him one quarter of his retainer. Nathan Lawrence, a company officer who had followed Atwood from Smithfield, also quit in disgust. Atwood owed him back salary, travel expenses, and re-payment of a loan.

Atwood was managing the company his own way. Rubwood had more orders than it could fill. He went around trying to get the orders cancelled. Edward R. Clark, Rubwood's general promotion manager and an investor, was with Atwood when he visited the U.S. Bobbin & Shuttle Company in Providence, Rhode Island, and tried to convince the president to cancel his contract. He lost more business when he offended an-other company with a large contract. Even though the company had loaned Atwood personally four thousand dollars (which he never re-paid), he sent the order C.O.D.

The list of creditors was growing much faster than the list of customers. There were more than one hundred creditors, a small telephone direc-tory of Monson and the surrounding towns, with debts ranging from fifty cents due Squier's Garage to $10,331 owed to Edward R. Clark, $4,000 to Markus, $1,500 to the pharmacist. Atwood was even on the list himself claiming nearly $9,000.

With many debts, a product that was in demand, and a company that had been courted by many who thought it could be profitable, the stock-holders met and agreed to file a voluntary petition for bankruptcy. On May 10, 1927, when the bankruptcy was granted, the four-year-old Rubwood Wheel Company had assets of $66,361.71 and a debt of $161,677.32. There was some office furniture, a safe, typewriters, one truck, $20,000 in machinery and cash on hand of $11.71.

Atwood had failed again, this time with a successful, highly praised product. His other ventures—the Williamsport aeroplane engine, the navy seaplane, the aviation schools—may have failed because of the diffi-cultly of the aviation marketplace or bad luck or lack of funds for further experiments, but this was a cave-in of his own making.

He was never interested in making spool heads or kiddie car wheels. He wanted to build airplanes, submarines, and even space ships. That's what he talked about: the revolution that the airplane would soon bring, and how we would next be traveling to the stars. He wanted to write epics, not invoices. He wanted to be the inventor of an epoch-making invention, not shoe heels and unbreakable toilet seats.

That glorious and fine feeling his stockholders felt gave way to anger. Markus was furious, as might be expected. Atwood had pumped him like a well, for stock, for cash for the company and himself, for thousands of dollars at a time when the bread he baked sold for a few cents a loaf. Men like the Thayers, Jordan, and Clark, were businessman and speculators. In any year, they could expect some losses. But such a loss for a baker (or a pharmacist or a hatter) cut into a family's savings.

Markus claimed that Atwood had once told him to stick with the company and he would profit: he would deliberately bankrupt the company, clear his debts, and divide the spoils with Kendall and Markus. He planned to use the holding company to shelter his assets, Markus said. The Thayers also believed that Atwood had used the two companies in a shell game to move money around, and had schemed for years to bankrupt Rubwood. When the windows were covered with whitewash at the factory, they believed he was secretly moving equipment out for a quick, off-the-book sale. He would have had bankruptcy declared sooner, Atwood told Markus, but his father had been handling some company money and he didn't want him involved.

This theory may be too elaborate. Atwood was an improviser. He had a different plan from moment to moment, and finally he had made too many conflicting promises. That's what Locke had witnessed as general counsel to the company. He had seen the willful destruction of a useful invention. "Atwood I firmly believe wasted most of the money that went into the Monson Company, much of which I believe he obtained on promises that he never intended to keep," he wrote to one of the bankruptcy referees. "He told me that he would be a fool to keep the various promises which I heard him make."

Katrina was a schoolgirl, but she had an insight that many of the stockholders would have coveted. "He brought up people to handle finances, but he wouldn't listen to them. I can remember discussions on that," she said. "No matter what your position was with the company—you could be vice-president, you could be treasurer—he didn't allow you to have your own say so. And if he wanted something such as that great big underneath garage or tunnel built, where did the money come from? The factory. So you're headed straight for bankruptcy.

"He milked the business dry.

"As father even used to say: 'I always went into bankruptcy because I had to run the whole show. And I shouldn't have.'"

Ten days after Charles Lindbergh made his solo 1927 flight across the Atlantic, a Boston newspaper had a stunning scoop:

"The *Boston Traveler* today gives first news of hitherto secret preparations for regular transatlantic airplane service using sky-liners carrying at least 100 passengers each," reported a copyright, page-one story.

"Boston will be one of the first ports in America to get the service . . .

"Not one cent's worth of stock in the organization is available to the public.

"The date of the start of the service is not divulged.

"On this day when the public pulse is kept a-flutter with thrilling exploits and adventure, comes a story seemingly fantastic at the outset, yet one that, told in even the most conservative manner, adds to human history a chapter of tremendous importance . . .

"Until now the plan has been protected by the utmost secrecy."

"Quick upon the heels of Capt. Lindbergh's triumph comes the *Boston Traveler*'s discovery of secret preparations that have been going on for 16 years without even a breath of it reaching the ears of a single person outside the powerful group of engineers and financiers and sportsmen who are making possible the gigantic undertaking."

By "sheer luck and not necessarily good reportorial work" the reporter had followed "the trail of this astonishing enterprise . . . from Boston to New York and Dayton and finally to the very heart of it all in an extremely interesting establishment on a lonely mountain top in Massachusetts." There he found, of course, Harry Atwood, but he was not named because the newspaper said, in boldface capital letters, the "designer shuns publicity." The reporter was Joe Toye. Sixteen years earlier Toye had been one of the reporters whom Atwood had flown into New Hampshire, and who later greeted Atwood's triumphal return from St. Louis to New York flight with a trophy.

Toye and many others had thought Atwood was dead—a misapprehension that happened a few times in his life. He had "disappeared from public life and has not been heard from since by many of his intimate friends." That helped him work in secrecy, said the mystery man, echoing his old dream of retiring to a farm to perfect the "art of navigating the air."

"This man of the mountain-top, the man whose exploits years ago were flashed to all parts of the civilized world, the man whom the world believed dead, is the designer of the great air-liner that will ply the air lanes over the vast Atlantic that battered the breast of the tiny flagship of the Genoese navigator of 1492."

However, after all that fanfare, the *Boston Traveler* couldn't print the plans—they were secret. The paper had the information "but as that information was given in confidence, this newspaper quite naturally will not violate the confidence given." At a later date the tale could be told.

This story, with its mystery airliner and mystery mountaintop man, is a classic of the breathless now-it-can-be-told school of amazin' science stories. The blue sky salesman had worked his spell on Toye.

"But," the story continued, "it can be told that the new plane, while adhering strictly to the exact science of aviation and following mathematical rules laid down after tests at the Massachusetts Institute of Technology, will be at the same time a craft that will astonish even the most airwise of all aeronautical engineers."

The airliner would cross the ocean in less than forty-eight hours, flying by way of the Azores. "Our air-liners will have more than one motor, more than two motors, more than three motors—how many more we would rather you would not divulge at this time," the unnamed inventor told the reporter.

"Our planes will be bigger than present planes—much bigger. You can tell that much. They will be much bigger. Our planes will contain cabins and berths and dining rooms and recreation rooms and promenade decks. They will be heated throughout. It will not be necessary in hot weather to use electric fans.

"We will be able to maintain a schedule. We will be able to give safe transportation so that women and children will not hesitate to fly to and from Europe."

The year before Lindbergh's flight, there was no regular air service in the United States. On the pioneering routes, a Fokker Trimotor was often used, which carried four passengers. The aviation business was almost dead in the first half of the 1920s. New airplanes and engines could not compete with the surplus from World War I. The "Lindbergh Boom" followed his great flight; in two years three hundred million dollars was invested in aviation. As he had when he ran the du Pont air school, Atwood was determined to catch the wave early. In his usual way, he overshot. In 1927 a determined passenger could patch together a thirty-two-hour flight across the country, in open cockpits and enclosed cabins, if he agreed to being dumped anywhere when they took on more mail. Regular commercial air service to Europe was twelve years away.

A week later the mystery man on the mountaintop was persuaded—"only at the strongest urging"—to reveal himself.

"If you insist," Atwood said.

"The man's abhorrence of publicity is very real. He has seen so many persons make extravagant promises only to have the promises unfulfilled," Toye reported. The week before he had refused to comment on Lindbergh's flight. "It would be a cheap attempt on my part to get publicity at Lindbergh's expense," Atwood said.

He was photographed seated in a wicker rocking chair, looking thoughtfully to one side. His crisp three-piece suit and grey temples made him look dignified, assured—the look that the important men of his generation wore, bankers, senators, statesmen.

No mention was made of Rubwood or the three-week-old Rubwood bankruptcy. His famous flights were noted, as well as "a strange coincidence": several years earlier, an aviator named Harrison Atwood had been killed in Japan, Atwood claimed. That man was also known as Harry Atwood, and when the news came through, many people assumed he was dead. He did not make any public announcements to correct the record. He had used his new-found invisibility to his advantage, he said. (The *New York Times* said it had no record of the other Atwood's death.)

He described the hundred-passenger plane further, saying he had "advanced a new idea which will permit the building of huge wing structures hitherto considered impossible . . . and also permits passengers to be carried inside of the structure, free from the inconvenience of the elements or even the noise of the engines." The plane would be built from the composite, laminated wood Atwood had been experimenting with since before he built the heavy navy seaplane—experiments that had given birth to thousands of kiddie car wheels and toilet seats.

He was describing a flying wing, one of the alluring dreams of aviation, thought to be the purest airplane; all wing, no fuselage, and, in some designs, no tail. There had been tailless designs since the days when Atwood had flown. In 1913 his old boss, Starling Burgess, had built a version of the British flying wing, the Dunne, its two wings swept back in a V.

The dream had taken on a new life, and a much grander scale, in the 1920s. In 1924 the German designer Hugo Junkers published his plan for a hundred-passenger flying wing with four engines. An Austrian engineer, Dr. Edmund Rumpler, was promoting a twin-hull flying wing in 1926, which would fly 135 and a crew of thirty-five in style: passenger cabins were housed in the leading edge of the wing, and separated from the ten noisy thousand-horsepower engines by a wide promenade deck. Rumpler tried for four years to get financial backing in the United States and Europe. His faith, like that of many flying wing designers, was unshakable: "Give me wings large enough and sufficient motive power and I'll take the earth for an airplane ride."

Atwood's flying wing would "be so much bigger than anything the public has ever seen that I feel the whole story would be almost incredible," he said. They would not "advertise the possibility of elaborate drawing rooms, dining rooms, bathrooms, swimming pools or other luxuries"; rather, the first plane would be simple. "Our plans have passed the tests of the most eminent of aviation engineers." Like a chant, the article repeated: "No stock is for sale. No stock will be for sale. Yet plenty of money is available for any need."

Other newspapers picked up the story, including the *New York Times*, the *New York Herald Tribune*, and, closer to Atwood's home, the *Springfield Republican*, which reported the details of a plan quickly taking shape. A smaller model, but "one larger than anything now in passenger use" would be built in a "comparatively short" time to serve Springfield and other cities in western Massachusetts. The big plane would have "as many as 100 engines, of light weight and small horsepower, distributed inside the wing along the whole front of the machine." The plane would be launched by electric tram and land in the water on "pneumatic pontoons." A factory in or near Monson had been "secured" to build the plane and land was being "considered" to build an airport to test the plane.

The *Springfield Republican* ran a picture of Atwood's navy seaplane flying, which they said had demonstrated the strength of Rubwood. "It is because of his income from his patents in Rubwood that he is now able to devote his entire time to aviation." The bankruptcy was not mentioned. The big flying wing was not a commercial venture, Atwood stressed. "Financing the project is being arranged for . . . among friends, who realize they may lose what they put into it," said the paper.

"Lindbergh's flight woke me up," Atwood said. "From now on I'm all aviation." The uncrossed ocean had come back into view. The Rubwood Wheel Company was newly bankrupt and forgotten. He was at the moment closely following the transatlantic flight of Clarence Chamberlin and Charles Levine, just weeks after Lindbergh. "Yesterday," said the *Springfield Republican*, "he was found with his hand on the dial of a radio set, and he could hardly eat his luncheon for fear that some announcement regarding Chamberlin and Levine would come without his hearing it."

"Lindbergh is glorious," he told Toye. "He is the man. I am water that has gone over the dam. I am a has-been. I am a member of the G.A.R. of aviation," he said, referring to the Grand Army of the Republic, the organization of Civil War veterans.

He would not seek any more headlines. "Those most closely connected with the plan" insisted "that only the most vague information be given to the public because 'so much bunk has been handed out by people saying what they were going to do' that they did not wish to make any promises that would not be fulfilled . . . Lindbergh did not have a lot of talk about what he was going to do—he just went ahead and did it." They will say "no more until such time as the group can demonstrate rather than talk." And nothing was ever said again.

"I could write a book for you telling you of the nice things he has done since you were around these parts, but at any rate you may be sure that from now on I intend to keep right on his trail," Joseph E. Kerigan wrote to Frank Broadhurst. Kerigan was one of the lawyers Atwood had not paid. Broadhurst, who controlled a large block of holding company stock, had returned to Smithfield, North Carolina, where he had first met Atwood. Perhaps, Kerigan suggested, "we might try to work out something to our mutual advantage." "I propose to stay right on his back until every means to force him to do what is right are exhausted," Kerigan said.

In the spring of 1930, things were rapidly unraveling for Atwood. His fourth wife, Mary Dalton, "Mother Mary," as the children called her, died from a severe infection following childbirth. She gave birth to Harry Jr. in February and spent the next months in two hospitals and a sanitarium. She died the day before Easter. She was thirty-four years old. A minister and his wife took in Harry Jr. and raised him to adulthood, but Atwood would never let them adopt him, despite their repeated requests.

Atwood was living on handouts. In the four years since Rubwood had folded, his principal occupation had been borrowing money. He had even sent his mother and one daughter to solicit his in-laws, the Satterthwaites. They had loaned Atwood money long after their daughter had died, but now they refused.

One former stockholder was giving him $100 a week. Frank M. Andrew had been President of Rubwood Inc. at its founding, and had held 46 percent of the common stock. He bought in for about $100,000 and sold out later for $150,000, making him the only one on record to profit from Rubwood.

He regarded Atwood as a "crazy inventor, a person with a very keen mind, a facile talker, and in many ways a brilliant person, but one who is irritable and lacks business capacity." Andrew took some pity on Atwood. The man's wife was sick and he had his back up against it, he said, so he loaned him money, not writing it down or asking for security, in all he guessed about six or seven thousand dollars. And in 1929, he bought the last of Atwood's shares in the holding company—54 percent of the common stock—for only fifteen hundred dollars, less than one-tenth of its former value, and at that he knew he was taking a gamble. Andrew had a buyer in mind, and would give Atwood part of the profits, but the stock market crash of October 1929 ended that. Rubwood Inc. was worthless.

"Things had gotten rough for quite a long time," Katrina remembered. "And I didn't think anything of it. We were a happy family. Give us money, fine that's great. None? Okay, so we don't have any. I would cut out new cardboards for my shoes. Sometimes I had to use newspapers—that was bad. That wouldn't last very long." She asked her father for the burlap that wrapped the large rolls of rubber at the factory. "So he brought home a lot of the burlap. I got out the needle and thread, and I made myself a skirt. I didn't know how to sew very well, in fact, I didn't know at all. But I would gather it, then I'd draw the great big thread and try it until I had a gathered skirt. And I smelled like rubber," she said, and laughed. "Couldn't get that odor out of it. I would wash it and wash it."

Her father, if he noticed, never said anything. "I couldn't say to him: I need a pair of shoes. He didn't have the money. Even for school lunches. Then of course the maid disappeared and then the chauffeur disappeared. Vera still stayed on and cooked, and she got no salary."

The bank moved to foreclose his house in December 1929, and may have waited through the spring while Mary Dalton was ill. The bank sold his house two weeks after her funeral. Merchants came to repossess a car, a truck, gardening equipment, and the house's electric power generators.

Two weeks after Atwood had lost his house, attorney Kerigan and his partner sent the sheriff to arrest him for unpaid debts. That night in the sheriff's office, Harry Atwood declared bankruptcy, and listed his debts from memory. He owed about three-hundred thousand dollars and claimed assets of three-hundred dollars, a pile of household furniture. He had lost all the land he once owned to back taxes and had nothing to show from Rubwood. He was forty-six years old. His newborn son was with another couple, he had long ago lost track of his first daughter, and now he was sending his three younger daughters off to their grandparents in Pennsylvania.

The three girls, at ages fifteen, thirteen, and ten, were coming home from the one-room schoolhouse on the bus, an open-sided truck with one board down the center and a canvas top. Coming up the hill, the bus halted and the three Atwood children were taken off. They were put in a car and driven to Springfield. The children were offered no explanations, no chance to say good-bye to their friends. Harry hadn't even met the bus. He had sent an uncle.

Their mother was dead, lost to them. "We couldn't even talk about our mother or ask about her or grandmother would still burst into tears," said Katrina. And now they were cut off from their father.

They hated him for sending them away. That day haunted them all their lives, and they recounted the tale as you would the misfortune from a tornado or other great storm: a sudden random fury, then the picking up afterward and the survivor's questions.

"We thought we'd been skipped," said Katrina—as if his children were another debt he ran out on. "We thought he didn't even like us."

"We never even went home," said Gene. "He was unloading." He dumped all three of them in a hotel to wait for a couple of days, she said. "Just like you dump garbage."

The original court documents are folded in three and the thick pile of these documents—official court forms, notarized contracts, and the most offhand bill—is wrapped with a ribbon. The outside of each document is stamped with the date filed and then, in ink, whether the claim was allowed or denied. There are as many as three or four kinds of ink on some and they feel like currency, like old handled bills.

These documents are a small Pompeii—Harry Atwood and the merchants of Monson caught at the moment the lava flowed in. Here are hundreds of transactions, the routine commerce of the day frozen at one moment: all the telephone calls made, electricity used, car repairs, each piece of fruit and box of Rinso from grocery orders (and always cigars), each vest, glove, and union suit.

There is the careful script of old farmers listing milk and cream delivered, the smudged and greasy receipt from a local garage, and long, typed ledgers from the grocer and the baker. Other bills provide the intimate details of daily life: the druggist, the hospitals for Mary Dalton's care, and the undertaker. The last bill is chilling because it is as itemized as the grocer's bill—grey plush dropside casket, chestnut outercase, preparation of remains, floral casket spray, funeral coach and limousine to funeral . . . $453.

He had built a towering debt. Promissory notes with his signature were like the currency of some small-time nation caught up in an inflationary fever: Harry N. Atwood promises to pay five thousand dollars in six months at 6 percent interest, three thousand dollars in three months, one thousand dollars on demand. There were a few larger borrowings: one hundred thousand dollars in cash secured with stock, due in five years without interest.

He signed each time with great assurance. As he had told the Wall Street lawyer, he would be a fool to keep all these promises. It didn't seem to weigh on his mind.

The list was long. He figured that he owed the attorney Kerigan and his partner twenty-two thousand dollars each, his father fourteen thousand dollars (which could have represented the sale of the family's Roxbury house and a large share of his retirement savings), his brother-in-law Frank Satterthwaite ten thousand dollars, the president of the Monson National Bank nine thousand dollars, and the bank itself ten thousand dollars. There was also his usual cast of creditors, Markus, Kendall, Jordan, Clark, and others.

If he had one pattern, it was this: he spent other people's money, spent it freely, and then convinced them to loan him more. Atwood regarded money theoretically; it was like light—both a particle and a wave, and it moved fast.

Kerigan and many others in Monson were sure that Atwood had hidden a great deal of money, three hundred thousand dollars in cash. So much money had crossed his hands—where was it? Markus said that once Atwood was drunk and confided that he had hidden money in New York. He must be holding some valuable contract or patent; why else, they asked, would a shrewd investor like Andrew "be so 'chicken-hearted' as to part with several thousands of dollars to this bankrupt." How could so many people keep loaning him money and yet his only assets were a pile of furniture and "two patents of uncertain value"?

They went after Atwood with great zeal and enthusiasm. "Since the bankruptcy we have been putting Atwood over the hurdles to endeavor to discover falsified bankruptcy schedules and concealed assets," Kerigan wrote Broadhurst in one of the letters he was sending almost weekly.

Atwood's trustee in the bankruptcy was James E. Murphy, an attorney in the same law office as Kerigan and his partner. He was not a "disinterested person" as the bankruptcy code requires. In fact, he petitioned the bankruptcy referee to join the pursuit: "I have a source of information concerning past acts of the bankrupt which would be of considerable help if I were employed as counsel in this matter," and, in league with another lawyer, "I believe we could discover concealed assets and enhance the value of the estate." Murphy was sure that Atwood had been worth four hundred thousand dollars in 1926, if not more. The referee refused his petition, but allowed him to hire a lawyer to pursue his leads.

They called in the FBI to investigate. The FBI listed Atwood's occupation as "inventor and stock promoter" and began visiting people, recording all manner of innuendo and hearsay as "fact": "Subject is known to have swindled people in Reading, Pa., and in North Carolina before he came to Monson, Mass." Or so Jordan told the FBI. He couldn't recall the town in North Carolina or any names in Reading, but he said he had good information from a traveling salesman who had been through those towns. The FBI did not pursue the leads.

Atwood's bankruptcy case was open four years—the lawyers refused to let it close after one year. The creditors met regularly like some sort of Rotary Club. They "interrogated the bankrupt," as he was now known, on seven different occasions. They had a mission, a treasure hunt. They would have enjoyed nothing more than taking Atwood to court, and then seeing him off to jail.

They looked for years. They found no El Dorado of cash or valuable contracts, but hidden in his neighbor's barn they found his prize possession: A Steinway grand piano, medium size (five feet, seven inches long), mahogany finish. He had not listed it as an asset. When it was discovered, he said he had given it to his neighbor as a gift. Here at last was something they could seize. Atwood loved to play the piano; everyone knew that. He tried to buy it back—it was the one thing he struggled to save—but he couldn't raise the $750 they asked. Until they closed his case, he was a financial nonentity.

The bankruptcy estate realized one other sale. Murphy wrote to the bankruptcy referee to say, with some evident satisfaction, that four years after Atwood had declared bankruptcy, Murphy had made an important discovery. There "came into his hands and possession a trophy given to the bankrupt by the *New York Times.*" When Atwood had flown from Boston to New York, the *Times* had made much of this trophy, repeatedly showing it to readers, even reporting the first time Atwood saw the trophy in the *Times* window: "Conquest of the Air," two figures dancing on top of a globe, one holding aloft a golden biplane. Front-page headline news twenty-three years earlier.

The creditors asked fifty dollars. The trophy sold for two.

In Monson they now believed that he was capable of enormous evil. In his every gesture, they saw malice. He was a sharper, a con man. Nothing more. Nothing he had ever said was to be believed. Had he landed a plane on the White House lawn? Did he ever intend to make anything with his Rubwood patents? And those investors who had ridden with At- wood as the Rubwood wheels hit the curb, what had they seen? "I don't know. Sometimes I think they imagined they saw the thing flexed," said Bill Stone.

Years after he had lost his house, when one of his creditors owned it, the house burned down. They suspected him of that fire. Rumors spread about Mary Dalton's death. He neglected her health, people said. And an affair he had with a clergyman's wife was the town gossip.

Around Monson, for years, even after all the talk had died down, he was known as "the man who robbed the town."

They built him into some kind of Jesse James, said Herb Murray, whose father, Robert, had worked for Atwood pouring cement up at the house, and driving booze down from Canada during Prohibition. Robert never had a bad word for Atwood. One time he heard someone say: "Harry At- wood was so crooked he used to steal the coins from the newspaper boxes."

"'That goddamned fool never knew Atwood!' his father said. 'If the guy knew Harry Atwood, he knew the truth of it: when Harry took out a paper, if the paper was a nickel, he put in a dime.'

"But they had all kinds of stories: how he swindled the people. My father never ever agreed with it."

All kinds of stories—missing money, missing stock, deceptive prac- tices—and the FBI, the creditors, and a deployment of lawyers looking to nail him with a criminal act. The FBI did discover a fraudulently obtained mortgage. In an attempt to save his house, Atwood had put his mortgage in his brother-in-law's name, without his knowledge. But nothing could be made to stick, as one lawyer wrote the assistant United States attorney: "I must frankly confess that though the testimony of the bankrupt taken appears to be considerably perjured, yet they are with reference to minor details, and do not go to the root of the evil itself . . . it would appear to me that this bankrupt can be shown to have been wholly unscrupulous, and if could be pinned down to a definite criminal act" he might find a way to pay his creditors.

No evidence was found. There was no violation of the National Bankruptcy Act. The FBI closed its case; the bankruptcy was discharged. Harry Atwood flew free. He always did. And he never looked back.

"I entertained them well," he said later. "Why should I pay them for being entertained? They had fun thinking they would get rich. They didn't and neither did I."

His creditors were left holding three hundred thousand dollars in debt. Some lives were ruined, others were hurt. Some never spoke about how much they had lost. The youngest shareholder, Bill Stone, didn't regret his hundred-dollar investment. "I had two trips to the mountains, so I got my money's worth out of it," he said.

Harry Kendall lost his job at the bank, and his house. He moved his family, two daughters and one son, to Springfield, and was last seen pumping gas.

Herman Markus lost his life's savings, more than twenty-thousand dollars. His wife died. He held on to his bakery, remarried, and led a baker's life, up early to open each day at 4 A.M. When anyone mentioned the Rubwood Wheel Company or the man who robbed the town, Markus would swear. He'd damn Harry Nelson Atwood up and down, and continue baking.

⫷ A Swinger of Birches

The birch is a tree of the cold north, thriving where other trees fail, bending where others would break. From its papery bark, the Abenaki fashioned canoes, bowls, tents, and even coffins.

From one six-inch-diameter birch, Harry Atwood said he could make an airplane that everyone could afford. With one birch tree he would soar higher than "a swinger of birches" launching out on an arching trunk, as Robert Frost had written: "I'd like to get away from earth awhile / And then come back to it and begin over." Harry Atwood was beginning again.

Whenever he got nervous, he went to the mountains. He had felt as free as a soaring bird in the mountains some twenty years earlier, the "bird-man" closing in on the record for the longest flight. The greatest sensation I ever had, he said at the time. Now he headed north to New Hampshire. He was staying at a small inn near Mt. Monadnock, one of the most climbed mountains in the world. He had no money, and sometimes no car. He was trying to keep a finance company from seizing his last car, a 1928 LaSalle Victoria, by transferring the title and talking someone into covering for him. Even so, the car was repossessed (after Atwood had evaded the company for two weeks). He borrowed money someplace to win it back.

At the inn he met a married woman who would finance his comeback.

She got him back on his feet. They would have an affair for years, and she desperately wanted to marry him. They each had the same license plate number, his in New Hampshire, hers in Rhode Island. She would visit him often in New Hampshire.

His dream this time was to build a small plane from the wood of one tree bonded with plastic. "Not a wire. Not a brace. Not a spar. Not a piece of fabric. Not a beam. Not a turn-buckle. Not a supporting metal fitting. Not a rivet. Not a welding. Not a single joint seam or piecing," as he would advertise. A dozen main parts, seventy-four parts in all. An average plane was made of thousands of parts. The "Airmobile" would be cheaper to make, safer to fly, the Model T of the air, one in every garage. Harry Atwood would be the Henry Ford of aviation. "Start 10 workers making that airplane at 8 o'clock in the morning and it could be in the air by 5 o'clock in the afternoon of that same day," Atwood said.

It was an audacious dream in the Great Depression, when people weren't buying cars or even shoes. Atwood was promising an alchemist's trick, turn a tree into an airplane, and then thousands of trees into thousands of airplanes, and turn hard times into prosperity for the factory that performed the feat.

In the fall of 1932 he convinced a staid and failing furniture company to take this gamble. The French and Heald Company had been making furniture in Milford, New Hampshire, since 1856; now there was little demand. They hired Harry Atwood to develop his new material, and in short order Atwood was chairman of the board and had written his own contract, and French and Heald, maker of chairs and tables, was in the airplane business.

Atwood had been experimenting with wood veneer materials before he had built his failed navy seaplane. He had a breakthrough insight some time in the last few years when he was going bankrupt and his wife was dying and almost anyone who knew his name was after him to collect a debt. If you could build a wood veneer and plastic structure like a cord tire, by wrapping separate layers or cords, you would have a strong, lightweight material.

He used birch veneer strips cut very thin, hundredths of an inch thick, layered with a cellulose acetate plastic, and then formed under pressure. Thin sheets were made of four to six layers. He called the resulting wood-plastic composite Duply, because he said he had been able to experiment at the DuPont labs at a time when he had nothing.

Duply was lightweight, stronger than aluminum of similar thickness, and fire resistant. The honeycomb structure developed for the Airmobile was designed to absorb the shock of crashes, and, Atwood said, was bulletproof.

The Airmobile would have a safe, slow landing speed. If there were a crash, "the occupants of the craft can all immediately step out of the airmobile, light up their cigarettes and go looking for the airmobile repair shop rather than the morgue," said Atwood's first convert, Emory Heald, president of French and Heald.

The early material was promising, but uneven. The first batches of Duply were tested at Atwood's alma mater, the Massachusetts Institute of Technology. There were great improvements from one sheet or tube to the next in the assembly of the layers. Maintaining a uniform heat and pressure created a homogenous material and improved the bonding of each part. But the tubes in particular were "not molded satisfactorily"; in immersion tests, moisture got in between the layers.

This was only one of the problems Atwood needed to solve. To go from the simple sheets and tubes to a complete airplane, "a certain amount of ingenuity must be exercised by the designing engineer to insure all areas of the structure being accessible to heat and pressure of the mold," Professor Joseph Newell, a leading airplane structures consultant, reported in December 1934. Some of the needed shapes would be challenging.

Even with the rough samples he tested, Newell found Duply "equal, or superior, to aluminum alloy in similar forms." "Duply offers the aircraft manufacturer a new material of great possibilities," he said. Newell expected that Duply would be produced uniformly, and eventually "by fully automatic or semi-automatic methods . . . If so, Duply possesses an important advantage over most other aircraft materials in that it can be produced in quantity by machine . . . at low cost."

If Atwood could perfect Duply, a dozen parts would be too many. He envisioned a one-piece airplane. From the nose to the tail, from wing tip to wing tip, the ideal Airmobile would be one seamless, streamlined piece, which would slip through the air. This was an early aviator's dream. Atwood had flown in a rougher, more improvisational era; he once had a plane, built by the best in the business, come apart in the air.

At the moment, though, he was producing inconsistent sheets and tubes. He had to develop the technology to make the basic plastic material and the more complex shapes, win patents, and as soon as possible get something airborne that the struggling company could market and sell.

Atwood and a small crew worked in secrecy in a closed part of the factory. No one had seen that before in the furniture business or in Milford. Any furtive activity implied guilt. New Englanders were open about their privacy. Secrets were shared, understood, and unspoken. There was something showy about doing work in secret. People began to talk.

A photographer came to Milford one day and was taking pictures of the town. The police chief peppered the stranger with questions. The photographer was annoyed that he was under suspicion just for showing up on a public street. The chief asked all strangers what they were doing in town. This was as it should be, said the *Milford Cabinet*. The innocent can answer, only the guilty stumble.

Milford was a cautious town of four thousand people, whose conservatism was enhanced by the Depression. A newspaper editorial looked with pride at a father and son who had served seventy-six consecutive years as clerk at the Baptist church. Around town everyone knew the original city-delivery postman who had walked his route twenty-two years before retiring. The *Cabinet* itself had been published and edited by the same family since 1809. The paper quoted an "acquaintance whose home has been in the west." Visiting New Hampshire, "he was impressed by the old family associations, the traditions that only come with years. In his region, he said, many of the towns are so new that there are few old people and the graveyards have just been laid out." Milford would stick with its old Yankee ways.

New ideas were resisted. A zoning committee was appointed in 1933, but no zoning laws were passed until 1970. The *Cabinet* was critical of the New Deal and dismissed any call to redistribute wealth or shake things up. People have to eat, said the editors, but this public relief and welfare is out of hand—it's driving taxes up. Far less radical proposals were discussed and rejected: several towns wanted to promote an apple blossom festival, but others said that tourists didn't bring jobs, just a blight of more cars and hot dog stands. Towns couldn't even agree on the right time; some 41 of the state's 235 towns and cities observed daylight savings time. Neighboring towns kept different clocks. In some towns, factories and houses were on "advanced" time, while schools and stores followed standard time.

Milford was the "Granite Town," which had given New Hampshire the name, the "Granite State." At the start of the thirties, Milford had fifteen granite quarries, and many mills and factories, like the French and Heald furniture company. Milford was a town that moved to the factory whistle. "We felt a little superior to the neighboring towns," said William B. Rotch, who came of age in the 1930s and later edited the *Milford Cabinet*. "They didn't have whistles."

Milford was like the granite quarries it took pride in; rock solid, a place where change could only be won by the skillful use of great force. A knowledge of levers, to move and rotate dead weight, was essential. This was not a town you would pick to pioneer a modern lightweight material, a thin veneer to take to the air. This was not a town given to experiments.

But by the mid-1930s, the big wooden sign welcoming visitors to Granite Town had fallen down; the quarries, losing out to hard times and concrete, were closing. The Depression settled over the town like a gray flannel fog. On the Milford common, the Oval, men would gather as early as six in the morning, hoping to be among the lucky few who would be hired for just about the only work there was, digging ditches for thirty-five cents an hour. There was no work to be had. In 1933, married women teachers were ordered to leave their jobs. Wages for teachers, town employees, and factory workers had been cut 10 percent in 1931. Farms failed. "Cows and Furniture by Auction," was a familiar advertisement. There were more deaths than births in town.

People made do; asking for help was admitting defeat. One out of eight people in the state was on relief—but that was only half of the unemployed.

The company that Atwood proposed to lead into the air age, French and Heald, was "the backbone of the town," said Rotch, and part of Milford's pride. There had never been a strike in the company's nearly eighty-year history. "Few industrial concerns have had such a close and confidential relationship with the public," said Rotch. Some twenty years earlier, in 1912, on a January night when it was twenty below zero, the factory had burned down. Within days the citizens of Milford had raised fifty thousand dollars to help rebuild the factory. In the 1930s, French and Heald was a furniture company with the demeanor of a Beacon Hill law firm, its main office marked by plaques honoring the founding family. There was a bronze one commemorating the company's founder, David Heald: "Beloved Parent, Consistent Christian, Useful Citizen, Painstaking Manufacturer, Honest Man." And another bronze plaque to his eldest son: "a lover of all mankind—his life was filled with accomplishments worthy of emulation by those who follow him."

A promotional booklet the company produced in 1931 said one thing: stability. Three generations of Healds, each shown in a formal portrait, had led the company. The last page of the brochure listed twenty men who had been employed twenty-five years or more, making "honest merchandise." The Healds had been making furniture since before the Civil War and would continue, guided by the Golden Rule. "With business competition constantly becoming more keen and the struggle for existence so much more difficult, the present officers of the Company are trying earnestly to demonstrate that real success in business can only be attained by the practice of those fundamental Christian virtues, —honesty, courage, optimism, love of one's fellow men, and an exemplification, in their relations with all mankind, of the practical application of the Golden Rule."

There are nearly twenty photos in the booklet, but only two show furniture. There is no hint of the smell of wood shavings; no photos of the men working in the shop, or close-ups of dovetails and joinery. There are no boasts about plentiful New Hampshire hardwoods or excellent craftsmanship. There are no boasts at all. That was the tradition in the extensive New England furniture industry. Quality was assumed; to sell anything inferior was dishonest. They were square dealers who didn't bargain; setting a price you didn't intend to charge was not proper. If the customer didn't like it, he could go elsewhere.

French and Heald was an unlikely incubator for a risky, experimental airplane venture, but these were desperate times. Aviation was wide open, a gambler's business. You had to develop a new technology and a new market at the same time. The varieties of failure were many. A plane could succeed but have no buyers; it could fail, frustrating waiting customers, and forfeit the market. Engineers and aviators in the young business were kind of like show business people, knowing that they could be riding a boom or a bust, be gone tomorrow, by business failure or flying accident. Those who succeeded in building airplanes, such as Glenn Curtiss, had a line of failed planes, crashes, wrong ideas. To outsiders it looked like folly, building something that might crash, but the aviators knew it was all part of experimenting.

Furniture didn't have these problems. There is no suspense in building a new chair. Provide four legs of roughly the same length, and perhaps a stretcher or two, and it will stand. No one has to be sold on the idea of sitting down or owning a chair.

The credo of Milford, and its backbone industry, French and Heald, could be expressed by something the *Milford Cabinet*'s editor had said when Atwood called a public meeting to explain the Airmobile. Though he was interested and encouraged people to attend, he might not be there: "We're old enough to control our curiosity."

The first time the men and women of the editor's generation had read about flying, it was most likely in a popular school primer poem, "Darius Green and His Flying-Machine." Darius Green is a "country dunce" who secretly builds a flying machine in the barn. On the fourth of July, when he believes his brothers have gone to town, he straps on his wings, planning to surprise everyone at the festivities. "I'll astonish the nation and all creation . . . Over their heads I'll sail like an eagle." He jumps from the barn and crashes, to the derision of his hiding brothers.

The poem was so well known that back when Atwood was preparing to leave St. Louis on his record flight, the *Post-Dispatch* ran a small sketch about a bent old man who had come a long way from New England to see Atwood's flight. "I tried to do it once myself," he said, and signed the hotel register "Darius Green." A year before, it was news when the poem's author had gone out to meet the aviator Claude Grahame-White who was then flying near Boston.

Darius Green was a lesson remembered by those who still had doubts about flying. *(If God had intended man to fly . . .)* The poem concludes:

> And this is the moral,—Stick to your sphere . . .
> Or, if you insist, as you have the right,
> On spreading your wings for a loftier flight,
> The moral is,—Take care how you light.

Duply was being measured and so was Harry Atwood. He was fifty years old with white hair, and when he posed for a newspaper picture, he had lost some of his polish. He did not wear his suit with the crisp elegance he had shown eight years earlier. His tie was crooked and hung over the lapel of his jacket. He dressed more like the small-town Rotarians and bankers he had to court. But his gaze was extraordinary. He sat in a rickety lawn chair with his arms around "Chub-Chub," his pet kinkajou, a South American raccoon-like animal. In the photo, this exotic pet is upstaged by Atwood's intensity. He stares right through the camera and beyond. He stares out as if from a dark cave—his eyes deep in the darkness of his furrowed brow and the rings beneath. He looks as if he has been up night after night, and will find no rest.

When people described him then, they referred to his enthusiasm, his drive, his ideas, or his manner. They never mentioned his age, never noted that here was a man starting over with a risky venture at an age when others have established reputations and know that retirement is in view.

Clarence Farr was a young aeronautical engineer just a year out of college when he met Harry Atwood in 1934. Atwood was hiring. Farr was a graduate of the highly selective aeronautical engineering program at

MIT: two hundred applied, thirty were selected. Like many in his generation, Farr remembered the first airplane he ever saw—a barnstormer
landed in his town—and that boyhood sight had set him on his course.
Airplanes were glamorous, they were the celebrity technology of the era.
Young people everywhere knew that the future was in the sky.

"By June 1933, when we graduated, the airplane industry was flat on its
back and on top of that the big Depression was on, which made two
whammies, not one," Farr said. "In February 1933 there was one guy of
our graduating class who had a job. The job was to go back and work for
the A & P store in Bennington, Vermont, where he had left four years before to come to MIT. And we envied him."

Farr did land a job one month after graduation, working on the design
of streamlined trains in Philadelphia. But airplanes were the thing, and
besides, Farr wanted to return to New England. He was anxious to get a
job in aviation. Atwood took Clarence and his wife Aline out to lunch the
first time they met. He did something Aline would never forget.

"Harry ordered tomato juice and so did I," Aline recalled. "And Harry
took a drink of his tomato juice and called the waitress over and said,
'There are maggots in the tomato juice.' I had been drinking it and I
hadn't seen any. She, of course, was flustered and took it away. We had
great service and great food. But Harry didn't pay anything for that one.

"From that moment on, I didn't trust him," Aline said. Her husband,
busy trying to get the job, didn't notice that Atwood sent back his juice.
Aline would keep an eye on this fellow for both of them. "I always watched
him very carefully," she said.

Atwood hired Farr and another young engineer, Tom Knox. He kept
his small engineering staff as divided as he could. For a long time, even
though Knox and Farr saw each other on the job and were the entire full-
time engineering staff, they had nothing to do with each other after work.
But after a few months, the Knoxes invited the Farrs to dinner, and the
Farrs returned the invitation. "We found out after we got together as two
couples: Harry had told us not to have anything to do with the Knoxes because they didn't like us. And he had told them the same thing. He didn't
want us to get together socially," said Aline. They became good friends.

Atwood never had the two couples up to his house at the same time.
"He'd call us on a weekend or a Sunday morning or one time it was
Thanksgiving and I was getting dinner," said Aline. "We had guests. And
he wanted us to come immediately. And I said no, we're not going up
there. Well you couldn't say no to Harry. When he called—he didn't give
you a chance to say no. He just said come." So the Farrs and their guests

had to troop up to see Atwood about some matter that could have waited. Farr figured that Atwood wanted to size up his employee's family and friends. The Knoxes received similar calls.

"He could be very charming, but he was very dictatorial. Ordered people around," said Aline. "Commanding. Never would say—like saying to Katrina—would you play the piano? It was: Play the piano. And: Let's see what you can do. It was his way of doing things."

Once when Katrina was home from college, "she was put in an awkward situation," said Farr. "Harry summoned her to play the piano." Katrina liked emotional music; she played a part from Liszt. "I was showy like father," she said. "Father was showy in everything." Next he summoned Farr to play. The young engineer was partial to Bach. "Then," said Farr, "he'd sit down and look around as if to say: See how it's done." He told Farr that his playing was too mechanical. (Farr said, "Harry played honky-tonk.")

This was an act Atwood had perfected in his childhood. His sister, Avis, studied music at a conservatory and practiced long hours. Her younger brother would sit down and play the same piece right through the first time by ear, winning praise. His sister resented the attention, as well as his treatment of the music. His music was all show and no depth, she said. He put notes and flourishes in where they shouldn't be.

Aline did not like going to the house. Atwood's kinkajou would be running along on a pipe overhead or some of his trained gray squirrels might be at play. Used to life in the trees, the kinkajou knocked things over in the house and everything below the animal was a potential latrine. Aline found it an unsettling place. In Monson, Atwood had experimented on his house; in New Hampshire he went further. The entire house was an experiment. He had entombed an oak-framed farmhouse in stone and concrete, covering the clapboards outside and inside, the paneling and floor, and even the dining room table. The roof was covered in several inches of concrete anchored with chicken wire. Atwood was trying to build up a thermal mass to capture the sun's heat. Snakes loved to sun themselves on the roof.

Alongside the house he had a tower built and planned to add a beacon to guide airplanes to an airstrip he had in mind. Until then, he used the tower to study lightning. He claimed that he could predict where lightning would strike. Out front he had a concrete swimming pool built, and, as in Monson, it was fed by a spring. Emerson Young's fine old place was transformed into what most everyone referred to as "the castle."

Atwood usually received guests in the great room between the house and his lab. At one end was a concrete and stone boiler larger than a car, big enough to burn logs four feet long. The boiler's thick mass captured the heat and radiated it into the room. He ran pipes from this steam boiler out under the driveway to clear snow, and also, in another experiment, under the house. He flooded the basement to heat the house with rising steam. (Fearing fire, he preferred humid places, though there wasn't a fire extinguisher to be found in the house.) All the wallpaper in the house fell off.

He experimented with insulation, building in layers of sawdust between the concrete. He had an idea to make a furnace like a concrete sponge: mix the concrete with sawdust, burn out the sawdust, and fill this sponge with oil. The concrete would hold the heat.

His pet squirrels slept in the pockets of his jacket, which hung at the foot of his four-poster bed. "He would play with his squirrels by the hour (he has tamed more than 1,000 of them during his lifetime) if business didn't interfere. He has been known to carry a pet squirrel into a business conference with him, the squirrel quietly asleep in a coat pocket," said the *Manchester Union*. His squirrel Jimmy was a particular favorite.

The story around town was that while he was addressing the state legislature, one of his squirrels awoke, climbed out, and sat his shoulder. "A magician always has to have an attention-getter," said Farr. "He was a showman."

He knew how to command center stage. When he had a new invention to announce, he met with only one reporter at a time, even if that meant hours of repeating the same stories to maybe half a dozen reporters. If he had owned the newspapers, he couldn't have more effectively controlled the reporters. Meeting Atwood, they were like deer at night frozen in a car's headlights, easy pickings. They lost their journalist's skepticism. They didn't even check up on anything he said.

In New Hampshire, Bernie McQuaid, a reporter for the state's largest newspaper, the *Manchester Union*, "adopted Atwood and made him front page news for months," the editor of a rival newspaper said. "Bernie did such a fine job of making Atwood the mystery figure of aviation those days that the other papers had to cover him for their own protection . . . And Bernie worked the mine for all it was worth." They said that Bernie controlled his source, but it was Atwood who had him tied up.

The *Manchester Union* and all the other papers mythologized Atwood. He was "the greatest of early aviators," the man "who holds more 'firsts' in early aviation than any other flier," the man who "took all the cups at a Belmont Park air meet." He was the "holder of more patents from the

U.S. Patent office than any other inventor of his time," some 280 patents. (Ten times more than he actually had then and far from, say, the more than 1000 patents owned by Thomas Edison.) Yet he resented being called an inventor. "I like to think of myself as an engineer rather than an inventor, for to me the term 'inventor' connotes a fellow who blunders upon something, perhaps quite by accident, while an engineer is a man who thinks a thing through." He was no fool Darius Green.

All the familiar Atwood stories were told: how he broke a record the first time he soloed when Orville Wright went to town; how the navy refused to take him during World War I because he jumped when they fired a gun behind him. There were new stories, too, including one about the "'mechanical man' which he got up for a vaudeville actor back in 1910 . . . which was actually the first of the 'robots,' made the vaudeville actor a fortune and is still remembered by old-theatre-goers as one of the most awesome contraptions ever devised by the human mind."

Atwood presented new versions of his recent past. The Rubwood Wheel Company had failed in the Depression (not years earlier). The navy seaplane was recast as the promising, though flawed, ancestor of the Airmobile. That seaplane was built in "one-tenth" the time used for regular planes and weighed less than half as much.

Like most of the stories Atwood told and the ones told about him, they are made up of truth and lies. But each truth and each lie is enfolded one over the other like so many things in nature—flower buds, onions, tree rings, certain rock deposits. Tightly bound layers of deceit and honesty. So tight that what Harry Atwood said was at once false and true. When Harry told a story it was composed much like Duply, thin layers of wood and plastic bonded under pressure until it was so strong it could stop a bullet. So it was when Harry Atwood talked. Falsehood and fact, exaggeration and honest report. A chemical formulation that might read: truth-lie-lie-truth-truth-lie.

In all things, Harry Atwood was an inventor.

At a dinner with some professors from MIT, employees and a reporter, the professors were discussing little-known flying records of early aviation, some that Atwood owned and some he falsely claimed, like the altitude record. Then Atwood spoke up. "Do you know how I happened to take the altitude record back along in 1911?

"Well, when I was a youngster, my folks and myself used to spend all our vacations up here in New Hampshire, and there was nothing I enjoyed so much as climbing the mountains. I suppose, in my time, that I've climbed every mountain in New Hampshire more than 3,000 feet high.

"I remember one time a chum of mine and I had climbed to the top of Passaconaway—way up to the very peak of it, high as we could get. We sat there, resting, and watching an old eagle wheeling around, high above us. I don't know what gave me the thought, because airplanes hadn't been invented then, but I was jealous of that eagle. Here we'd climbed all the way up, and he was still higher than we were. I said to my friend: 'Some day I'm going to find a way of getting above that eagle.'

"My chum laughed, but I said, 'just you wait and see.'

"Years later I was flying one of my first ships up through New Hampshire. Up near the base of Passaconaway, or maybe it was Whiteface, I spotted an eagle, and that earlier scene came back to me. I headed for the eagle and say, it couldn't have been, and yet he looked just exactly like the old fellow I remembered, up there above Passaconaway.

"The eagle saw me coming and started to climb. I climbed too. I chased that eagle all over the mountains. I chased him until he quit, and I got above him, and do you know, it wasn't until some time afterward, on the return flight, that it occurred to me that to get above that eagle, I had to get above those mountains, and to do that, I had by far exceeded every airplane record in existence."

The *Manchester Union* reported it all under the headline, "Atwood Broke Altitude Records Chasing Eagle."

Harry Atwood was gathering believers. He assembled a remarkable team to design, develop, and promote the Airmobile: Clarence Chamberlin, second across the ocean after Lindbergh; Ruth Nichols, holder of three women's flying records; and Otto C. Koppen, who had designed Henry Ford's small plane, the "Flivver." They were united by faith: everyone should fly. They believed the day was approaching when everyone would own an airplane.

"The trend of the times is skyward," Chamberlin wrote in 1930. "The rising generation will take to the air with nonchalance and impunity." You only had to look at the history of the automobile to understand what was coming. His father had purchased the first automobile in their Iowa town. The neighbors complained, and farmers from miles around gathered at a mass meeting to protest. They voted unanimously to boycott his father's business. His father was never comfortable driving, even after many lessons. "I don't think he ever did entirely conquer a sort of terror inspired by this new and strange device," Chamberlin said. But his son, the future aviator, took right to it without a lesson and was soon a better driver than his father. He had grown up with the automobile. The same was true for airplanes. "I have had youngsters of sixteen or less in the air with me who handled a plane as well after a few minutes of instruction as I did at the end of two or three hours' despairing effort on the part of my instructors," said Chamberlin. They took right to it; they had grown up with flying.

They would need airplanes. "It has been my ambition for a long time to produce in quantity" a plane anyone could afford, Chamberlin wrote in 1928, shortly after his transoceanic flight, when instead he could have listed another great flight as his goal. "I think the United States is ripe for a medium-priced, reliable, reasonably 'foolproof' airplane of small size and good performance. If I can contribute this to American aviation I will feel that my jobs of flying have not been in vain." His description of that airplane, its weight, airspeed, and handling characteristics, anticipated the Airmobile.

"Ten years from now, filling stations all over the country will be so located as to serve both the driving and the flying public," Chamberlin predicted in a 1928 article, "Shall We All Fly Soon?" Many shared this belief. Once his Airmobiles were filling the sky, Atwood said, sections of major roads could be widened for landing strips, twenty-five-hundred feet long and three-hundred feet wide.

Chamberlin made his prediction in the great excitement following Lindbergh's solo Atlantic flight in 1927, the "Lindbergh Boom" that saw a rush to invest in aviation. Chamberlin was one of the stars of that season. He made the next crossing of the Atlantic, just two weeks after Lindbergh. He could have easily been the first, but he was undermined by his financial backer, Charles Levine, a millionaire junk dealer. Chamberlin had the better plane, a Wright-Bellanca, the plane that Lindbergh had tried to buy for his flight, and one that would be used in three Atlantic crossings. Chamberlin also had the experience. He had established a world endurance record in the Bellanca, flying in a circle for fifty-one hours and thirty-one minutes with a co-pilot, an achievement that signalled that at last airplane engines could be trusted for a nonstop Atlantic flight. He had also been instrumental in getting this plane built. But he was the last choice of his backer, because Levine didn't think the slightly built pilot was the "movie type." Levine kept changing pilots, second-guessing Chamberlin about equipping the plane, antagonizing everyone until they quit. Finally the plane was attached in a messy legal battle. Chamberlin was grounded and had to watch Lindbergh fly to Paris.

When Chamberlin finally took off, Levine jumped in the plane at the last minute as a surprise. (Levine's wife, it was reported, cried out and was "almost overcome.") Chamberlin flew more than 3,911 miles in forty-two hours, landing just outside Berlin, a new distance record. He was front-page news. Atwood, listening in Monson, sat by his radio for the latest on the flight. Chamberlin literally flew over Lindbergh, who was sailing home, a hero. (Chamberlin would also follow Lindbergh in death by two weeks.)

Chamberlin had missed his moment, one of the greatest of the twentieth century, but he never held it against Levine. He was a quiet Iowa boy whom the promoters and money men overlooked. He had the classic flyer's biography of his era. Growing up, he tinkered with engines in cars and motorcycles, learned to fly for World War I, barnstormed, flew odd jobs here and there, always looking for backers, trying for years to obtain an airplane to cross the Atlantic. When he was in the fifth grade, around 1903, he had written that in 1930 he would fly an airplane around the world.

His flying stories, as he tells them in his autobiography, *Record Flights*, are self-effacing, but still show his pride in his handling of Bellanca's planes. There were people who did not serve him well—a business associate who never paid (he had no written contract) and Levine—but he never once settles a score in the book. Chamberlin was a gentleman to the end, a teetotaling Iowa boy, but with a gently mischievous sense of humor.

While he was preparing his plane for the Atlantic flight, increasing numbers of the curious came out to the airfield. A woman asked, "What happens if a plane runs out of gas while in flight?"

"Ma'am," Chamberlin said, "that is one of the tragedies of aviation. The good Lord only knows how many pilots are up there, out of gas and unable to get back to land!"

Chamberlin was a good friend and mentor of Ruth Nichols, a pilot who shared his faith in flying and his problem of getting the best planes to fly. "For me it seems that *all life flies*—protons, planes or people," Nichols wrote in her autobiography, *Wings For Life*. "There is no living without flight."

She lived this credo and was a tireless promoter of aviation. "Mothers, grandmothers, brides, Campfire Girls, Junior Leaguers, debs and sub-debs—you must fly! You will have to fly! You have no choice," Nichols implored in a 1933 magazine article. "Think of me as a monomaniac, if you will . . . But in a decade, when flying has become as commonplace as taking the morning train to town, don't say I didn't tell you so."

The press called Nichols the "society girl flyer" and the "debutante aviatrix." She was from a well-off Westchester family listed in the social register, a member of the Junior League, raised on country-club tennis, polo, and her father's love of horsemanship. Her father was a member of the New York Stock exchange who had been a Rough Rider with Theodore Roosevelt in the Spanish-American War; her mother was a Quaker.

She set her first flying records while still a student at Wellesley College, as a co-pilot on the first nonstop flight from New York to Miami, and as the first licensed woman seaplane pilot. There followed a career of firsts, including the first woman airline pilot (for Chamberlin's short-lived airline) and the first woman executive in the aviation business. With her friend Amelia Earhart, she founded the first women's pilot organization, known as the Ninety-Nines in 1929, when there were only 126 licensed woman pilots in the country.

It was a career of much hardship. "I have piloted a plane in a plaster cast, and a steel corset, too impatient to wait for bones to knit from the last crash," Nichols said. "I have frozen my tongue sucking oxygen at sixty below zero, six miles up. I have escaped twice from burning planes. I have clung to a life raft in cold, mountainous seas. I have had most of the bones in my body broken. And after each disaster came the command from something deep within me: Get back into the air . . .

"Maybe it doesn't make sense. I have been told this so often that it has become a kind of background drumbeat to my life. Family and friends have urged me to keep my feet on the ground ever since the first time I came home in an ambulance." She had six serious crashes and she counted fifty-five narrow escapes in more than thirty years of flying. "The only people who haven't tried to change me are flyers. They comprehend.

"On fair days over the usual run of homeland country, plane flights arouse in me a casual happiness. A sense of well-being and contentment. Often times I find myself winging through space, my voice in happy competition with the motor's roar."

Chamberlin guided Nichols on her greatest quest, to be the first woman to fly solo across the Atlantic. He helped select and modify the airplane, a Lockheed Vega she named the *Akita*, and plan a training course that included Nichols's setting two international women's flying records. In March 1931 she set an altitude record, reaching 28,743 feet, almost blacking out as her oxygen supply froze. The following month in the same plane she beat Amelia Earhart's speed record, flying 210.754 miles an hour. In June, with her financial backing, physical training, and airplane modifications ready, she flew from New York, intending to crown her record-setting year by crossing the Atlantic.

At St. John, New Brunswick, Nichols crashed. She crushed five vertebrae. The doctor told her she would be bedridden for a year. Chamberlin flew her home in a stretcher a week later, and supervised the recovery and rebuilding of her plane. She was in agonizing pain. It took four nurses to move her to change the bed sheets. From her bed she began to plan her next Atlantic attempt. Soon she was walking, then riding in a car.

Only four months after her crash, she set a transcontinental distance record, flying in a "surgical steel brace." This was her third international record of 1931, but that flight too ended in a fiery wreck. Wedged in by her parachute, corseted by the steel brace, flames shooting up around the cockpit, she barely escaped. Once more Chamberlin came to her aid, flying out to the accident site only hours later, and again he helped rebuild the *Akita* for the Atlantic challenge. Nichols scrambled to raise money. Even with her family background, it was always difficult for a woman pilot to find support.

But while she was still rebuilding the *Akita*, Amelia Earhart beat her, making a celebrated solo crossing in May 1932. Like Chamberlin, Nichols had lost out on her moment. She gave up on an Atlantic flight. She began raising money for a flight around the world—a trip that Earhart would take on before her and die trying to complete. One of the many jobs Nichols took on to raise funds was promoting the Airmobile. She brought Duply to the attention of many, got Chamberlin involved, and may have helped line up the largest potential contract.

Chamberlin and Nichols were savvy flyers and headline heroes, but the third expert Atwood hired was a quieter figure. Otto C. Koppen, an associate professor at MIT, had devoted his life to designing a safe airplane, pioneering stall- and spin-proof designs. As Henry Ford's aeronautical advisor from 1925 to 1928, he had designed Ford's Model T of the skies, the "Flivver," a small monoplane. Ford's pilot had set a world distance record for light planes, flying the Flivver nearly one thousand miles. "As soon as we know as much about [airplanes] as we do about automobiles—and that will not be long—then they can be built by the thousands or by the millions," Ford said in 1924. Koppen's design for the first Airmobile would be similar to the Flivver.

At MIT, the students called Koppen's class on aerodynamics "The Miracle Hour" for his deft use of long equations to calculate the characteristics of airplane flight. He was *the* aerodynamics authority at MIT. "The Miracle Hour" could be an appropriate name for Atwood's Airmobile project.

After a year and a half of work, Atwood lifted the secrecy surrounding his plans. The secrecy had been "lamentable" said the *Milford Cabinet*. Patents were granted or pending, and Atwood was finally free of his Monson bankruptcy. A newspaper photo was published to show that Duply was a reality. Five honeycombed Duply beams supported eight men without a sag. (Left unexplained were the three boards of what appears to be ordinary lumber underneath the Duply beams.)

When Chamberlin and Nichols came for their first visit to see the Airmobile, Atwood arranged for them to speak to the boys' club in his town. Word spread and the entire population of Greenfield—396 people—turned out. They were "all agog over the presence . . . of two of the most famous figures in modern aviation," reported the *Manchester Union.* "In happy astonishment, townsfolk, more than one of whom had never seen an airplane at close hand, listened to Colonel Chamberlin tell of his transoceanic flight and when they recovered from their pleased bewilderment, bombarded him with questions about aviation for almost an hour, all of which he answered with the utmost good will and good humor." Nichols's talk was received with the same enthusiasm.

The two aviators cautiously endorsed Duply. "What we have seen and heard since our arrival in New Hampshire today," Chamberlin said, "indicates there is a good prospect that the price of aircraft will be lowered, and the safety factor increased in the near future." Nichols agreed: Atwood and his colleagues "have something which in my opinion is going to make aviation safer and less expensive."

In hard times, aviation had proved itself a miracle worker, a conqueror of oceans. Just thinking about flying was a wonderful escape, like going to the movies. Chamberlin told his audience how amazing it was to have lunch in New York, "the world's biggest city," and then arrive after only a two-hour flight some 250 miles away at a small town in the foothills of New Hampshire.

"Twenty-five years ago in Milford a favorite Sunday afternoon thrill for Elm street residents was holding a watch and counting automobiles," said the *Milford Cabinet.* Sometimes as many as eighteen or twenty passed in an hour. The figures were reported to the newspapers. A ride in a motor car was an experience and a thrill. "Today we look up when an airplane goes over. We wonder how it would feel to be up there in the sky.

"Henry Ford made his motor car commonplace. Somebody will do the same for the airplane.

"It is by no means impossible that right here in Milford the start will be made toward putting airplanes within the means of all but the poorest families.

"It's not a joke."

The newspaper editors supported Atwood, famous flyers came and went, but Milford was just not convinced. One of the first rules for reading small-town newspapers is to read the paper as an outline, a series of talking points to go find out what really happened. The sharper edges of gossip, subtext, and motive never get into the paper. Even so, it is clear that the Airmobile was under fire early. By Atwood's own admission, he was confronted with "opposition which at times amounted to widespread popular disapproval."

Atwood offered the prospect of jobs, the romance of flight, and a boom-town promise of a gold strike. But what of it? The attitude of many in town was: Oh yeah? Stop the foolishness. Build furniture.

The creditors were pressing for their money, demanding that the company make furniture and not waste itself chasing this airplane dream.

Harry Atwood was facing the greatest blue sky selling challenge of his life. He had to hold off the creditors, win over the community, get the plane into the sky, and get contracts signed—all within in a few months. It was like one of those old cliff-hanger movie serials they used show at Saturday matinees: the small airplane struggling to take off as the walls totter and start to fall in all around.

When they closed the factory at the end of February to get ready to build airplanes, and wages went unpaid, local opposition became heated. The company pleaded for support almost weekly in long newspaper advertisements, open letters to citizens, employees, and bond holders. "Nothing can be more destructive to the proper exploitation of a new product upon a new market than a local whispering campaign which broadcasts doubts," said one advertisement. "Let no one believe that this new product is going to bring millions of dollars into the community without tireless and unflinching efforts to develop and make known the merits of Duply products to a National market."

The factory was closed to clean house and "remove the debris of a depressed industry and depression." The company would still make furniture; it would stay loyal to Milford. The secrecy once necessary was lifted—"let everyone from the local farmer to the local manufacturer, who questions the soundness of the Duply development, come directly to the French & Heald factory and he will be given every opportunity to make his own investigation and satisfy himself thoroughly that Duply and its possibilities are all that is claimed and more."

"WE ARE ENTERING THE AIRCRAFT BUSINESS," said another ad. "It is the major object of this message; to convince our local townspeople that we are not chasing any rainbows."

Harry Atwood turned to a New England tradition, the town meeting. He would stand up, face his neighbors, and try to sell them the future. "Tomorrow evening, many of you, and I hope all of you, will gather together with me to listen to my friend who came with French and Heald at my calling almost three years ago," wrote company treasurer George C. Langdell, in an advertisement. Few men were more respected in town than Langdell, said the *Cabinet.* "Milford knows George Langdell, his ability, his loyalty, his good judgment and sound common sense."

"I do not know what he is going to tell you," Langdell wrote, "but I do know this much—that he has been my friend, French and Heald's friend, and yes, a true civic friend of all Milford. And furthermore I feel sure that you are all going to agree with me when you leave the meeting tomorrow evening.

". . . You yourself, at the meeting, ask him why we are 'fooling around' with 'fantastic' airplanes; why we are 'neglecting' the furniture business; why we are maintaining a 'costly' laboratory which is developing shoe-heels as well as airplanes; why we may profit suddenly and arise from the depression without waiting for the production of a single airplane or shoe-heel; why we hope and expect to employ more labor at increased wages at a time when we are now unable to maintain a skeleton payroll; why he remains in Milford at this time when the industrial struggle is so great and particularly when there are so many more prosperous industries which are now requesting and bidding for his services . . . YOU ask the questions at the meeting. I assure you that there will be no evasion of any questions and no question of doubt as to his meanings. He has particularly requested all of us in French and Heald to save front row seats for his most severe critics."

There were no seats left in the Milford town hall the night Atwood spoke. People packed the hall until there was no place left to stand and the crowd backed up outside on the steps had to be turned away. After Langdell opened the meeting with a short history of French and Heald, he introduced Atwood and took a seat on the stage next to the company president and grandson of the founder, Emory Heald. The newcomer began his sales call. This was a summation of his life—the stranger in town with a scheme.

"The man who tells you there is no market for low priced aircraft is stating the facts in reverse," Atwood said. "As a matter of fact, there is no low priced aircraft for the market." In 1934, only five hundred planes were sold for civil use at an average of eight thousand dollars each, he said. "How many in this audience would be buying automobiles today if they cost eight thousand dollars each, or even five thousand dollars?" (He didn't mention that the typical light plane cost from fifteen hundred to twenty-five hundred dollars. With maintenance costing about eight dollars per hour of flying time, one third of all owners sold their planes after just one year and didn't buy another.)

The four-passenger Airmobile would sell for eight hundred dollars, about the price of a new Chevrolet sedan. "I have no doubt that there is a market for these low-priced craft—craft which are safer, lighter and stronger than any yet known—right here in New Hampshire." The blueprints were complete and the first Airmobile would fly in thirty to sixty days.

This airplane was unlike any they may have ever seen, he told them. It would be built from one six-inch diameter birch tree, plastic, and seventy-four parts, not two thousand parts. This was the talk he would repeat often in the coming months, sometimes with different numbers reported; a three-inch tree, or an eight-inch tree. No matter, the picture was the same. If his listeners didn't understand the Duply process, they knew that trees were being transformed into airplanes, and New Hampshire had plenty of trees. But did people want airplanes?

Duply had so many other uses: furniture, canoes (50 percent lighter), baby carriages, coffins, shoe heels, life preservers, small balloons, hot drying kilns, refrigerator insulation, heavy engine bases, and wood-grained walls for buildings, with air-conditioning ducts molded-in. There were inquiries from Europe, Russia, and Canada. All this would eventually help the furniture business, though that part of the factory was still closed.

He met their doubts head-on. There was a "whispering campaign" against the Airmobile, "under-cover attacks" by the "misinformed and uninformed." Snap judgments were harming the business. People said that developing a new airplane was too big a project for such a small town in a small state. This was absurd, he said. French and Heald "is the best conceivable place in the country" for the Airmobile. He invited them to come down and see (but make an appointment first—the lab was too busy to have people just wandering through).

He told them how he had arrived in Milford, giving as was his habit a fresh version of his recent history. The Rubwood Wheel Company had failed because of "law suits which he won, but which were so costly and drawn-out that they put him out of business."

The floor was open to questions—the critics could fire away—but people wanted to hear about his days as a pioneer aviator back in 1911 when he was a summer's hero.

In the weeks following, Atwood continued to campaign in the community. He hosted forty members of the Manchester Lions Club for lunch at the Milford Inn, gave them his sales talk about the birch tree and the market, and took them through the laboratory. Over in Nashua, the closest city to Milford, he started the Aero Club of New Hampshire, with his friend, "the live-wire" mayor of Nashua, Alvin A. Lucier. Although he didn't have a pilot's license, Lucier was an aviation enthusiast who helped establish the city's first municipal airport. When Atwood played the piano, Lucier sometimes accompanied him on the violin. They gathered fifty members at the first meeting (just a few licensed pilots among them) for Atwood's tour and a short talk by Ruth Nichols. The club's sole purpose was "to rouse public interest in flying," and create "air mindedness." There had been a terrible plane crash in Nashua back in 1929, which had left people afraid of flying.

Atwood called in the reporters and sent them away with the glowing prospect of the revolution to come. "We'll Soon be Skylarking in a Wooden Plane," said one headline in the *Boston Herald.* There were photos in many papers of the aircraft workshop, showing one worker measuring a gathering of birch ribbons, while another examined some finished square tubes. Another photo showed an airplane model in a wind tunnel, which was "believed to be the only one in the state."

The press was fed new developments weekly. Army engineers were visiting; a millionaire aviator and financier was flying in; Ruth Nichols and Clarence Chamberlin, pictured again at the airport, arriving with interested investors. Factory representatives were visiting important officials in Washington. Twenty-one "signed orders with deposits" had been received for an early delivery of Airmobiles. The engines for the first planes would be purchased from Chrysler. The first Airmobile was "rapidly nearing completion."

His greatest sales call awaited; some 375 creditors were pressing to be paid more than one hundred thousand dollars—suppliers of wood and plastic, and more than 100 men who were owed wages, a source of Milford's disenchantment. The company called the creditors to a meeting. Atwood asked them to hold their claims for ninety days, until July 1. They would be paid in full from the Duply profits. "Valuable contracts" for Duply were in the works, Emory Heald said. He believed that the creditors would be paid off before the July 1 deadline. "Much hope was attached to the new Duply development," reported the *Cabinet.* "Many products can be made of it, and no doubt some can be made to show large profits."

If they pressed their claims, they could lose everything, Atwood warned them. Under his contract, if the company was in bankruptcy, or otherwise hindered, he would walk away with Duply and the profits. If the creditors cooperated, he'd stay. "Without going into too much detail he outlined how he proposed to bring material help to the company," said the *Cabinet*.

Atwood had publicly declared his loyalty earlier, addressing the mortgage bond holders in an advertisement. Reacting to reports that "he intends to remove the Duply development from Milford," he said that he did have an offer, was "empowered to make such change" and would profit from the move, but he had "no idea of forsaking his French and Heald associates." Local people were the "sole investors" in the company's mortgage, which Atwood had arranged. "In plain English, the writer desires to place himself on record that he is going to see the Bond Holders' issue through to a finish; not run away because of difficulties that are only temporary."

The creditors were "friendly," reported the *Cabinet*. "It was generally acclaimed in the open meeting that the developments were sound," said the minutes. "There was the unanimous acclamation of the creditors that they would cooperate." They would wait for their money.

But they didn't know that Atwood had tried to "run away" just a week before their meeting. He had declared his contract void due to the company's financial problems. The creditors also believed that the company owned the patents, which was the usual arrangement.

The ninety-day moratorium was Atwood's window of opportunity. If the Airmobile were going to be sitting alongside the family Ford in everyone's garage, it had to fly through that window in ninety days.

As another winter of hard times receded, things were looking up, the *Cabinet* said in the spring of 1935. "It's easy, right now, to take an optimistic view of conditions in Milford," the paper editorialized. Labor disputes had been settled in the granite industry, several mills in the valley were busy, some important public improvements were about to receive funding, and the "French and Heald factory appears to be right on the edge of an era of activity, in both furniture manufacture, aircraft production and perhaps other lines." The *Cabinet* could see blue skies ahead. "We are not threatened with ruinous dust storms or hurricanes. Baseball and trout fishing are here. Soon we'll let the furnace fire out, plant the garden, and get set to enjoy life.

"But a lot of warning is needed . . . Many of the things that look good are not actually accomplished. They are only strong hopes." A fine definition of a blue sky promise.

The adze is an ancient tool, with origins in the Stone Age and refinement in the Bronze Age. For Roman carpenters and military engineers, the ax-like tool was indispensable. Without the adze, the Airmobile couldn't be built. Frederick Wetherbee was an expert with a wetted adze. While Atwood was out selling the future, Wetherbee was slowly shaping the form on which part of the plane would be built, a mandrel. He worked the wood into the shape of a fish, the streamlined shape of an airplane fuselage. The mandrel was much like a dressmaker's form, and, once finished, the project moved from the Bronze Age to the twentieth century.

Three weeks into the credit moratorium, and two and a half years after Atwood had arrived at French and Heald, the company began to build the first Airmobile. "The construction process was unconventional and ingenious," said his engineer Clarence Farr. Birch strips, .015 inches thick, were bound with cellulose acetate, chosen because it was an easily worked thermoplastic (requiring heat to soften). It was moisture-resistant, relatively uninflammable, required no additional finishing, and was available in a choice of colors.

The mandrel "was first wrapped with cellophane to avoid adhesion and to permit the form to be withdrawn later. Over the cellophane was a wrapping of thermoplastic sheet. The next layer was a spiral wrapping of birch veneer strips. Next was another layer of plastic sheet. Next was wrapped a layer of veneer strips applied 'cross-grain' to the first layer. And so on until we had the desired number of piles of wood. The last wrapping was thermoplastic sheet, for external sealing of the wood, and for coloring the finished product," said Farr. No additional sanding or painting was needed. The Airmobile's fuselage was a light blue; the wings and tail were yellow.

"Over this mandrel and wrappings we custom-built an airtight rubber bag, tightly fitted to the composite form. Then we put the rubber bag and contents in a pressure vessel or autoclave, closed the vessel, and applied compressed air." This was a "king-size pressure vessel," seven feet in diameter and twenty-six feet long, which sat on concrete cradles alongside the factory.

"Now with the inside of the bag vented to atmospheric pressure, the compressed air forced the bag and all the wrappings tightly against the mandrel and drove out the air pockets. The next step was to replace the compressed air with live steam at the same pressure. The steam, of course, softened the plastic. To solidify the plastic we again replaced the steam by compressed air and dripped cold water on the bag. Then we were ready to exhaust the compressed air, open the autoclave, strip off the rubber bag, remove the mandrel, and—voila—the finished product," said Farr. You could drop the fuselage and it would bounce, said Wetherbee. The wings had been tested with eighteen hundred pounds of sand, and six men had stood on a wing while one end was held in a press.

There had been some problems along the way. In one batch, steam had leaked through the rubber covering on the wings, spoiling them. The first ailerons had warped. Variations of wrappings and coatings had been tried until a consistent Duply was achieved.

Professor Joseph Newell, testing Duply again two years later, found it to be uniform, and still advantageous, though he was more cautious in his praise. "The margin in favor of Duply, though small, is nevertheless substantial when one considers that the Duply has sufficient bulk to give a smooth surface on a wing without requiring the addition of stiffening members or extra thicknesses of sheet, as is frequently necessary with aluminum alloy or stainless steel."

Twelve parts had to be built this way to make the Airmobile: the fuselage including the vertical tail fin, two half-wings, two ailerons, two landing gear 'boots,' the rudder, and the two stabilizers and two elevators that comprised the horizontal tail. No additional interior framing or supports were used.

This first Airmobile was a small, one-person, open-cockpit plane with a wingspan of twenty-two feet, and a length of sixteen feet. It weighed, with engine, gas, and pilot, only eight hundred pounds.

The Airmobile, reported impressed newspapers, is "as much a unit as a one-piece bathing suit." From the shop floor, however, the plane of the future looked like a large, involved, basketry and woodworking project. "There was too much handwork," said Wetherbee. In one version, they coated the birch strips with liquid acetate by running the strips through something like a clothes wringer. There was a spark from the electric motor and they "damn near lost the whole factory in the process of making parts." This technique was dropped. As Wetherbee saw it, this was no way to compete with a nuts-and-bolts assembly.

Start ten workers at 8:00 A.M. and the plane could be flying by dinner, Atwood had said. His claim was "a little far-fetched," said Wetherbee. "It was made out of how many strips? Each strip had be handled. A hell of a lot of work. Anything a man touches gets to cost."

But this was the prototype. They were still making it up as they went along. Each process was part of an experiment. They were working toward a technology, a new way of assembling an airplane. To build a conventional airplane required fifty different trades and seventy-five industries. Visitors were surprised at the low labor cost for the Airmobile. Duply could be produced for a fifty cents a pound, said Atwood, and sold at one dollar a pound.

When the fuselage was finished, Atwood had one man walk out of the shop and hold the fuselage aloft for a newspaper photographer, the man standing there with his arms upraised, like a *V* for victory.

The plane received steady publicity. Duply was proving to be lighter, stronger, and cheaper than first anticipated, Atwood told the press. Ruth Nichols was flying in with visitors to see the Airmobile. Dr. Michael Watter came to examine the product for Victor J. Burnelli, a leading designer of "flying wings."

The Airmobile was assembled, awaiting its first flight. Creditors expected their money in one month. Dr. Watter checked the wings with a straight edge. "It seems to me that they are unable to control their shapes as closely as desirable because the wings, for instance, had flat and hollow spaces resulting in a loss of profile to the extent of even as much as one-quarter inch from the contour desired." Watter believed that, in time, they should be able to perfect the shapes. "The thing is so novel and ingenious that it is hardly possible to form a definite opinion from one short visit but it is unquestionably something worthwhile looking into for anyone who is interested in smaller and cheaper planes." But he thought it had "no future" for the large commercial planes that interested Burnelli.

"Mr. Atwood," Watter took care to report, "stressed the point that the thing is still in the laboratory stage." Atwood was running out of time. The Airmobile would fly in two weeks.

✐ The Miracle Hour

Late on a June afternoon, a crowd was gathering at the Nashua airport. There had been no big announcement, headline, or advertisement. Word had spread since late morning, when workers at the factory were told to load the plane on the truck to go to the airport. As the *Cabinet* said, "it isn't possible to move an airplane through the streets without anybody noticing it." The Airmobile was going to fly.

It was getting on toward supper, and the plane had not flown. The engine wouldn't start. Unable to buy the engine they needed, they had borrowed one from a plane in for repairs. The small thirty-six-horsepower Aeronca engine was underpowered for the Airmobile. Atwood and his crew milled around the plane. Ruth Nichols handed Clarence Chamberlin, the Airmobile's test pilot, a parachute. She wanted him to wear it.

This was a scene from Atwood's earlier days: an expectant crowd waiting for an exhibition flight, while the mechanics tried to coax an engine to life. He had never left the exhibition business.

Chamberlin taxied back and forth, trying the engine. In front of the crowd, now grown to two thousand, he stopped and discarded his parachute. The reporters took note of the "world famous transatlantic flyer" at this historic moment.

From a far corner of the field, the blue and yellow plane started a long run. The tail lifted up, then the plane bobbed and bounced and he cut off the engine. They were losing daylight. The mechanics resumed work. The engine was running weak and rough, "in uneven pulses and spasms, and the rev indicator was jumping all over the scale," Chamberlin said. The sun had set.

"A three-quarter moon was shining brightly overhead when the plane finally took the air, and the sight of the little machine silhouetted against the bright blue sky of early evening was one which aroused the enthusiasm of many a watcher," said the *Manchester Union*. It was "an occasion which many felt to be epoch-making." They would be telling their children this one day: I saw the first Airmobile fly, June 13 it was, the day the Depression ended for Milford. When the plane banked and turned, the "golden" wings "flashed brightly," and the crowd cheered.

Chamberlin flew ten laps of the field. Even with the engine not running at full power, the Airmobile reached a speed of 120 miles per hour, judged a record performance for such a small engine. He had flown for only twelve minutes and thirty-seven seconds. If you didn't believe that this was the future you were seeing, then this was just another small plane puttering around an airfield.

A shout went up when the plane stopped and the crowd rushed toward Chamberlin to congratulate him. Atwood was the first one to reach the plane.

"Christ Harry, it's nose heavy," Chamberlin said.

"We can fix that, don't worry," said Atwood.

The press and the crowd caught up.

"She handles wonderfully," the *Boston Globe* reported Chamberlin's saying. Gave him a "feeling of security and control better than any new plane he'd taken aloft," reported the *Milford Cabinet*. The Airmobile handled with "watch-like sensitivity," reported the *Manchester Union*.

Actually, it was not unusual for an experimental airplane to be out of trim on its first flight. "It would have been a miracle if it wasn't nose heavy or tail heavy," Farr explained years later. "It's a dynamic thing. You don't know how it's going to fly." It is an easily solved problem, but who wants to explain that and have the headline, "Plane Nose Heavy, Engine Erratic, Short Flight, Call it Success."

What the banner headline said in the next day's *Manchester Leader* was, "State Boom Seen On Atwood's New Plane. Invention Likely to Revolutionize Entire Industry." Mass production was "assured." Orders had been received. The flight "demonstrated in conclusive and breath-taking fashion that Harry N. Atwood was right" when he began to develop Duply, said the *Manchester Union*.

The stories in Boston, New York, and elsewhere were just as celebratory, all using the word promise. ("Promises flights for the multitude.")

"The man who pioneered in the aviation field 25 years ago with such world renowned figures as the Wright Brothers—Harry N. Atwood of Milford—stands ready to be classified as the 'Henry Ford of that industry,'" said the *Nashua Telegraph*. "From signs already manifested within the aircraft building industry 'duply' is bound to shake it to its foundations," said the *Christian Science Monitor*.

In triumph, the whole crew lined up in front of the little airplane, one row in front kneeling, as in a team photo. The twelve people included the young engineers Farr and Tom Knox, professors Newell and Koppen, Heald and Langdell, Mayor Lucier, Chamberlin, Nichols, and Atwood.

Like most people, the editors of the *Manchester Union* had cheered each successive flying record, but "most of us have not thought that aviation had personal application. We have smiled at jokesmiths who have written about a plane in every garage. Exaggeration, we have said, is the keystone of American wit. New Hampshire now knows that the humorists were prophets."

The Milford Civics Club paid tribute to Atwood at a special meeting. Emory Heald praised Atwood as "a man who never knows defeat and who thrives on doing things that folks say can't be done." Clarence Chamberlin praised Duply: "This is the only material I know anything about which offers any real hope for the inexpensive aircraft." And Charles Emerson, one of the town's leading businessmen, rose to "speak for the citizens of Milford." Atwood's Duply had "brought a bright ray of hope in the hour of darkness, and the future of the town depends in large measure upon this product."

History had been made, said the *Milford Cabinet*. "The little ship may never fly again. Larger ones are to be built, and the original Duply Airmobile may eventually find its way to some museum along with the first locomotive, the original Wright biplane and the first sewing machine."

Atwood turned the acclaim a notch higher. He took out a full page ad in the *Union* and a large one in the *Cabinet*. "The multitude of people on the field did not have the slightest conception of what was actually taking place," he insisted. He wanted everyone to understand that the Airmobile was not just an ordinary airplane.

He made the most of a short test run. Chamberlin "was instructed to bump the craft to pieces over the rough field, as far as he dared. He was instructed to fly, or not fly, as his discretion dictated. The ship was all his." The first Airmobile "contained no bumpers, shock absorbers, springs, or other cushioning elements. Not even a cushion on the passenger seat. It was a dead-weight structure with a dead-weight load, upon a dead-axle.

"The AIRMOBILE in this condition, plus a 100% overload, was bumped over a rough field at speeds greater than a mile a minute. Every hump in the field was a powerful hammer, and the force of the blows delivered to a dead-weight DUPLY structure, at a mile a minute speed, were beyond computation.

"When the hammering ground-tests were terminated, a thorough inspection revealed not a break, not a tear, not a crack, and not even an abrasion . . . And let it be understood that this first test-AIRMOBILE comprised parts which came out of the first 'heats' of DUPLY fabrication."

In the ad, Chamberlin said he was impressed with how little engine vibration there was, how quiet it was in the cockpit—"I could have easily talked to a passenger in an ordinary tone of voice"—and how well Duply acted as a shock absorber upon landing.

There was encouraging news almost daily. The government of Colombia wanted five planes. A New England Airline operator was submitting a design for a six-passenger transport plane. Atwood said they would also build his own patented design for a seaplane. Mayor Lucier pushed for Nashua to be home to an Airmobile factory. The Airmobile would make a flying tour of New Hampshire, and Ruth Nichols proposed that Atwood provide her with an Airmobile for a promotional tour of the United States. Atwood was in demand to speak to civic and commercial organizations throughout New England. It seemed now that he had the greatest invention of all: jobs.

Atwood announced the biggest news in the advertisement: "The two-place AIRMOBILE with a special automobile engine, and with luxurious fittings, is under way. The four-place family AIRMOBILE is under way. One large aircraft manufacturer has contracted to produce in his factory, two thousand DUPLY AIRMOBILES in the next sixteen months. Much of this production is contemplated for New Hampshire. Other industries are in the making. Jobs are in the making.

"The safe aircraft; the lowest possible priced aircraft; and the best material in the world for aircraft, has been born in New Hampshire; without government funds or recognition; without State assistance or recognition; without banking help; and without the endorsement of one single aviation industrial organization. Even the public was led to believe that the task was impossible; at least impracticable and foolishly visionary. Yes, it can truly be said that the DUPLY AIRMOBILE was born IN SPITE of everything and everybody."

The ad showed a photo of the Airmobile sitting alone, at sunset, in the lengthening shadows of all who stood outside the picture.

"We believe we have accomplished a miracle," Emory Heald wrote to the creditors two weeks after the flight. "We have not raised $100,000 cash at this hour. It will be miracle #2 if we do so before July 5.

"However, we are not depending upon miracles to state that the prospects of our paying one hundred cents on the dollar to all creditors have become tangible, and we know that you will join with us in your gratitude to the one man who has turned the tide." Atwood was negotiating contracts to license Duply. The factory shut down again, this time for a month.

One creditor was angry. The Blair Veneer Company in North Troy, Vermont, had originally recommended Atwood to French and Heald, loaned Atwood money to get him started, and invested more than fifteen thousand dollars in the Duply development. But now the company turned on Atwood. After weeks of negotiation and delay, Atwood had offered to pay all outstanding debts from 25 percent of the expected Duply profits. This was not what he had promised back in March—or was it?—when he referred to "sums of money which would automatically be converted into paying off all creditors," who "would automatically receive the benefits derived from all contracts." But he did not define the "sums" and the "benefits," and no one is on record asking him. As he had done with the shareholders at the Rubwood Wheel Company, Atwood had floated some promises, which he intended to honor in his own manner.

The other creditors accepted his offer, but Blair Veneer wanted more—ownership of the patents until the debts were paid in full. Indeed, back in March they believed that French and Heald owned the patents, which were, after all, the security behind all the promises.

Atwood withdrew his offer. Once again he was fighting for control of his patents. "French and Heald have no claim on patents, and they make no claim," Atwood said. Since he had "been placed in a strong position by the success of Duply," he would deal with each creditor individually.

This was a complete circuit of mistrust. The more Atwood feared losing his patents and schemed for control, the more he was mistrusted by others. It is hard to say where such a circuit begins—who is the first to doubt—but once started, it is a circuit wired for failure.

Atwood's attitude toward negotiations could be seen in how he drove the back-country roads at night. Roberta Window remembered a visit to Greenfield. "When he was driving us home, he had a startling habit of turning off his lights whenever he approached a corner on the narrow dirt road. This, he said, was to allow him to see if there was another car coming towards him. I was not completely sold on his experiment!" He would give the other driver no sign he was there. The safety of both cars was his responsibility. For Harry Atwood, even the traffic laws were not a two-way street.

The veneer company took him to court. Many of his inventions led to court. The other creditors had no dispute with him. Just one investor stood between Atwood and success.

This dispute over the division of future Duply profits, reminded the *Cabinet* of "soldiers fighting among themselves about the division of spoils in the city they expect to capture tomorrow. While they squabble the city is rapidly burning up."

Once more Emory Heald called for Milford's support, in a full-page advertisement. "We are now literally deluged with inquiries and solicitations for business. There are included offers to finance us; requests to purchase our business; solicitations for us to grant manufacturing licenses; and propositions for reorganization and re-financing. Coincidently, our furniture business has taken on new life . . .

"The difficulty which confronts us, we regret to say, is a lack of confidence in us and in Mr. Atwood; in our combined abilities to save our industry for Milford.

"We state without qualification that we could have paid off every one of our creditors one hundred cents on the dollar before July 1, if we could have shaken ourselves free from lack of confidence and interference . . . May we state, the interference is not imagined. It is real and forceful . . .

"We also desire to make clear at this time that Mr. Atwood has by his brilliancy placed us in a position where we cannot fail to make a fortune for ourselves and our associates."

"It is with great regret that we hear from time to time comments about him almost amounting to ridicule.

"That he continues to work in our interest, in spite of this humiliation, means that his integrity and loyalty is of the very highest. There are some who have questioned his sincerity in trying to bring any business to Milford, and yet his efforts are tireless to establish us so we may pay our creditors in full . . .

"Our financial condition was growing weaker and weaker at the time we sent for Mr. Atwood, and through his patience, work and loyalty, we have been saved in crisis after crisis. For three long years he stood the brunt of rushing a development in time to save our company from disaster and many times in face of almost overwhelming odds . . .

"Failure is unnecessary, ridiculous, unwarranted . . . Let it not be said that the people of our town failed to stand united behind us at this most important period for us and for them."

Atwood appealed directly to the creditors. The factory workers were among those who heard his appeal. "He gave us a pep talk, along with Alvin Lucier," said Frederick Wetherbee. "If we would just sign off, give them another few days, everything would be lovely. We had a claim for wages not paid. Harry worked up the group's enthusiasm. The group said, oh yes we're all for you. They finally gave him an extension, just a few days was all he was asking for. But they didn't know that a few days put their mechanic's claim beyond the statute of limitations. If they wanted money, they would have to get in line with everyone else. It was a ploy by Harry. I didn't sign it, but I lost just the same."

In court, the veneer company said, essentially, that Atwood had talked circles around them, just as he had done with the workers. They wanted the judge to appoint a receiver to run French and Heald, and they wanted ownership of the patents until the debts were paid.

The Airmobile was sucking the company dry, they said. Back in March, Heald had told the creditors' meeting that the furniture business was draining the company. "After some difficulty," they obtained two balance sheets. In the three-month grace period they had given Atwood, the company's assets had shrunk by nearly one-third.

At the beginning of the debt moratorium in April, the company had assets of $98,000 and an almost equal amount of debt, $102,000. Three months later, the assets had been drawn down to $70,000, and the liabilities had increased slightly to $109,000. One thousand dollars a week had gone into the Airmobile and the salaries of the company's officers. The furniture company's investment in aviation now stood at more than $80,000.

The company's only substantial asset was the Duply development, but the company didn't own it. Without the patents, Blair Veneer contended, Duply was "valueless, causing irreparable loss and damage to said creditors, and causes the said company to be hopelessly insolvent."

Atwood, while a director and general manager of the company, had rewritten his contract three times, each time with terms more favorable to him. The more French and Heald spent, the less they owned.

In his first contract, in May 1933, Atwood transferred "all of his rights in any patents, patent applications, inventions, developments, secret processes, formulae and any other rights he had pertaining to Duply" for $10,000, and a royalty of 5 percent based on the sales price of all Duply products. French and Heald would pay for the development and experiments, and pay Atwood an impressive monthly salary of $500—much more than the company president who was making $375 a month.

Once Atwood had applied for his first patents, and the secrecy around the operation was lifted, he negotiated a new contract, more than a year later in August 1934. Now he owned the patents. This contract was "extremely detrimental," said Blair Veneer. French and Heald continued to pay the entire cost of development as well as the cost of all patent applications. Atwood's salary was reduced to four hundred dollars a month. He would still collect a 5-percent royalty on Duply sales (payable the first day of each month).

This was a sweetheart deal for Atwood. He was "not obliged to devote his entire time" to the company. And if French and Heald went bankrupt or was placed in receivership, he was free to sell Duply elsewhere.

After risking eighty thousand dollars, the company had earned only the right to manufacture Duply products. But the company's officers, and treasurer George Langdell, who signed the contract, must have believed that this alone would be worth much—Atwood had convinced them that Duply was going to be that profitable.

Even this contract wasn't good enough for Atwood. A week before the creditors' meeting in March, he had declared his contract void because of the company's financial troubles, yet he continued to receive his salary and the company continued pay for the Airmobile. Then he had a third contract written and signed in June 1935, during the debt moratorium. The terms were never revealed. The creditors were refused the information. This contract may have removed French and Heald's exclusive right to manufacture Duply and left Atwood free to sell his invention to anyone, with limited benefit to the company.

Blair Veneer also alleged, and never proved, that company's finances were "handled in a peculiar manner," and that in the last month Atwood's salary had doubled to two hundred a week. They hinted at fraud.

Atwood's attorney, Alvin Lucier, responded by charging Blair Veneer "with a conspiracy to tie up the patents" just as important deals were pending. "The next 30 days will produce startling developments" Lucier said. The Blair Veneer Company was blocking the contract negotiations: it is difficult to sell something when its ownership is in doubt.

A compromise was reached. Atwood was granted three more weeks. He was saved again. He and his lawyer had talked their way past another deadline. The court appointed a manager to watch the company, and rolled Atwood back to his second contract. Atwood still owned the patents, but with one important caveat: the manager was given the right to approve any contract Atwood made.

The next thirty days did produce "startling developments," just as Atwood's attorney had promised. August 1935 would turn out to be as fateful a month for Atwood as August 1911 had been.

Atwood was about to close a contract that would be an ideal match. Earlier in the summer, he had dropped banner-headline-sized hints. "Plane Wins Atwood $150,000," the *Nashua Telegraph* announced the day after the test flight. "Reliable authority is that within a few days, or as soon as the material has been tested sufficiently, Atwood will be handed $150,000 by one of the better known plane building concerns as part payment for the right to use his material."

A small Pennsylvania company, Taylor Aircraft, was also struggling to produce a low-priced airplane. In 1931, it had introduced a plane called the "Cub." It quickly became a leader in the field; more than two hundred of the high-winged two-seaters sold at $1,325 in 1935. The Cub's fuselage was built with a steel tube frame and a fabric covering. The wings were formed by aluminum ribs meeting wooden spars made from expensive sitka spruce, which was becoming scarce. ("The most expensive pile of shavings in the world," Bill Piper said of the wood lost shaping the spars.) They were determined to lower production costs, and sell the Cub for less than $1,000. They had visited the Milford plant and were impressed.

C. Gilbert Taylor and his brother Gordon had designed their first light plane, the Chummy, in 1927. The Lindbergh Boom brought them financing to start a company. Gordon was killed in a Chummy in 1927, the boom fizzled, and Taylor went bankrupt in 1930. William T. Piper, a Pennsylvania oilman, made the only offer for the company: $761. He gave Taylor a 50-percent interest in the company, and the presidency. Piper was the treasurer. They set to work on a new plane, the Cub. They had laid out the first Cub following a chalk outline on the floor, and now, after years of refinements, they believed they had the airplane everyone could afford.

Clarence Farr was sent to Bradford, Pennsylvania, for a week to work out the production details. Taylor and Piper were "head over heels" about Duply, said Farr. "Taylor pinned his hopes on the process." He and Atwood had agreed that a contract would be drawn.

At the same time, Duply had attracted the attention of someone else who wanted to see the "mile-a-minute, penny-a-mile" cheap airplane built. Eugene Vidal was the director of the Bureau of Air Commerce (a forerunner of the Federal Aviation Administration). In November 1933 he proposed a "New Deal for Aviation" to do for the airplane what "mass production did for the automobile; convert it from a rich man's hobby" and allow the average citizen to enter "the kingdom of flight." His agency would back the development of an airplane that would sell for seven hundred dollars. "It was my father's dream to be the Henry Ford of aviation," said Vidal's son, Gore.

"The forgotten man of aviation is the private flyer and his brothers are legion," said Vidal. "They work at manual training branches in high schools and at engineering tables in colleges, and each dreams of the day when his inspired design will revolutionize aeronautics. They build model planes by the millions and trudge out to local airports each weekend to worship their idols from the ground and long for the day when they will have saved enough . . . to buy a hop."

His agency surveyed pilots, student pilots, and mechanics. Of the eighteen thousand who replied, thirteen thousand said they would purchase the seven-hundred-dollar airplane. Vidal sought one million dollars from the Public Works Administration to develop the plane and help the industry tool up to make ten thousand metal monoplanes by the following spring, which Vidal termed an "easy task." (There were only seven thousand licensed airplanes in the country, compared to more than twenty million cars.) He was granted half his request, five hundred thousand dollars, but this still left him far ahead of Atwood, who was trying to do the same thing with eighty thousand dollars. It would be the largest government program ever for private flying.

The aviation industry reacted with a "shrill yelp of suspicion, terror and ridicule," said *Time* magazine in a cover story on Vidal. They said it couldn't be done and would cause pilots to delay purchasing existing planes, which cost three or four times more. "Broadcasting the statement that one can 'build' a 'cheap' airplane and sell it for seven hundred dollars or anything near that price indicates a pathetic ignorance of the problem at hand," said the noted inventor William B. Stout, a designer of all-metal airplanes. If they had been given one thousand planes free, Stout said, they couldn't deliver the plane to a customer for seven hundred dollars. Others said that it cost seven hundred dollars to overhaul a typical airplane motor. "A considerable segment of the aircraft industry thought it a joke—and not a particularly funny one," said *Aviation* magazine. *Aero Digest* dismissed the entire bureau as a "conglomeration of half-baked undigestible ideas." Atwood had heard similar objections over the years. They succeeded in having the PWA money cancelled just five months later in March 1934.

Vidal retreated to funding a competition for a safe airplane design. Five designs were built, and one was flown by ten-year-old Gore for the newsreels. With his friend Amelia Earhart, Vidal came to Milford to see if Duply could be used in his safe plane program. He was impressed. The next week he sent an airplane to New Hampshire to fly Atwood down to Washington.

Atwood was "hard at work with the foremost designers in the country, improving and modifying the design of a new plane which the department of commerce plans to build with Duply," said the *Cabinet*. Vidal and Earhart returned to New Hampshire, this time with a group of technical experts from the leading aircraft companies. With the government's interest and the pending Taylor contract, triumph seemed just days away.

Farr returned with Taylor and Piper, each "full of enthusiasm" for a Duply Cub. Taylor, Piper, and Atwood went into a room to negotiate the final contract. "I was not in the smoke-filled room when all this negotiation went on," said Farr. "All I saw was the ashes afterward."

The deal was off. Taylor, like Atwood, was no compromiser. Even people who respected him found him difficult to work with. "C.G.," as he was known, "was not a businessman. He'd work his way into a corner. He just had trouble working with people," said one close to him. When confronted, he'd say, "Don't confuse me with the facts." He was "never at ease." Once when he was helping his daughter-in-law make up a bed, he took out a small tape measure to precisely align the sheets.

C.G. was a determined man, who hid a foot crippled by polio, even running on it in baseball games. And he was so shy he had a hard time making phone calls. He could be bullied into tears. "If he got with Atwood, forget it." Atwood and Taylor were a bad match. But Farr blames Atwood. "I think he wanted it to fall apart. There's no doubt it was deliberate," said Farr. "And I know sure as I'm a foot high—although I wasn't in the room—that Atwood deliberately harangued [them] to the point that they gave up and said: This guy's impossible. We can't possibly sign a contract with him."

Atwood had wrecked the deal. When he had his third contract drawn up, he was scheming to own the Taylor deal himself. But the court-appointed manager had ruled that the Taylor contract belonged to French and Heald. This was unknown to Farr, and to almost everyone else. They just looked on in disbelief as things fell apart. Atwood may have also thought he had a hidden ace with the government's interest. But after the initial excitement, that too went nowhere.

Once again, Atwood had wanted to control it all. "He wanted to be the Henry Ford of the airplane industry, who had invented and developed and test flown and promoted and now had in production, the poor man's airplane," said Farr. Farr saw his paychecks diminish and then stop altogether. He began to ask around about Atwood's past businesses. He found his way to Frank Andrew, the investor who had backed Atwood in Monson, and loaned him money when he was at his lowest.

Andrew told Farr about the Rubwood Wheel Company and other Atwood schemes. "The history had the same color to it of fantastic imagination, fantastic innovative talent, and hyperactive promotional efforts which wound up in collapse," said Farr. Harry Atwood was following a pattern, Andrew told him. But how long ago had he established this pattern? At the Saugus air school in 1912? In Sandusky and Toledo in 1913 and 1914? At the Williamsport airplane engine company in 1916? Or when the Carolina Aircraft Company built a plane for the navy in 1918?

It was all so disappointing. The Airmobile had flown. Duply had tested well. "It was an unqualified technical success," said Farr. But Atwood didn't know when to hand his invention over to others. "With great skill he conceived the idea, patented it, convinced a factory to produce it, and he got a test pilot who was good box-office. He singled out the one plane manufacturer for his market" (Taylor). And the rest, well, it should have been the successful beginnings of a new airplane.

He had "constructive, progressive ideas and ran them into the ground," said Farr. "Everything good he came up with had a spark of genius and nothing good happened." Once more, Harry Atwood had willfully destroyed a useful invention. "I can't help but feel that if a person like that would channel his efforts in more conventional ways, he'd be unbeatable," said Farr. "But he's always trying to beat the system and he comes up short."

Like many in Milford, Frederick Wetherbee felt deceived. "He was a con man—I shouldn't say that. He had the characteristics of a con man. He was a super salesman. He could sell anything. He had this bright idea. They bit.

"The impression I had: he was just for himself."

C. Gilbert Taylor lost his company. He was thirty-six years old, sick, and in despair. A couple of months after leaving Atwood, he was hospitalized for what was reported to be appendicitis. But he may have also been terribly shaken by his encounter with Atwood. Gene said her father terrorized

Taylor, making him cry. Taylor was out of work for two months. He sat by the window in his house, looking out at the runway and the factory. Relations had long been tense between Piper and Taylor, and now the two weren't talking. Without Taylor's approval, Piper had the Cub redesigned. Taylor first saw it out his window; he fired the small engineering department. Piper told Taylor he was through, he would have to leave. "Piper didn't hold a gun to my head, but he might as well have," Taylor said years later. "He offered me five thousand dollars for my half of the company, paid at the rate of forty dollars per week. He said that if I didn't accept the offer he would bankrupt the company and 'then where will you be?'" Taylor did not receive fair payment. Some called it the Great Plane Robbery.

Piper risked his fortune and rode through many hard times. He was a smart marketer and a hard worker. By 1940, four out of five pilots had learned to fly in a Cub, and by 1974, Piper claimed to have made one-quarter of all aircraft in the world, more than any other single producer. He was called the Henry Ford of aviation. The day of the Model T of the air never arrived, but the Piper Cub was the closet thing to it: forty thousand Cubs were built.

Henry Ford had given up the quest early, after his test pilot and family friend was killed in a crash shortly after setting a record in 1928. Only three versions of his Flivver were built.

Taylor regained his health, started a new company, designed new planes, and never looked back. The Cub became famous—as the Piper Cub. Taylor was unknown outside of aviation. He kept working long days—twelve hours or more, at the drawing board late into the night. His last designs flew when he was eighty-one years old.

He and Atwood were in many ways similar: inventors driven by their dreams, stubborn men who never compromised and were terrible businessmen, who just walked away from bad deals and companies.

That fall, Ruth Nichols joined Chamberlin Flying Services. Chamberlin had bought three Curtiss Condors from Eastern Airways, and barnstormed New England taking passengers up for a one dollar a flight. The Condors were big twin-engine biplanes, seating eighteen passengers, plus a crew of a stewardess, ticket taker, and mechanic. At a stop in Troy, New York, in October 1935, Harry Hublitz with his co-pilot Nichols, flew from ten in the morning to eleven at night, carrying a total of one thousand passengers. Taking off the next morning, the left engine quit. The plane hit an elm tree and exploded in flames. Hublitz crawled out of the wreckage, blinded and on fire. He died later at the hospital. Nichols was snagged by the tree and thrown to the ground. Her leg was broken in nine places, her back in five places. She was badly burned and the doctors were not sure for days if she'd live. She recovered and walked with a limp, but it took some time. This was Nichols's worst crash.

Chamberlin barnstormed for two more years with his remaining airplanes, gave that up, and ran five aviation schools between 1939 and 1943. "Then I retired to the farm. And I had more trouble trying to be a farmer than you can imagine." He gave that up.

French and Heald was declared "hopelessly insolvent" in January 1936. The company was under court control for one year while it was reorganized and refinanced with a loan from the Federal Reserve Bank. Forty percent of all furniture factories had folded by 1936. The survivors hoped to end up with a bigger share of the market.

The furniture company righted itself, showing a thin profit some months. The Depression wore on, and Milford was left to wonder if it had missed a grand opportunity or just shed a con man. For years after, people would discuss what they had seen.

When the veterans returned home from World War II, they told their neighbors about this airplane the British had, the DeHavilland Mosquito, one of the outstanding airplanes of the war. Used for reconnaissance, and as a fighter and a bomber, it was the world's fastest operational aircraft in its first two and a half years of service. The Mosquito didn't show up on radar—it was a wooden airplane. Parts had been built in a furniture factory, although it was constructed in different manner—a lamination of cedar ply and balsa wood. It left people wondering if there may have been something to that Atwood airplane.

After Clarence and Aline Farr's first meeting with Harry Atwood, on that day he sent the tomato juice back, they asked each other: What do you think? Clarence spoke first. "I said, 'Well, I think he's a genius.' And she said, 'I think he's a four-flusher,'" a card cheat. "We were both right. Because if he weren't a genius he couldn't have done what he did. If he weren't a four-flusher, he couldn't have done what he did."

And Farr thought back to some advice Clarence Chamberlin had given him. Before the test flight, when they were loading the plane for the trip to the airport, Chamberlin, he recalled, "was walking around the factory floor, hands in his pockets, deep in thought."

"Clarence, what's the good word?" Farr asked him.

Chamberlin paused and said with a grin, "Save your money and buy a farm." And they went out in the last of the morning light to fly the airplane that was going to revolutionize aviation.

⤳ Life with Father

Harry Atwood's daughters returned in the summer of 1935. He was fighting for his invention, the Airmobile, and did not want distractions. Five years earlier, he had sent his three daughters away to their grandmother's. He was broke then. They had left as schoolgirls, and now the two eldest were young women of eighteen and nineteen. For Harry, they belonged to a time back in Monson when he would pull their toboggan uphill, when he was Poppa Harry and would sit with them after dinner at the family meetings they called the Atwood Family Fools. Nice memories, but he had little use for memories. They belonged to the past and Harry Atwood did not look back. He sent the two eldest away to barnstorm for a month with Clarence Chamberlin and Ruth Nichols; when they returned, he sent them all away.

"He didn't want us for the rest of the summer. He didn't care," said Katrina. In the middle of the Depression, he gave them a few dollars and told them to look after themselves.

"He said, here, I'm giving you girls ten dollars a week each. That's thirty dollars. And don't come back for three weeks, four weeks, whatever it was. And that's what we got," said Katrina. They had a hard time living on the money.

"So I was the oldest and I said, all right, we'll take the train from Russell Station where we lived in Greenfield down to Boston and we'll go to the YWCA because that's cheap. And then we'll get a newspaper and hunt for ads.

"Now we could have gone back to our grandmother, but she had kicked us out for the summer, I mean nicely. We knew she needed a break from us. We realized we were awful to handle." Grandmother Satterthwaite was seventy-five years old, and for almost nine years had managed the girls by herself. Her husband was dead, and she had minimal help from an uncle. She died a year later in 1936.

"We went from Grandmother and we never had to think about money with her; now we had to think. Well, we thought we would like the ocean. In the newspaper ads, the cheapest I could find would be ten dollars a week at a summer place. It was in Plymouth, Massachusetts. A horrible little place, but it was on the ocean, or in an inlet or bay or something. Somebody Cove. I don't know what it was called. And we rented this horrible little cottage for ten dollars a week. And that left the balance for food.

"It was pretty awful." Her teenage sister Gene "picked up with this guy—*whoo whoo whoo*—well that was a lot to handle. He was, what I think of as a gangsterish type. And that's about the type that were living in that place."

Katrina "learned a lot that summer. We went to lovely places to eat with the gangster's money. And we'd then go back to father's to collect our thirty. By that time the gangster would be broke and so he'd disappear for a day or two, and then he seemed to have enough. You didn't question it. I think he drove for some other gangsters or something. He wasn't allowed to talk too much.

"This guy was also an alcoholic. So there was a lot of drinking on the beaches and stuff." But, she adds, "there wasn't a lot of cheap stuff going on." They watched out for themselves. Katrina dated a deaf-mute. He was nice and they went to dances. "I confined myself with him because that was safe and I wanted just to wait and get back to my grandmother's."

At their grandmother's they had led had a proper upper-class life, had engraved calling cards, and danced at the country club's debutante parties. "It was a very closed society," said Gene. "I mean we were not allowed to mingle with people out of our class. Several times I brought friends home from school and they were immediately thrown out. They taught us: you don't talk to Catholics, you don't talk to Italians, you don't—oh it was such a prejudice. I couldn't take it . . . You lived up to society. You did not do this, you did not do that, because it wasn't up to what society called for."

"Then Ruth Nichols came back to father's house," said Katrina. "And so she said, 'Harry, what do you mean you sent those kids out there in this? May I go down and see where they live?' He said, sure. He wasn't interested.

"She came down and she pulled us all out immediately. And she came back and she really gave it to father. She said, 'What do you mean sending your daughters down to a place like this?'

"He said, 'I never saw it.'

"We didn't see her after that.

"You see," Katrina explained, "he'd seen us. That was enough. He sent us off with Clarence Chamberlin. We came back; he couldn't take it."

One time I asked Katrina flat out, "Did your father ever say he loved you?" She was off in the kitchen savoring a cigarette. I could see her at the counter. Her voice boomed back, "Oh no! God no! Oh forget it!" She came back into the living room.

"Did we love him?" she said, asking the next question for me. "Yeah we loved him until we awakened. We thought whatever he says, that is the *truth*. And it was a rough awakening when we realized what he says is not the real, real, real truth."

For about five years we had been discussing her father in stories that rose and fell like a roller coaster—the playful Poppa Harry of Monson, the tyrant of New Hampshire. Katrina and Gene had told me so many stories of their return to him in New Hampshire that I was surprised when we nailed down the dates: a summer for Katrina, a year or so for Gene and Ruth. A few months that cast a long shadow. We had been going round and round in these stories, and at the center was the question of his love. A child shouldn't be left standing alone for half a century asking for her father's love.

When they had all found their way to him in New Hampshire, they were at a critical moment in their lives. Their grandmother, in her last year, had sent them off into the world. She had done what she could for them. They were in need of ordinary things in the right measure: guidance, advice, attention, love. But their father was not ordinary. He sent them away, not only off to live on their own, but emotionally, as well. They were on their own now.

Back in Monson, their father had paced the enclosed porch that wrapped three sides of the house. "He used to pace a lot," said Katrina. "He would pace up and down while he was thinking. He was not to be interrupted. If anything got in his way, he'd kick it aside and just would pace. We had our playthings all over. We had a chauffeur, gardener, maid, and men for the fields. We were never trained to be neat."

Her sister Ruth "had gotten this very severe punishment which she didn't deserve and we all knew it."

"She watched for him and she got her chance. She knew he was going to be out pacing on the porch. So she took this hat, one of his I guess, and put a brick under it, and put it in the middle of the floor.

"I wouldn't dare do something like this. And then she hung back at one of the windows. We were all there looking. Ruth said: 'Watch him now! You watch him!' Father came along and he was all absorbed in his mind and he gave the hat a great big kick. And he broke his toe.

"We, of course, ran away. And he never once admitted it and he never said anything about it. He tried hard as hell for days not to limp. Nobody got hell or anything. He wasn't going to admit that he was so damn mad he kicked the hat out of the way and got his own dose of it. And if he could think up things, believe me, he taught us to think up things to pay him back."

Like the brick hiding under the hat, behind the good times and games in Monson, there was much family unhappiness.

Gene is the youngest daughter. She was just one year old when her mother, Ruth, died. Her earliest memories are of her father's furies. She remembers Harry arguing with Mary Dalton, his fourth wife, whom the girls loved and called Mother Mary. She was pregnant. "She had a great big stomach and he would leave the house nights and just leave her alone with us three," Gene recalled. "She was so frightened to be alone. And I remember the fights he instigated. I had a place in the bathroom, where we had the old claw-foot tub, and you could hide in the back. Now that's how small I was. And I remember hiding back there every time they'd fight. He was very abusive. He just wanted to unload her.

"His anger was just horrible. One Christmas, Grandmother sent us a lot of gifts . . . He would burn them in the fireplace. Right in front of us," said Gene. His daughters have many stories about his temper. One morning, Katrina remembers, he was throwing oranges at her bedroom door and yelling at her that she was lazy: "Get up! Invent something! Get into the laboratory! Design something!"

Gene's stories preserve a child's horror at terrible forces unleashed. Harry Atwood is a monster, a man who didn't care about his daughters, who once tried to marry her off in order to get a rich aunt to invest in one of his inventions. A man who was dishonest, who mistreated and used women, who bullied her sister Ruth to tears. Her father is a child's nightmare monster at the window, something snarling, something threatening, growing by the minute outside the window and soon filling the window.

"If anybody showed any weakness, Dad jumped on it," and he would "try to embarrass them, try to completely humiliate them, and he was excellent at this. I know he did it with me a few times . . . He was very cruel."

"My sister Ruth was a very timid person," said Gene. "And Dad just picked on her morning, noon, and night. She despised him. I can remember as a young child at the dinner table, she almost always left in tears. Katrina and I, of course, were just about as pushy as he was. And he didn't dare push us around too much." Yet his pull was so strong that Gene had run away from a Quaker school in Philadelphia at age fifteen to be with him in New Hampshire. Ruth, age nineteen, soon joined her, as did Katrina, age twenty, when she was home from college, since their grandmother had died. Ruth was sweet and sympathetic, said her sisters, a very trusting person—"All things father wouldn't understand," said Katrina. She was also troubled. "If you were a little mixed up, father would see to it that you would be very mixed up," said Katrina. Just as Ruth had placed a brick under the hat in Monson, she fought back in Greenfield, too.

Once an important investor had come to inspect one of Atwood's inventions. Harry had just kicked Ruth out after another fight. She arranged to be on the same train out of town as the investor. She told him not to believe her father, he was a con man. She killed the deal. Another time, after Harry had provoked her, she took a shotgun and blasted away at his Cadillac. She shared a room with Gene. "And she kept a .22 rifle on the end of her bed in case Dad might come in and decide to abuse me," said Gene. He never had, he never would hit a woman, but the girls felt threatened.

Grandfather Atwood, a kind gentleman of the old school, lived with them in New Hampshire. After one of Harry's "rampages," he said to Gene: "How could I ever have a son like this? Your grandmother and I were such normal people."

"Dad was so temperamental that Grandfather and I would sort of eye each other and we would disappear," said Gene. "We'd take one of the cars, fill it up with gas. We always had a little money between us. And we'd disappear when Dad got in a bad mood. We'd go to little country inns and just travel around for maybe a week."

Harry Atwood hated snobs. He had contempt for the assumptions of inherited wealth. Though he often surrounded himself with the rich, and at times lived in a high style, he resented privilege. He always lived among farmers and laborers, even if he did not live as they did.

When Amelia Earhart's husband, George Palmer Putnam, visited, "Papa nicknamed him Putt-putt," said Katrina. "He took an aversion to the man, which was too bad. And that's because he arrived in a long limousine with a chauffeur and was formal and polite and all that stuff. And father really didn't like pretense. That really knocked him down. So by the time it was lunch, he invited the chauffeur in. Gave him a great lunch. And Putt-putt he sent outside. That was father."

(But then, everyone hated Putnam. There were just degrees of hate. He is a villain in so many memoirs of the era; a snobbish, overbearing schemer who bullied competing women aviators, trying to buy them out or threatening to freeze them out. He was powerful and he was feared. Many thought he pushed his wife too hard, packaged her like a product, lining up an exhausting series of lectures, publicity, and endorsements—sunglasses, luggage, and even an entire Amelia Earhart kitchen.)

Atwood did not like what his daughters had become at their grandmother's house. They were putting on airs. (When Katrina was going to play a piano recital in a new dress, he sent her off in a dirty pickup truck, not his Cadillac.) If they learned a few things about the world when he sent them off on their own, then good.

"We were brought up to be snobs," said Gene. "My father was so different when I went up to see him. He saw the snobbishness that had been put into me, that I was trying to get rid of. He got rid of it." Gene, by her own account, looked down on other people. She thought farmers "were uneducated, stupid individuals. That's the way I had been brought up. Dad taught me to listen to them and learn something from them," including their neighbor Arthur Taylor, a farmer who worked for her father.

Taylor came to one party at the house, said Katrina. "The governor of—I don't know if it was Massachusetts or Maine—was sitting down in a chair. And Arthur Taylor came by and there weren't any chairs and he was kind of lame and Father turned to him and said: 'Arthur are you hurting tonight?' And he said, 'Ay-ell, Mr. Atwood, I sure am.' And father turned to the governor and said: 'Would you stand please.' The governor got up, and he said, 'Arthur, that is your chair.' So the governor stood for the rest of the evening."

He taught them another lesson when a couple of boyfriends had come from Pennsylvania to visit Gene. "And they were too high-toned for Father," said Katrina. "He called them drones. Well, one had been kicked out of college and was going to another. Things like that. My sister was not interested in the boys. She didn't want them here. But they came.

"We knew something was going to happen, but we didn't know what. Father sent word: go out by the pool. You will be served by the butler, drinks and cocktails. So Father went in, got a white jacket, and he was the butler. And he served. Everything he did was so off-key that it was all we could do to contain ourselves. He would tip over drinks, stumble into people, did all kinds of things. And just had fun. He was going to teach the boys a lesson.

"The boys began saying, 'My God why do you have a man like that working for you up here?' And, of course, Father heard this choice little thing. Finally, the one boy that he really didn't care for was standing near the pool, so Father gave a great big stumble and the guy went crashing into the pool, and came up swearing and was terrible to Father. All hell let loose and Father just told them off.

"He did her right that time.

"'Well,' father said, 'You wanted to get rid of them.'

"She said, 'Well, yeah, but not quite that way.'"

Their father was many things to the girls: saint and tyrant, hero and tormentor, court jester and teacher. They never knew how long they had his attention or how it would be shown.

He played favorites, pitting one sister against the other. "He played people unmercifully," said Katrina. He did it often, with the young Airmobile engineers, his wives, his mother, and a legion of investors. "Every day could be a new heaven," she said. Or it could be hell.

"Sometimes he'd wake me up at three o'clock in the morning and say, 'Get your bags packed, we're going to New Jersey.' And away we'd go," said Gene. She was sixteen or seventeen years old. "We had more fun. I think he had a girlfriend in New Jersey. And I was just permitted anything at all. We saw plays and had a ball and he put me at a hotel room and he went over to his lady friend's. We just had such a good time. And then all of a sudden he would turn and want to get rid of me—as he did with all his girlfriends."

"I adored him," said Gene, "and then I could turn right around and some of the things he did to me, I could hate him.

"When I first went up there I was fifteen, I think. I loved him so much. I wanted to get away from Grandmother, away from bigotry . . . And I just didn't see anything wrong with him. I knew there was something wrong later on . . ."

He was disappointing—as a father, as an inventor, as a businessman. You can still hear the disappointment in the voices of people who haven't seen the man for thirty, forty, or sixty years. It was so exciting, they say. We were building this airplane, he had such good ideas, he was fascinating to be with, and then it would all come apart.

It was if they had met Harry Atwood in the desert when they had only a few drops left to drink. He told them he could bring forth an oasis—if they gave him their last water. And when they did, they were only sorry they didn't have more to give him. He would produce a small oasis, a glimmer of the great day to come, and as the thirsty entered, it would vanish. Only then did they realize they had never gotten a drop to drink. Harry Atwood led you forward, conjured miracles, and left you thirsty. He created some extraordinary things, happy times for his children, and then destroyed everything and moved on. "He would kill his own invention just out of spite," said Katrina.

When Gene announced that she was to be married, he promised to give her the wedding. They would have the ceremony and reception at the house in Greenfield, and he would look after everything. A few days before the ceremony, Gene went to the house. He had not done one thing. "He said, 'No, the hell with it,'" said Katrina. "You couldn't trust him if he gave his word." He was at none of his daughter's weddings.

The daughters' later lives were difficult. Gene married six times (she told her father she wanted to match him). She lived forty years in Las Vegas and hated each year. There were some hard years, taking in laundry, living in an old trailer in a trailer park. Katrina married twice, the second time happily. All three had to face their alcoholism. Ruth killed herself at age fifty-four, three years after her father died.

"Look," said Katrina, "he turned himself on and off with his own kids. We weren't necessary to his happiness. When we were, he would surround himself with us. But not long. He'd get completely bored with us."

An absent father is a terrible presence. "In my older age I've tried to figure him out and sometimes I come up with a blank," said Gene at age seventy-two. "He'd be so horribly moody. You could not be around him. I know he didn't love us. I just wonder what he did love."

Gene and Ruth were living in Las Vegas when they heard of their father's death. "I said to Ruth, here it is that Father is dead and we feel nothing. It's sad. Just terribly, terribly sad."

⇝ Talking Infinity

The last time William Rotch saw Harry Atwood was around 1938. Atwood had dropped in to see Rotch's parents. He was talking about the wars of the future. "Guns would become obsolete in the fighter planes of the future, he said. Instead, planes would be armed with some sort of rocket, with a homing device which would draw it toward the plane at which it was aimed. Evasive maneuvers would be useless. The rocket would follow the plane until contact was made and it exploded.

"He told of small planes that would be launched from big planes high in the atmosphere . . . He foretold the day when 'space platforms' would be put into orbit, manned with weapons or used as observation posts, circling an earth far below."

Atwood went to Washington in 1939 with a design for a robot-guided missile he called the Air Weasel, which would knock down incoming airplanes. A weasel in pursuit of a rat follows it relentlessly to the kill, he explained to the *Boston Sunday Post.* If bombers were coming toward the United States, the missiles would find them "using electronic eyes, ears and feelers tuned to sounds, vibrations, light, and all disturbances given out by planes" and blow them out of the sky. Atwood was convinced that Hitler had his scientists working on such missiles, which would shoot down planes and sink ships with "ghastly precision." He offered to develop the Air Weasel for a dollar a year.

"It makes my heart sick to think of the vehicle to whose development I have devoted all my adult life, made the instrument of such inhuman, barbarous slaughter of innocents. It seems to me that the greatest contribution to decency that we, who know airplanes, can make is to develop the mechanism that will make them useless for warfare," he said.

"What happens when a fleet of bombers attacks a city and the defending squadrons go aloft to battle them? A handful of warriors meet a merciful death, though most return to their bases safe and sound. But down below, in the city streets, thousands of women and children and aged civilians are torn and shattered by flying shrapnel, blown to pieces by high explosive, stricken by poison gas. If I am made the means of stopping this savage slaughter of non-combatants, I'll deem it a greater triumph than sending a plane out in limitless space to voyage between the planets."

But the army told him that if it could have been done, they would have done it. At that moment in the fall of 1939, as Germany invaded Poland, Hitler's rocket scientists had advanced far in developing the V-2 rocket, but had yet to create a guidance and control system.

Harry Atwood always had an eye on the long voyage: fly across half the country, the continent coast to coast, the ocean. Now he looked to the ocean above, the stratosphere, and beyond. He looked to infinity. He believed in infinity. Infinity was his religion.

"There was a preacher at the Congregational church in Greenfield," said Nellie Pickens, who was hired in her teens as Atwood's housekeeper. "He used to come up to the house and sit half the night. He and Harry would talk for hours and hours and hours. He said he had to get away from the petty stuff of the church, and get out and talk about infinity and time and things beyond.

"Harry never went to church, as far as that goes," said Nellie, but "he made several speeches to different ministerial meetings as to the reason why he didn't go to church." Atwood believed in God, but he had his own doctrine. "You sit up there on top with your feet hanging out of an airplane in space and looking over the world. You can't help believe in a god," said Nellie.

"They talked infinity and life goes on forever" and Nellie would keep the coffee coming.

"Like Harry always said: there's no beginning and there's no ending. It's infinite. Phases come and go—that's all. There's no end."

And when you die? "It's just like opening and closing a door. It's just like closing one door and going into another room. Um-huh."

After the successful test flight, Atwood had been invited to Dartmouth College to talk about the future of aviation. But he did not talk about the coming triumph of the Airmobile. His eyes were on the stars.

"Not many days ago," he said, "I visited the Chief of Staff of the U.S. Air Force, to obtain permission to build a new type of air-vehicle that I believed might point the way for mankind to soar beyond the atmospheric limits of the earth." Atwood's friend from the Wright brothers flying school, Hap Arnold, was the assistant to the chief. "I did not hold forth immediate possibilities of flights to the moon or to other celestial bodies. I merely maintained that it might be of vital importance, in this era of international turmoil, for Americans to obtain facts about the ether.

"There were several days of conferences. My project was disapproved. The U.S. technical staff gave me its reasons. They stated they had made a thorough survey of all matters relating to man-flight into space, and could assure me that it was an impossible thing to attain. They said that space was predominantly a realm of Nothingness. They estimated the absolute limit of man-flight towards space, at 21 miles above the surface of the earth. They computed the temperature of the atmosphere at the 21 mile altitude to be close to absolute zero. They said that the unshielded lightrays from the sun in combination with the chill of space, would cause structural collapse and failure of craft constructions and power-plants. In brief, they aimed to prove that mankind could never soar away from this earth, and that posterity was doomed to become extinct when the earth became cold and barren. I left Washington knowing that our Air Force was not going to monopolize space transportation in the near future.

"However, a few weeks later, a member of the technical staff paid me an unexpected visit at my New Hampshire home, and remained for several days. When he left to return to Washington, he advised me that my theories and developments merited serious consideration by the government. I have not received further word from him.

"My friends, you have asked me to give you my vision of the future of aviation . . .

"We shall be journeying through interstellar space before the advent of another generation. We shall find it the most perfect roadbed we have ever traversed. We shall learn that it is a universal transmission line of energy and substance, that can be tapped at any point or time, to serve our demands. We shall soon know that it's a life-sustaining atmosphere, and not a death-dealing Nothingness. In fact as we roam further and further into the great outdoors of Nature, it shall be revealed to us there is nothing lacking in interstellar space to prevent us from journeying onward forever.

"If you should feel inclined to scoff at these fabulous predictions, please ponder the lessons that have been taught throughout the ages, about a supernatural realm of Nothingness. The day is about to dawn when these teachings shall be hurled from the halls of science.

"My humble mind cannot conceive of a concoction of Something and Nothingness. I cannot conceive how men and stars 'pull' each other by means of a 'rope' of Nothingness, with a toehold upon Nothing. I cannot conceive how wave actions are transmitted through a realm of void. In other words, I cannot conceive how we are here tonight, or how our universe holds together, or how it ever got together, if any part of Nature was an aeriform emulsion of Something within Nothingness.

"The constant and nonwave-action exertion of the force of gravitation upon anything and everything, is positive evidence that there is a definite Something of Continuity throughout Nature; and that Nature is boundless. I am quite convinced that the theory of relativity is on the road to identifying it.

"If Nature is boundless, and embodies an infinite domain, it is actually a hermetically-sealed container. Nothing can get out of it. Everything in it has been endowed and sealed by infiniteness, with infiniteness and for infiniteness . . . Energy, substance and life, are already in the container. Nothing can escape from it. There shall always be a place to go.

"I am not talking in terms of religion. I am speaking within the vision of science. Clergymen are qualified to show the way to the eternity of immortality. Scientists should be qualified to show the way to the survival of posterity. When we learn to fathom the relativity of nature in terms of infinity, we shall know that creation is not a finite institution."

Behind closed doors, Atwood continued to work. He had looked at birch trees and had seen airplanes, and now, looking at bushel baskets, he saw what he thought was a path to the stars.

Seeking to improve Duply, Atwood had found himself staring at an ordinary woven bushel basket. An empty basket could be lifted by one finger, yet it could carry one hundred pounds, and, upturned, make a seat for a heavy man. "The old-fashioned basket weave was one of the strongest structures for its weight ever known, though it could be pulled to pieces or unwoven rather easily," said Atwood. "But the addition of plastic holds the locked ribbons in place; it's like locking a door and then cementing up the lock."

His new patented material was, essentially, a woven Duply. "He had built a plastic rowboat, light and tough, which rested in the swimming pool beside the house," said Rotch. "In winter, youngsters used it as a sled, and he was proud of the fact that ice failed to scratch its tough hull."

He was also working on "plastic skis, built to any desired degree of springiness, and which would not need wax for downhill running, and this in a day when everyone knew that the best skis had to be made of hickory," said Rotch.

John F. Coggswell, a reporter for the *Boston Post*, visited Atwood when he was experimenting with the skis. Nellie "braided a full-sized pair of skis in less than two hours. A half-hour later they were out of the presses and cooling. Three hours after the start, they were on the side of the mountain, sliding. Harry Atwood grabbed one of the skis, while I was there, hurled it clean across the workshop against the cement wall. It hit on the tip, bounced off like a rubber ball, clattered to the floor. It didn't have a scratch or a break on it." Some of Gene's friends gave the skis a demanding test on Mt. Washington at Tuckerman Ravine. The skis were hard to control. Atwood gave up the idea.

He told Coggswell that a "Massachusetts subsidiary of one of the largest corporations in the world" was paying him "a goodly sum" for a license to use his patented material in "more than 60 different articles, running from cigarette cases to caskets, from handbags to indirect lighting fixtures." The Parkwood Company, one of his licensees, made lightweight, woven, wooden bowls. The company was known for its line of Amelia Earhart luggage.

But Atwood's ambition wasn't to pioneer waxless skis or other such products. He was at work on something much grander, which his experiments only hinted at: a "metallized Duply," a weave of wood and metal threads, gold in some trials; and a woven wood with a special airtight rubber coating. He had constructed several models, burning them, to measure the interior temperatures. He was "aiming at something else, looking beyond, seeking further to enlarge man's mastery of the air," said Coggswell. He led Coggswell on, letting him do the figuring, never stating it outright.

"We're building a hermetically sealed fuselage, by weaving the regular wood ribbons with special plastic," said Atwood. "The fuselage under construction weighs no more than the standard metal fuselage of the same capacity but it will withstand an internal atmospheric pressure five times greater than it would be subjected to in an absolute vacuum. It would hold together with an inside pressure of 75 pounds to the square inch and no pressure outside."

"Whew!" wrote Coggswell. He did some math. The airplane designer Igor Sikorsky had figured that a pressurized cabin at an altitude of twenty-five-thousand feet would have to withstand 787 pounds of pressure per square foot just to maintain cabin conditions as though flying at ten thousand feet. Atwood was claiming a design to withstand a 10,800 pounds per square foot.

"He'll hint of this ambition of his, but won't reveal it yet, nor his reasons for being sure that he'll pull it off," Coggswell wrote. "But it's my guess that he is planning on taking an airplane where man has never flown before. He did a lot of that in aviation's fledgling days, you'll remember."

Atwood was selling the thinnest blue sky, ten miles up and more, above the clouds, where the atmosphere shaded into space.

Since French and Heald had gone into receivership, Atwood had rented part of the factory where, in secrecy, he was developing airplane floats and skis and his new airplane, which he hoped would be the first of a series that would eventually fly up to the stratosphere and beyond. But even his presence was a sore subject for the company's new directors. Atwood and his lawyer Lucier protested at a shareholders' meeting held to reorganize the company, and after a stormy argument, they walked out. A few weeks later, Atwood was ordered to quit the premises. He had no money, but he owned the Duply patents.

Eugene Vidal was on his own, too. He had left the Bureau of Air Commerce in 1937. He wanted to build his own airplanes and he remembered the Duply Airmobile. Backed by the industrialist Vincent Bendix, he set out to buy the Atwood patent. Vidal had a poor record spotting investments; he had lost money in Florida real estate, and in a silent toilet flusher that wasn't. But Bendix was a titan of industry who had parlayed the electric self-starter for automobiles into an industrial empire in fifteen countries, producing automobile brakes and other parts, as well as aircraft instruments. "The King of Stop and Go," as he was called, was worth more than fifty million dollars. He spent lavishly on houses, parties, and art. He bought an entire Buddhist temple in China and had it shipped to the United States. By 1939 he had spent himself into personal bankruptcy, but the Bendix Corporation was thriving. Bendix had become rich by buying patents and developing them. His company owned fifty-five hundred patents.

"They came to the house in Greenfield, two lawyers and Vincent Bendix," said Nellie, who was now his girlfriend as well as his housekeeper. Harry had been back and forth to New York to see them. "They argued and argued and argued. And finally Harry sat down and played." He had a grand piano. "He'd sit up two, three hours a night, in the middle of the night, playing the piano. He always said, everything he ever did, he did at the piano first. Vincent Bendix sat down at the edge of the piano bench and said, 'I didn't know you could play.'

"Then one of the lawyers said, 'We can't pay much for a paper patent.' Well, there is nothing more insulting you can say to a research scientist. That means you just write something down," with no testing or product behind it.

"He stopped in the middle—something he never did. 'This is one New Hampshire lamb you're not going to fleece. You can go back to New York.' He didn't want anything to do with them. And believe me, we didn't have enough money for breakfast."

Nellie had seen Atwood's anger worse at other times. One time he put his fist through a window. He was arguing with his patent attorney. "Harry was real upset. He had his hand back to put his fist down: 'I will not do it.' His hand went through the window." He told Nellie to call Mayor Lucier over in Nashua, and let the hospital there know he was coming in. Then he wrapped his hand in a rag and drove himself to the hospital. He wouldn't allow anyone to drive him.

"If he'd get angry, he'd destroy something that meant a lot to him," said Nellie. "He destroyed that cup," a trophy he'd won back in 1911. "He threw it and mashed it."

At the hospital they wanted to take off his fingers to prevent blood poisoning. He wouldn't let them. "I can't play the piano without fingers," he said. He wouldn't let them give him anesthetic, for fear they would take his fingers off. He made them reattach his tendons.

"I remember waiting for him. We didn't hear anything. After the doctors worked on him, he sat and talked with the doctors for four or five hours. He returned at 4 A.M. By 6 A.M. he took the splint off. And he did get blood poisoning. Every day for two weeks we had to sterilize a jackknife and open the wound. The skin was healing faster than the inside wound." Two months later he was sitting at the piano slowly moving his fingers, and gritting his teeth. It hurt so much. Talk about a stubborn person." He slowly regained his ability to play.

"Bendix told the lawyers to go sit down on the other side of the room and not say a thing. Let him handle it.

"So Bendix left him with a check for ten thousand dollars that night."
Atwood had sold Duply.

Vidal prospered with the patent.

"Today, a dozen factories here and in Canada are making tails and
wings and fuselages and other parts out of wood by Vidal's cooking process," reported the *Saturday Evening Post* in July 1942, six years after
French and Heald had given up on Duply. "Factories licensed by Vidal are
making pontoon boats, deck housings for PT boats, and auxiliary gas
tanks. They are making training planes and fuselages for twin-engined
bombers out of cooked wood. They are swinging into production on a secret combat plane and other highly secret military projects. Hundreds of
Army and Navy planes now flying have parts made of molded plywood, either by Vidal licensees or others. At least two experimental non-military
planes made entirely by this process—except, of course, for the engine,
propeller shaft and such parts—are now flying around. The Canadian
government has ordered parts cooked out of wood for hundreds of
planes, and the Chinese government has a Vidal license."

There was an aluminum shortage. President Roosevelt's call for
125,000 airplanes to be produced in 1942 and 1943 could not be met
with available aluminum. Duply had been a solution awaiting a problem,
and now its moment had arrived. "The Army has issued a directive that
plywood be used wherever possible in training ships," said the *Post.* "The
procurement sections of the Army and Navy are buzzing about it." One
industrial designer was visiting the navy on behalf of his clients, mostly
furniture makers who couldn't get raw material due to wartime restric-
tions. "Why don't you look into this cooked wood stuff," a navy officer
told him, and sent him to Vidal.

Vidal had set out to make the $700 airplane and prove his critics
wrong. "The war has interfered with that. In any event, he can console
himself with the million dollars or more he seems likely to make from the
process," said the *Post.* The Vidal Research Corporation was said to be
worth at least $800,000, and that was before it boomed with the alumi-
num shortage. Vidal had big money behind him. One major oil and
shipping family had invested $1.5 million in factories to build products
under his license.

He did not acknowledge Atwood. He did mention seeing Clarence
Chamberlin fly an experimental airplane in New England. It was built
"out of a striplike tape of wood veneer, wound round and round, with

plastic sprayed on it and rubber bands over that, all covered with thick green paint. It was a freakish thing," said the *Post*, which portrayed Vidal as the sole inventor heroically bringing forth a new wonder. "Why not, he figured, start with the thin slices of wood and wrap them, with alternate layers of plastic, around the form, and then steam the whole thing into a rigid shape?" This was a succinct description of the Duply process, but now it was known as the Vidal process. A picture showed a single woman holding up the fuselage of the Summit, identified as the "first all-molded-plywood-and-plastics plane."

The designer the navy had sent to Vidal was ecstatic. "This is it," he rejoiced. "This is a designer's dream of heaven. American homes will never be the same again." He began designing futuristic bicycles, tennis rackets, typewriter frames, lightweight bus bodies, beds, and bathtubs.

Atwood was paid royalties "for one year and that was the end of it," said Nellie. "They'd learn what they could, change some little thing, and say it was a new patent. It was so cruel. No sense in fighting it. Nothing you can do about it. They'd spend millions to get around patents when they could have just paid him. They still do it.

"There's nobody going to pay one little man anything. It used to make me so angry."

The Airmobile was floating in the swimming pool in front of Atwood's house. Harry Atwood had loaded two tons of rocks into the plane and there the Airmobile floated for eight months, right through the winter. He told visitors he was testing the water resistance of Duply. The Airmobile had sunk only two inches after all that time afloat, he claimed.

Others saw the plane of the future adrift and had another explanation: "He's a kook!" They had spent all that money to build that one plane at the factory and now look at it. Hard to see what all the fuss was about. There was talk that he wanted to make sure the plane could never be flown again. They looked at the house behind the pool, all covered in stone and cement, and the man within who talked of space travel, sometimes while a trained squirrel sat on his shoulder, and they said, "He's a kook!"

To the fifteen-year-old Bob Whittier, Atwood was a hero from the pioneering days of flying. Whittier lived in a town near Boston. His teacher, a family friend of Atwood's, asked the partially deaf boy if he would like to visit the airman. ("Would I? Wowee!") On a hot Memorial Day weekend in 1937, Whittier traveled by train and bus to Atwood's Greenfield home.

"Always there was an air of restlessness" about Atwood, Whittier said. Once while explaining something technical, he grabbed a pencil to make a sketch and finding a broken point, threw it across the room."

Whittier listened eagerly to Atwood's flying stories, told—as usual—with a new twist. (Literally. He said that his only injury from flying was when he had landed in a pine tree and had to climb down, spraining his ankle.) He showed the boy around the house, the tower he used to study lightning, the workshop filled with ribbons of veneer, and the lab with "a dozen or more small hardwood airplane models, most under a foot in span and most done in blue and silver. They had all manner of unusual shapes." One was a flying wing design, "another was of canard or tail-first design," models Atwood had made when the government was interested in Duply.

"Noting my interest in them, Atwood let me look at them and think about them for a while. Later he handed me a pencil and asked me to sketch any ideas for dream planes that I might have in my head. I promptly dashed off a squadron of racy-looking ships after the fashion of the Ryan ST and Bill Barnes' fictitious 'Stormer' as shown in the old 'Air Trails' magazine adventure yarns. I got the feeling that Atwood was a little disappointed with my efforts and I have always suspected that in asking me to sketch some dream planes, he was hoping that a boy's active and unfettered mind might hit upon a configuration of merit that the trained minds had overlooked . . .

"After a night of dreaming about Burgess-Wright biplanes and flying my own Airmobile, I awoke and eagerly accepted my host's suggestion that we go to Concord Airport for a plane ride . . . I was all excited about flying with the pioneer airman and somewhat surprised to find myself being invited aboard a gull-wing Stinson" to fly with a local pilot, Nellie, and another passenger. They flew over Greenfield and circled Atwood's house.

"Riding back to Greenfield, I asked Atwood why he had not flown too. To my puzzlement, he said he had in fact done some flying in a yellow Aeronca-K I remembered having seen at the airport. So I naturally wanted to know why he had not gone with us." Atwood replied, "So that some of us would still be left if something happened to one of the planes."

The Airmobile itself was out of the pool and sitting in a grove of pine trees, "somewhat faded and weather-checked." To show the strength of the plane, Atwood stood on one wing tip and had Whittier stand on the other, and the boy and the old inventor proceeded to jump up and down on the wings of the airplane.

Harry Atwood owed money all over town for groceries, for car repair, for the cement used to build his "castle." Companies sent out bill collectors. They would return with the most amazing stories—and no money. The Blair Veneer Company, having shut down the Airmobile and forced Atwood from French and Heald, was still after him.

Six years earlier, on a small sheet of hotel stationery, Atwood had written:

$1683.17   Nov. 26, 1932

Six months from December first for value received I promise to pay to Blair Veneer Co. on order the sum of sixteen hundred eighty three dollars and seventeen cents, with interest at 6%.

Harry N. Atwood

This promissory note had been the start of the Duply development in New Hampshire. He had not paid it and had no intention of paying it. In January 1939, the sheriff attached Atwood's estate for twenty-five hundred dollars and summoned him to court. Other claims followed. He owed one electrician eight thousand dollars.

Harry Atwood had lost big this time. Ever since his twenties, he had been coming to a new town with a new invention and all that it promised, selling the blue sky of a revolutionary seaplane, automobile wheel, or Airmobile. He was always able to go to a new place and attract money with a new idea. He had come back and come back for nearly thirty years, since his first venture, the Saugus air school, folded.

But he was no longer young at age fifty-five, and a different era was coming in aviation, one in which big corporations and teams of engineers tested and produced expensive airplanes. Things were changing rapidly. Even if you spend your life looking to the future, trying to bring it on, you can be left behind.

Atwood hid his grand piano with a neighbor, buried the Airmobile, tore up the water lines leading to the house, and fled with his housekeeper, Nellie. The court delivered summonses to a Chicago hotel and they went unanswered.

Nature was infinite. It contained everything: Atwood, his past, and his future. There were always places to go.

III

When caged and near at hand, the lark's song is positively dis-
agreeable, it is so loud and full of sharp, aspirated sounds. But
high in air above broad downs, poured out without interruption
for many minutes together, it is very agreeable.
—JOHN BURROUGHS, *Birds and Poets* (1877)

⤳ Fog

Harry Atwood disappeared into the fog of Vancouver, British Columbia. The fog settled in so thickly that fall and winter that he and Nellie
would often be lost trying to find their way home. They crept along some
nights following the trolley lights. One night, they followed a trolley all
the way into the car barn.

Now look what you've done, the trolley driver said.

Harry said they were lost.

Oh you're that Yankee inventor, the driver replied. Everyone in Vancouver knew who he was.

He was working on a small airplane for a little company run by a husband and wife, which is all Nellie can recall. They may have been under
contract to the Canadian government. Atwood was going back and forth
to Ottawa all the time. Years later he told a story about smuggling some secret technology through customs during the war.

It was a time when all the talk was about King Edward's abdication, said
Nellie. "It was very British there. You went to someone's home and you
didn't say a thing until they said something. One house might be high
royal and the next thought it all should be done away with.

"Work stopped at ten, twelve, and at two for tea. There was nothing for
me to do, so I went to the movies a lot."

Before they had left New Hampshire, Harry's father, Samuel, had gone
to live with his daughter. He wrote Nellie every week, she said, in his careful penmanship. One week he didn't write. There's something wrong,

said Harry. And they got in the car and left Vancouver. It was February, and they couldn't cross the mountains. In the time before interstate highways, they faced a long drive down the West Coast and across the desert Southwest.

His father, at age eighty-four, was in the hospital, fading, and the family was trying to reach Harry. They drove for three days, and, as Nellie tells it, Harry arrived to comfort his father on his deathbed.

Samuel Atwood was buried in a small cemetery in Carver, Massachusetts. The family was gathered at the grave when Harry arrived. "He drove up in the car, and we turned around and looked, and Mother said there's Harry," said his niece, Barbara Conway. "He never got out of the car, and when the service was done, he drove off."

The Purest Airplane

"I'll tell you what: I bet I've poured more concrete than anybody in the world," Nellie said, and laughed. "Did it by hand. But it was fun. I enjoyed every minute.

"We never had a dull moment. I'll guarantee you. For thirty-two years I never had a dull moment," she said of her life with Harry Atwood. "Sometimes we were up and sometimes we were down. And we'd go years without any income at all. And then we'd sell, either get a contract of some kind or you know . . . And we're rich, what'd we do? We have to pay back what we lived on for those five years, you know," and she laughed again. "That's research for you. More stuff goes in the wastebasket than goes anywhere else.

"For years we didn't even know if it was Christmas, Thanksgiving. Nothing. Never knew a holiday. We just kept on working. When we had a project we were working on, we just didn't stop for nothing. Worked day and night on 'em."

Harry married Nellie in Las Vegas. It was his fifth marriage, and by far his longest, longer than all his other marriages combined. "I loved him from the first time I saw him," Nellie said. She remembers exactly where he was standing when they met. "I was just a kid, I went up to work for him. I fell in love with him on sight. He didn't know it for years—several years."

When they left New Hampshire, they went west. Vancouver first, then a couple of years working for different veneer factories in the Midwest, just different flat places, as Harry Atwood saw it. He didn't care for it. He would find them a new place to live.

"He went to Chicago. The next day I got a call from Arkansas." He told Nellie he had found a place. "I said well, does it got this? does it got that? You know how women are. What about electricity, what about this?

"'Oh we could have it, we could get it.' And all that stuff. That's as far as he'd tell me. Got out there and there were no electricity within ten miles, I guess," she said, and laughed.

"It was just country—wild country. The place we went to was way out, fifteen miles from anywhere. I mean the town . . . the little-bitty town of Berryville was fifteen miles from where we lived. To get to our land we had to ford a creek. We were kinda' sittin' there on the bank and I said, if this is what you want, this is okay with me. I was always willing to go along. We got it for sixteen hundred dollars: forty acres. We enjoyed it—we really enjoyed it, living there."

Berryville was in the Ozark mountains, just ten miles from the Missouri border. Atwood's place was off in its own valley behind Pension Mountain, where the cattle grazed the open range. It was "a long ways and kinda' crooked," as one native remembered. The roads were dirt back then and the "road was rough. You seldom ever find an automobile that go up it in high gear. He was out with the snakes—rattlesnakes, cottonmouths. He had an awful nice dog out there, got killed by one." They had no telephone, but they did have a piano. The neighbor who had hidden Atwood's piano back in New Hampshire shipped it to him. It was the only thing he had from his years in New Hampshire.

Thirty years earlier, when he was famous, he had announced that he wanted to go away, give up the headline-making flights and settle down on a farm to experiment with perfecting the art of flight. This was the fullest expression of his desire. "True to my unchanging form, I am once more located in the midst of a jungle, surrounded by mountains, encased in a newly-built cement house, and living in the midst of isolated but colorful conditions," he wrote an acquaintance.

In Berryville, Nellie had Harry's last child, a daughter, Nelda. He was fifty-eight years old and Nellie was twenty-six. They lived too far from school, so Nellie taught her at home.

At first, "he built like two little bitty rooms. The whole thing was like twenty-four feet by, I guess, fifteen. Just enough to get into was all," said Nellie. "We had moved into it one Sunday and the next Sunday there was about fifty people came by. They came on horseback, they came on foot, they came everywhere, from all through that area to welcome us in. They were the friendliest people you'd ever meet in your life."

The family added to the house, and built three houses in all, each with

Ruth Atwood, in the year
of her death, with Ka-
trina, 5, Gene, 1, and
Ruth, 4, 1920. (*Courtesy of
Katrina Atwood Copeland.*)

Poppa Harry with Topsey
the bear. (*Courtesy of Katrina Atwood Copeland.*)

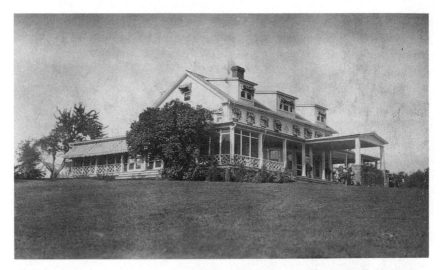

The good life: the Atwoods' house in Monson, Mass., in the 1920s. (*Courtesy of Katrina Atwood Copeland.*)

The 90-day marriage. Harry and Helen Satterthwaite and children, Marcia, Katrina, Alfred, Ruth, and Gene. (*Courtesy of Katrina Atwood Copeland.*)

Five shares of Rubwood Wheel, Inc. (*Monson Free Library and Reading Room Association.*)

1,422,813. LAMINATED COMPOSITE WHEEL. HARRY N. ATWOOD and GEORGE B. BAINS, 3d, Reading. Pa. Filed Dec. 24, 1920, Serial No. 432,939. Renewed Nov. 16, 1921. Serial No. 515,695. 10 Claims. (Cl. 301-63.)

1. The method of producing a composite laminated structure of complex contour which comprises providing a flat body surface with an outstanding portion substantially defining the contour desired, applying to the built-up surface, a ply of vulcanizable material, and subjecting the assemblage to a molding operation attended by heat and pressure whereby to effect union of the ply to the built-up surface and cause the same to conform to the contour of the said surface.

1,477,025. METHOD OF PRODUCING VEHICLE WHEELS. HARRY N. ATWOOD, Boston, Mass., assignor to Rubwood, Inc., Lawrence, Mass., a Corporation of Massachusetts. Original application filed Nov. 21, 1921, Serial No. 516,766. Divided and this application filed Nov. 29, 1922. Serial No. 604,074. 4 Claims. (Cl. 18-56.)

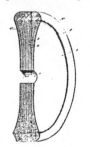

1. The method of producing a vehicle wheel which comprises assembling veneer plies and intervening bonding plies of rubber, building up a tread of rubber stock about the periphery of the assemblage, and subjecting the whole to a process of vulcanization.

1,458,379. VEHICLE WHEEL. Harry N. Atwood, Smithfield, N. C., assignor to Rubwood, Inc., Lawrence, Mass., a Corporation of Massachusetts. Filed Nov. 21, 1921. Serial No. 516,766. 9 Claims. (Cl. 152-29.)

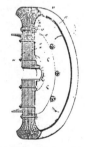

4. A vehicle wheel comprising a body and tread, the body being made up of plies of veneer and intervening bonding plies of rubber, the veneer plies being outwardly curved at their peripheral portions in the direction of the relatively adjacent sides of the wheel and with gradually increasing degrees of curvature and the bonding plies being gradually increased in thickness at their peripheral portions to correspond to the increase in width of the spaces between relatively adjacent veneer plies, the tread being intimately incorporated with the said bonding plies.

Three of the many patented wheel designs. (*Official Gazette, U.S. Patent Office: July 18, 1922, p. 416; December 11, 1923, p. 389; and June 12, 1923, p. 368.*)

Harry's daughters in exile: from left, Uncle Frank Satterthwaite, Ruth Atwood, Gene Atwood, Katrina Atwood, and Grandmother Satterthwaite, circa 1932. (*Courtesy of Katrina Atwood Copeland.*)

Atwood and Clarence Chamberlin studying the plans for the Airmobile. "The trend of the times is skyward," Chamberlin said in 1930. (*Courtesy of John Titus.*)

Before and after: the Greenfield, N.H., house when Atwood bought it in 1933, and today after his stone and cement work. (*Courtesy of Katrina Atwood Copeland.*)

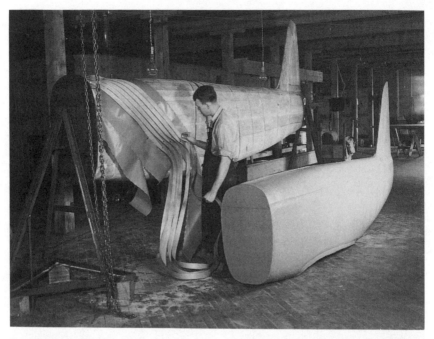

The building of the Airmobile, the Model T of the sky. Wrapping the mandrel with the thermoplastic sheet and the birch veneer strips. (*Courtesy of John Titus.*)

Some of the components of the Airmobile. (*Courtesy of John Titus.*)

A fuselage light enough for one man to hold up. (*Courtesy of John Titus.*)

The completed plane awaiting engine and test flight. (*Courtesy of John Titus.*)

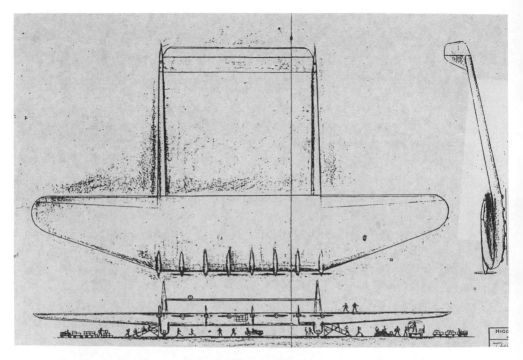

The Higgins Air Freighter, a 150-ton flying wing with 10 engines and a 300-foot wingspan, World War II. (*Courtesy of Nellie Atwood Pickens.*)

Harry Atwood at 83 in Hanging Dog, N.C., with the medal awarded to him by President Taft 56 years earlier. (*The Chattanooga Post.*)

a pool, the last indoors. "We cut our own pine logs and even Nelda, at five years old, helped peel logs. The pine poles once dried out, they look just like mahogany. I loved to lie on the floor and look at the poles in our living room. The pine in that part of the country were not like pine in any other part of the country."

Harry Atwood did not build ordinary houses. He built fortresses against tornadoes. The house was constructed with a double palisade of logs, with concrete poured down through the center of the wall and on top of the roof. "Tornadoes went over us many times and all it would do would be take out some windows. The building was actually poured into the ground."

A tornado leveled about half of Berryville the day Nellie's friends were giving her a baby shower. She was late to the party. When she arrived in that part of town, there were people and refrigerators up in the trees, and her friend's house was demolished. "It was nothing but kindling wood. And the whole group of people were just standing arms around each other in the middle—the house was taken up and landed somewhere else.

"I've been in so many of them," she said. "Those things are terrible—you don't have any idea. Just like a freight train: you could hear it coming for miles. And debris would come. There'd be metal come for ten, fifteen miles.

"He'd make us go in the house—in some of the houses we had our log beds built into the walls and he'd make us get in under the beds before it ever got there. And he'd stay out just to the very last minute. To watch it," just as he had watched lightning back in New Hampshire.

"Daddy knew what side the tornado would be on. Daddy knew the weather. People would ask him what it was going to be," said Nelda.

For Nellie and Nelda, Harry Atwood was wonderful. No doubt. Not a hiccup in their faith. "I did everything he told me," Nellie said. "His favorite saying was 'Nellie will take care of it.'"

"Daddy would call like five o'clock in the afternoon and say we're not going out tonight, there will be fifteen of us at the house for dinner tonight," said Nelda. "Mama would have a big dinner ready. She was a great cook." Nellie and she would go out and quickly pick blackberries and Nellie would bake two or three big pies.

Nellie's Harry is generous, always helping others. But "he didn't give charity. He'd find something for you to do, even though he didn't need it," chores like chopping wood.

On Sundays, they'd go walk in the mountains, or go help a neighbor, such as a widow they knew with three small children. "Daddy said it was a waste of time to go to church and sit in the pews," said Nelda. "At least two

Sundays a month we would go check on her and we would cut wood. The whole family . . . do whatever had to be done. And there were old people we would go by and see. That was Daddy's way of worshipping on Sunday. Was doing for people. Daddy helped people seven days a week if they needed help. He would give the shirt off his back."

He's a good family man, always thinking of his wife and daughter, a good neighbor. Their portrait of him is all sunlight. Nellie glides past stories of hardship, only letting a few details slip out about, for example, a dispute with neighbors who jumped Harry, knocked him out, and were looking for his gun to shoot him with, when Nellie came upon them. She had made him leave his gun at home that day. She dismisses the story with a few incomplete sentences, and is on to the next good time.

In his Piney Creek Laboratory, Atwood was still chasing the plastic future. As he had always done, he slept four hours a night, smoked twenty cigars a day, and worked without ceasing. Tomorrow—that's what engaged him, said Nellie. "What are we going to do tomorrow?"

"Plastics are going to be the answer for high-altitude flying," he wrote in 1943, answering a letter from the War Manpower Commission. "The chemical and physical formations must be of unusual make-up. Commercialized plastics of today do not meet the specifications." He was running a farm in "conjunction with a plastic laboratory." This "may be an original institution of value in this specific work. Science is not confined within commercialized laboratories. Washington should pay strict attention, confidential attention, to private researchers, right now."

He was growing weeds, or, as he grandly phrased it, "a species of weed-vegetation that matures in approximately sixty days with little attention," which, when combined with "certain plasticizers can be formed into a cellular, non-porous, structural material of great strength and tenacity." It was lightweight and withstood "temperatures of less than −60 deg. Fahrenheit without a material changing of strength properties."

This was "valuable right now to a war effort," he said. The war was heating up, there was a huge demand for new airplanes, as well as talk that there wasn't enough aluminum and other metals to build them all. He decided to show his plastic-plywood to a large company, either to Howard Hughes out in California, or to a shipbuilder down in New Orleans.

He flipped a coin and went down to New Orleans to call on Mr. Andrew Jackson Higgins, a local legend who was becoming nationally celebrated as the "Shipyard Bunyan" for his feats of production. "Many folks in New

Orleans are serenely confident that Andrew Jackson Higgins is going to win the war," said *American* magazine.

Higgins had a "regal disdain" for "business routine and squeamish ears," said *Fortune* magazine. "He radiates belligerent authority. When President Roosevelt told Higgins he wanted to talk to him, Higgins is said to have rapped back, 'That won't do at all, Mr. President. I want to talk to *you*.' He has a stocky build, a pleasantly malicious expression, and ruddy visage; and he always wears dark, tailored gabardine shirts. He drinks bourbon almost exclusively, and swears beautifully and easily. People he dislikes or considers obstructionists—among them some of the most important men in New Orleans and Washington—he simply addresses as s.o.b.'s." He had punched a few people in anger.

Higgins's twelve thousand employees called him "The Boss." He addressed them over loudspeakers, said *Fortune*. "Whenever there is a victory . . . or whenever he cannot contain himself, his rich bass reverberates through the clerestories of the factories." "Don't relax," was his watchword. His workers appreciated his frankness and his union shop. He was a cross between Huey Long, the Depression-era Louisiana demagogue, and Henry Ford, thought *Fortune*. New Orleans aristocracy thought him a crass opportunist. He had made many enemies in high places. "Higgins has been gratuitously insulting and gratuitously truthful, which often amounts to the same thing," said *Fortune*.

But he had designed such good ships that the navy had to use them, even though "many persons both in and out of the Navy used to regard Andrew Jackson Higgins as an uninhibited madman with a special gift for introducing into official correspondence the earthiest items of stokehold and mule-skinner idiom," said the *Saturday Evening Post*. When dictating one letter, he had rattled off twenty goddamns, said biographer Jerry Strahan.

Working in the lumber business for years, Higgins had developed shallow-draft boats that could jump a log and crawl up on beaches and back down. One design could move through only nine inches of water. These were the predecessors of the landing boats that made possible the invasions of North Africa, Italy, and, on D-Day, France. General Eisenhower praised Higgins, calling him "the man who won the war for us."

He had badgered the navy with his designs, writing on the blueprints of the navy's own design for a landing craft to carry tanks, "This is lousy." The navy consented to visit his factory and see his designs. He asked them to come in three days. They arrived to see not drawings, but to watch a running "tank lighter" jump over a mud bank and climb up a sloping cement sea wall to deliver a heavy tractor. Higgins and his crew had worked two days and two nights straight, cutting up an existing boat and designing it as they went along.

The navy ordered fifty boats, and asked if they could have nine in two weeks. "Why not," said Higgins, even though his plant was full and he had no steel and no engineering drawings. To the neighborhood's horror, he seized a city street and set up an assembly line to work around the clock, talked his way into some steel, and, to move it, persuaded a railroad president to hitch flat cars to his passenger trains. He moved and rebuilt seven railroad bridges to deliver the boats. The last of the boats were painted en route.

The Higgins boats outperformed the navy's own design, but the navy chose its own boat. Higgins raised hell, forced a competition, and his design became the standard for landing craft. Harry Truman's committee on wartime procurement chastised the navy for "negligence or willful misconduct."

Higgins became one of the world's largest shipbuilders, at peak turning out more than seven hundred small boats a month. By the war's end, Higgins had designed 92 percent of the navy's ships. He was "one of the great production geniuses of modern times," said a wartime commissioner. "Higgins is an authentic master builder, with the kind of will power, brains, drive and daring that characterized the American empire builders of earlier generations," said *Newsweek*.

He loved to develop new products. He possessed "an almost frantic hospitality to ideas," said *Fortune*, spending nearly one million dollars a year on a large staff of almost one hundred men.

Higgins "will take a chance on practically anybody with a plausible idea," reported *Life* magazine. A gas station attendant he hired later invented a semiautomatic clutch, which vastly improved the maneuverability of the landing craft, and brought the inventor royalties greater than the boss's own salary. His staff was credited with many successful products. "I'd hire a gorilla if I could squeeze an idea out of him," Higgins said.

He had big plans for after the war: a Higgins helicopter for everyone, a Higgins prefabricated house for the Negroes of the South, Higgins boats for the world. "I'm in the market for ideas," he said.

Harry Atwood had knocked on the right door.

"He didn't have money enough to rent a hotel room," said Nellie. "He came home with two thousand dollars at the end of the week."

Atwood was back in the news. He was pictured with Higgins on the deck of a torpedo boat. Higgins looked like an extra from *Guys and Dolls* in his double-breasted dark pin-striped suit, black shirt, light tie, and white, wide-brimmed hat with a black band. Atwood stood next to him, a thin reed, with a new Higgins-style suit flagging off his frame. The suits were cut large in that style, and here, with a black shirt and light tie, he looked as if he were a poorly cast understudy.

I was his "personal protege," Atwood said, "his number one favorite," a company vice-president with a twenty-thousand-dollar-a-year salary. "He is very much like me, at least in disposition and eccentricities. He is wealthy occasionally, poor frequently, bankrupt once, and always overspends."

Higgins was fifty-six years old. His newly assembled aviation staff were men of his generation—ancient by the standards of an industry younger than they. They were already teenagers when the Wright brothers flew at Kitty Hawk. Among them was the history of aviation: early aerodynamic theories, form-giving designs, brave record flights. Higgins had bought a fine historical collection, a real G.A.R. of aviation, as Atwood had said of himself years earlier. Along with Atwood, he had hired Giuseppe Bellanca, Alfred Victor Verville, and Dr. Max Munk. All the younger talent was under contract elsewhere. *Time* magazine called this living museum, a "spotty-looking aviation staff," but Higgins saw it differently. "They're nuts, they're geniuses," he said proudly.

Giuseppe Bellanca, age fifty-six, had achieved national fame in 1927 for his airplane designs when his friend Clarence Chamberlin flew a Bellanca across the Atlantic just weeks after Lindbergh. Bellanca grew up in on the coast of Sicily where he spent hours watching seabirds. "I can see air," he said. He built his first (unsuccessful) airplane in 1909. He emigrated to the United States in 1912. Bellanca spoke of attaining "pure streamline" in his designs. By 1922, he had designed the most efficient airplane of its day, an enclosed-cabin, high-wing monoplane. That plane won races and awards, and was the basis of the transatlantic airplane. His friends called him "the professor" for his shy, distracted manner, his genius, and his lack of business sense. Bellanca was left behind in the 1930s as all-metal airplanes and other design innovations were adopted. During the boom times of the war, he could get no work.

Fred Verville, age fifty-two, had started out working for Glenn Curtiss, preparing the seaplane *America* to attempt the first transatlantic flight (which was thwarted by World War I). Verville designed his first airplane in 1915. His 1922 Verville-Sperry Pulitzer Racer was a breakthrough low-wing monoplane with retractable landing gear. It was hailed as an engineering achievement, a design that showed the way to World War II fighter planes. In 1960, it was honored by a distinguished panel as one of the twelve most significant airplanes of all time.

The soft-spoken, polite Verville had also known frustration. In 1929, just as he had won a large army order for training planes, his company folded. He drifted through small jobs in the 1930s, and worked for the Curtiss-Wright Company before coming to Higgins.

Dr. Max Munk, also age fifty-two, had written some of the aerodynamic formulas that had become common currency, particularly for wing-tip-induced drag in biplanes. He also developed a linear theory that simplified airfoil calculations. Munk emigrated from Germany in 1921. Working for the government, he invented the variable density wind tunnel, which allowed for more realistic tests. Like Bellanca and Verville, Munk had done his most important work twenty years before Higgins hired him.

Higgins had other nuts and geniuses on his staff, like Preston Tucker, the maverick automobile designer, and Higgins's assistant, George Rappelyea, who had engineered the Scopes monkey trial, by talking a young high school teacher, John Scopes, into challenging the Tennessee law on teaching evolution. (Rappelyea signed the complaint that led to Scopes's arrest.) "He was a master propagandist. He fabricated, and Higgins knew he fabricated, but he let him," said Strahan. He got Higgins great press. ("Hold your breath for the stupendous wartime deeds of this Paul Bunyan strongman of the South," said one magazine.)

Atwood brought Higgins the latest generation of his woven plastic-plywood. Higgins was impressed. The entire log could be used, and they could use locally grown Southern wood, bypassing wartime shortages. Atwood had also brought Higgins his plans for a 150-ton, ten-engine flying wing with a three-hundred-foot wingspan. (One-third larger than a 747's wingspan.) Atwood had revived his flying wing dreams from his Monson days, and presented it as the solution for flying cargo. A flying wing just looks good, a "pure" airplane; the stretch of wing is what we respond to when we see a soaring hawk or a seabird. Higgins took up the cause: "I shall build planes without outside privies on them," he said.

Airplanes are the future of cargo, said the shipbuilder. "I much prefer being in the air cargo carrier business to building surface carriers, because the airships are so much less vulnerable."

He set up Atwood and Bellanca and a staff of engineers in a mansion on a lake, a fine place with nice old trees on the grounds and grand rooms (with golden doorknobs, which Nellie never forgot). There was a cook on the premises. Higgins had housed his other research geniuses in mansions around New Orleans, all reportedly under guard.

The Atwood-Bellanca project was separate from Higgins's other aviation business, a "super secret off-shoot devoted exclusively to research and experimenting. Atwood has developed a sensational kind of woven plywood and an even more sensational cargo plane design. Both are cloaked in secrecy," wrote one aviation magazine. "Remember this," said a company vice-president, "Mr. Higgins is in aviation for keeps."

They were at work on the Higgins Air Freighter. The cargo would be carried inside the wing. As the design evolved, it was no longer a pure flying wing. One slightly smaller version had eight engines on the leading edge of a 240-foot wingspan, with a twin, 80-foot long tailboom supporting a horizontal stabilizer. For its day, it was a Paul Bunyan–sized airplane, about double the size of the B-29, then the largest plane flying.

Two wartime shortages and the politics of a cancelled contract had made this outsized dream seem attainable. There was an urgent need for air transport planes. "Not a single plane originally conceived for cargo is in service in the Western Hemisphere," reported the Office of War Information in June 1943. German submarines were sinking supply ships. Some planes were grounded for lack of spare parts. Bombers were diverted to ferry troops and supplies. Other planes converted to cargo, such as the DC-3, could carry at best two and a half tons. "At present American air transport needs are being filled by operations that show considerable ingenuity but which cannot be called efficient," said the Office of War Information.

The War Production Board called on the army to double cargo plane production. The head of the army's air forces, Lt. General "Hap" Arnold, said the cargo planes should be built of "noncritical materials." Steel, aluminum, and other metals were in short supply. Wood was in fashion again for airplanes.

On the West Coast, Higgins's arch rival, the shipbuilder Henry J. Kaiser, was granted a contract to develop a 70-ton cargo plane. Kaiser also formed a partnership with Howard Hughes to build a 140-ton, eight-engine cargo plane. Built of plywood, it would come to be known as the Spruce Goose.

Higgins was trailing Kaiser, but he was about to turn a big setback into a political advantage. In 1942 Higgins gained and lost the largest ship contract in American history. One hour after receiving the $385 million order for two hundred Liberty ships, he dispatched a bulldozer to start to clearing the site for the factory. He was building a two-mile-long floating assembly line for ships, the world's first. A ship would be built in 5 days, instead of the usual 150 days. One ship a day would come off the line, a rate that would match the country's *entire* ship production. "It can't be done," said other shipbuilders. "The hell it can't," said Higgins.

Four months later, the contract was abruptly cancelled. Higgins had spent ten million dollars blasting and dredging twelve hundred acres of swamp for the factory where upwards of sixty thousand workers would build the ships. The steel shortage had worsened; there was not enough steel to build the factory, let alone the ships. Other shipyards had cut back, some Detroit assembly lines had shut down, and armament production was threatened.

Higgins roared. With "fortissimo publicity," said *Time* magazine, "he raised enough rumpus to start several Congressional investigations, to snag thousands of headlines, and convince many people that he was a victim" of, as Higgins phrased it, "those smart bastards in the East." He made so much noise that President Roosevelt came to visit, the only Louisiana stop on his cross-country tour. Roosevelt had been secretary of the navy and knew Higgins, and recently Higgins had stood up at one of Eleanor Roosevelt's rallies and pledged to hire Negroes at equal pay (for which he was criticized). Roosevelt toured the plant for an hour, and invited Higgins to Washington. The uncompleted shipyard would be put to use.

For five weeks, Higgins and Atwood met with the president, the War Production Board, and army officials, including Atwood's old friend Hap Arnold. They displayed a three-foot model of the Higgins Air Freighter, and outlined their plan to build it with Atwood's woven plywood, which contained metal. "I call it a wood alloy," said Higgins, adding apologetically, "I had to coin a name for it which is not very good, but the best I could do." It was twice as strong as duraluminum of the same thickness, he said, but it was made primarily from noncritical materials. The Air Freighter's construction would make it virtually unsinkable, should it be forced down in the ocean, he said.

He wanted to build an untested type of airplane at a colossal scale with a new, untested material. The army was wary. "Mr. Higgins' proposal to build his planes of plywood—an unprecedented use of such material in planes of the contemplated size—aroused a storm of controversy," said the *New York Times*. "It was pointed out, however, that the Russians had built their best fighters, the MIG-3, out of plywood. The British have also used plywood in a combat plane known as the Mosquito."

Kaiser was already building a huge cargo plane, and there were many critics who said the plane would not be ready in time. The army needed production.

Higgins left Washington with a contract for twelve-hundred cargo planes of a conventional design, to be built with Atwood's "wood alloy." The two-hundred-million-dollar contract was larger than all the rest of his business, and one of the largest airplane contracts in American history. He would have to hire fifty to sixty thousand workers—80 percent women and 50 percent Negro, he said—and build a factory large enough to house a dozen football fields and a half dozen baseball fields.

He had not given up on the Air Freighter. He would build a demonstration plane with his own money. He had done that with the landing boats, and now they were in use all over the world. He would do it again with the great flying wing. Mr. Higgins was in aviation for keeps.

For Harry Atwood it was a glorious moment. He had come out of the backwoods of the Ozarks with only his ideas and had won over Andrew Jackson Higgins. He still had the touch, he was still a master blue sky salesman. With over one thousand cargo planes flying out around the world sheathed in a wonder material, and a flying wing coming along that would revolutionize aviation, Atwood would be vindicated. There would be stories in the national magazines about the inventor who never quit, who had kept at it since his first plywood airplane, the World War I navy seaplane, and since the Airmobile flew for only twelve minutes in New Hampshire. It would be just the kind of pluck-and-luck, Horatio Alger story that Higgins's propaganda wizard could peddle: the inventor who was trained by the Wright brothers, leading us to victory.

There was a big party at the Willard Hotel in Washington in a ballroom hung with model airplanes. Army brass and various wartime commissioners and congressmen toasted the success of Higgins. He'd show them how to build cargo planes in a hurry.

But he never got the chance. Higgins built his large assembly factory, set up Preston Tucker in a factory to build engines, and built a plywood sawmill, veneer mill, veneer plywood and molding plant, and a "wood alloy structures plant."

A month before the airplane factory was completed, the contract for the Curtiss C-76 was cancelled. There were problems up the line. Higgins was a subcontractor, and, unfortunately, he had been yoked to a disaster.

The Curtiss C-76 Caravan deserved the title of "Worst Aircraft of World War II" in the estimation of aviation historian Walter J. Boyne, who called the plane "the basketcase bummer." The Caravan had a few problems in "weight and balance, structural strength, stability and control."

"In simplest terms, the C-76 could not be flown empty," Boyne said. "To get the center of gravity in reasonable range, the plane had to be ballasted beyond its maximum permissible gross takeoff weight . . . At any speed, in any gusts at all, the elevators would flap back and forth violently." In static tests, "the wing structure had failed eight times, sometimes at as low as 40 percent of the design load factor." The fuselage and the vertical tail had also failed tests.

Curtiss scrambled to fix the plane. No two planes that came out of the plant were alike. "As in a seven-door French farce, the Curtiss engineers met themselves coming and going," said Boyne. "On the one hand, they were frantically trying to reduce weight by reducing the size of structures," and on the other hand, they were trying to strengthen the plane "with numberless stiffeners, reinforcing straps, fillets, spoilers."

When the tail sheared off a test plane and it crashed, killing the crew, production of the plane was cancelled. Curtiss had built only twenty-five planes. Higgins was sitting with an empty factory. The army directed him to build metal planes.

He retooled. By war's end, in a factory big enough to cover a dozen football fields, he produced only two metal cargo airplanes. Cost: twenty-three million dollars. "One of the Army Air Force's more expensive failures," said an official air force history.

The Curtiss Caravan was another black mark against a plywood or wooden airplane. The basic cause of the Caravan's failure "was in the woodworking. The meticulous skills which had once produced a generation of aircraft jewels . . . had simply vanished," said Boyne. "American industry could not meet a rather basic technological challenge. Galling all concerned was the phenomenal success of the wooden DeHavilland Mosquito, admittedly a small aircraft, but subject to much higher load factors."

The Caravan, said Boyne, "confirmed for all time that wooden aircraft were more difficult to manufacture, maintain, and overhaul, and that it was impossible to achieve the load-lifting capacity available in a metal airplane."

Harry Atwood had for years been on the losing side of a technological struggle. Duply, and his subsequent "wood alloy," were materials that were both too early and too late. Duply was a composite in an era when that was new and little understood. It was an early plastic, but it was also wood at a time when wood was rapidly losing favor. The future belonged to aluminum and other metals.

The crash of a Fokker Trimotor in March 1931 signaled the end of the wooden airplane. The Fokker F-10 was a difficult plane to fly; pilots noted its disconcerting wing flutter. Caught in a prairie storm over Kansas, the wing iced up and snapped off the plane. Later investigation showed that moisture inside the wooden wing had weakened some of the glue joints. (Several years before the crash, a textbook, *Modern Aircraft*, had praised the "thoroughly proven" wing design for its "flexibility, which permits deflection . . . no rivets or connections can be strained." Through ten years of service, "the cost and time expended on repairs and maintenance work on wings of this type have been conclusively proven to be lower than any other type of construction known at the present time . . . and normal maintenance year after year is practically reduced to occasional varnishing.")

Eight men were killed, including Knute Rockne, Notre Dame's legendary football coach. The "Rockne crash" was front-page news—the *New York Times* called it the year's big story—and the public never again trusted wooden airplanes. The Fokker F-10s were grounded, then pulled from service, and Fokker Aircraft was soon out of business. The first of the all-metal airliners, the DC-2 and the Boeing 247, debuted two years later.

The aluminum shortage had given Atwood a second season, but the moment that shortage passed, metal design ruled. Giuseppe Bellanca's career also sank with his allegiance to wood.

Even during the metals shortage, wooden planes were suspect. Inventor William B. Stout had served on the committee that drew up the design specifications for the Curtiss Caravan. He was opposed to building it out of wood. Stout was a pioneer of the all-metal plane. In his autobiography, Stout gets in a shot at Anthony Fokker, designer of the Fokker Trimotor. Fokker, he said, refused to fly in one of his own planes because it had been crated in storage for three months. Why? Stout remembers Fokker's answer: "'While the plywood airplane may be just as strong, and just as fast, and just as light, and cheaper than the all-metal airplane, and while the veneer may be just as beautiful in appearance, it has one basic difference which none of you can overcome no matter how you build it. Any plane of that structure after six months' time will start developing a 'veneer-eal disease.'

"This statement was so unexpected and the laughs so spontaneous that, in effect, the plywood airplane died right there." Rockne crashed several months later, added Stout.

Not all historians agree with Stout and Boyne. World War II aircraft built from a process similar to Duply (Duramold) are still flying fifty years later. And with the Stealth Bomber, composite materials are said to be coming of age. Still, the last wooden plane built for World War II became a fossilized monument. Howard Hughes's Spruce Goose was about the same size as the planned Higgins Air Freighter. Built to evade German U-boats, it was not finished until two years after the war, costing the government eighteen million dollars and Hughes seventeen million dollars of his own. The Spruce Goose flew just once, for one mile at an altitude of seventy feet. Wooden airplanes were antiquity.

Another aviation dream had failed. "We both exploded and didn't even say goodbye," said Atwood. "He still maintains that I was the greatest genius that he ever knew, but that I was an uncontrollable son of a ———. I do not deny the allegation," Atwood wrote later.

He went back to his Piney Creek Laboratory in the Ozarks. "I shall never abandon my explorations into things that can't be done," he wrote in 1944 to T. E. Andrew, the investor who had backed him in Monson, and had supported him when he was bankrupt. After the big defeat, Atwood was looking back. "What an opportunity the French & Heald company really had, years ago, when I wanted them to make plastic aircraft. My patents would now be letting them sit upon the 'top of the world.'

"Have you forgotten about the 'flying weazel?'" he asked Andrew, referring to the robot-guided missile he had brought to the army.

"Everyday the radio tells about the German developments of self-propelled aircraft, tanks and undersea craft. Where are ours? I wonder if Senator H. Styles Bridges, 'Hap' Arnold, or any others, remember my developments, writings and predictions about the 'coming war.' Well, I will make one more scientific prediction—and it is as sure to come to pass, as science is accurate. The next war, perhaps with Russia, perhaps with who knows, will be a war of little brainless demons, clashing with each other, in the air, on the land, and under sea, and they will devastate everything, until civilization is a quagmire of human debris . . . I always aimed to defend, but never to aggress. So what? The world fights on. I cannot stop the fight . . . This time the world is crazy—not me."

"I love retirement in my jungle retreat, where I can practice humanity, and live in peace." His remote, wild valley was a good place for old age, and death. He might even have enough money to see him through. A new industrialist wanted to buy his patents, and he was ready to sell. My patents "have 12 years to run, (I have not)."

"It may be my destiny to terminate life's journey in the isolation of a strange land," he wrote to the one group to whom he was loyal, his fraternity brothers. He had sent a message to be read at the 1949 reunion. He was at work on new type of coffin, he said, made from plastics he had hoped to use on spacecraft. "I wish that I could be with you today. I cannot . . .

Good night,
Harry Atwood."

⤳ Jailbird

Lester Boss was eighty-five years old, able to laugh at the young man he was when Harry Atwood talked him into driving him across the country and then stole his car. "He could just get to you is all I know," said Boss. "He a pretty sharp old rascal."

Atwood "happened to come in one day in the filling station," the Phillips 66 that Boss owned, "and wanted a little work done or something. Found out I could fix most anything on an old automobile." And he could weld, build tools and machinery. They got to talking and soon Boss, who was so busy at his own garage that he worked nights too, would "just drive over there and fix this stuff, fix something else, and take him some gas, well, just first one thing and another. And do work on his car. One thing and another." Atwood lived twenty miles away, over hard-traveling dirt roads, a place that seemed remote even to an Arkansas native like Boss.

Boss was good-natured, trusting, used to dealing with folks on a small-town scheme: you judged someone by their family, by what kind of people they came from, and by how long you had known them. You had points of reference. Atwood was a planet, a wandering star in his own orbit against that firmament. Boss had a disposition that left him open and a curiosity that drew him in. ("I think he flew one of the first airplanes up there that they made," said Boss.)

Atwood was working on his inventions and Boss "got to helping with some of them, building them. First one thing, then another." He built him a press for veneer and plastic—"put an air outfit in there so you could put the air to them or steam to them, blow them up, tighten up the press . . . His wife could weave that stuff about as pretty as you ever seen.

"Anyway he got to owing me quite a little."

And that may be the best explanation of how Lester Boss found himself one day in August 1953 driving Harry, Nellie, and Nelda from Arkansas to New Hampshire. First one thing, then another. The Atwoods had lived in Berryville, Arkansas, for twelve years, all of Nelda's life. Harry was looking to start over again in New England. It would be a homecoming and a reunion with a part of the country he loved.

He wasn't planning on returning to Arkansas. Not that they had packed much. They left behind clothes, papers, furniture, his grand piano, and the house they had built. "He just walked off and left it," as he often did, Nellie said with disbelief. "In New Orleans we had baby cribs, strollers . . . He didn't want to move it. 'We'll get new ones. Leave it.' It seemed crazy to me."

"That was their biggest argument, was when they moved," said Nelda. "The least he could take. And she had boxes of stuff, clippings and papers she wanted to keep. He would make her leave a lot of stuff behind."

It was a long trip in those days on the numbered routes that ran through cities. Atwood did some of the driving and he was a good driver, said Boss. They drove by the Grand Ole Opry in Nashville—that's what Atwood said it was, a "great big outfit"—and in Washington, D.C., Boss got to see the White House for the first time. They went around by the South Lawn, tourists at the fence, and Harry Atwood pointed out where he had landed in a Wright brothers biplane forty-two years earlier, before two world wars and a depression.

After seven days, they arrived in Peterborough, New Hampshire. The Atwoods were visiting one of Nellie's brothers, and Harry was trying to get investors for a new invention. Boss let Atwood use his car, a 1953 Ford, as long as he stayed in the Peterborough area. One day Atwood didn't return the car.

This was pushing Boss too far. He would give Atwood free gas and repairs, head way over to his house to build him things, and drive him across the country and pay for the trip. But this was one thing too much. "I don't know what you'd call it, stealing or not. Anyway he just borrowed it and didn't bring it back. I guess you call that stealing, don't you?" said Boss.

He went to the law for help. He reported the theft to the Peterborough police. They arrested Atwood and held him in the local jail on "probable

cause." Harry Atwood's homecoming had put him back in the news. The
car was found in another state. Atwood, for his part, told the newspaper
he didn't steal the car. He had given Boss a $610 down payment. That
number—$610—was so definite that it had authority when seen in print.
If Atwood had said he put down "a couple of hundred dollars," his story
would sound dubious. But $610, who would make up a number like that?

For more than two hours the court tried to sort out what, if any, deal or
promise had been made. He had talked his way out of tighter spots than
this.

Atwood's attorney said that Boss and Atwood had a deal. Boss had offered to sell the car, and Atwood had given him $610 as the down pay-
ment. Atwood said he had parked the car forty-five miles from Peterborough, in a different state, on a lawyer's advice. He was driving without
registration, which wouldn't do if he were stopped by a cop.

"No, no, no, he didn't try to buy the car, he just did it. He didn't give me
any money. Fact of it is, he owes me several thousand dollars," Boss said
years later. "Even that trip, why, I paid for that trip. Got up there and run
out of money. Went to the bank there and they wouldn't" cash a check.
"Went to the federal bank and told them where I was from and everything
and they cashed a plenty big enough check for me to get home."

Boss's story was simple: "He just borrowed the car from me and didn't
come back."

Atwood's story, which had kept the court busy, did sway some. "I don't
think Atwood was trying to steal the car but he appeared to be trying to
buy the car on his terms," said state police sergeant John Conti.

The judge didn't see it that way, and charged Atwood with "larceny of
automobile," a felony. He was committed to the Hillsborough County jail
in Manchester when he could not raise the eighteen-hundred-dollar bail.
Harry Atwood had talked his way out of Arkansas and into jail in New
Hampshire.

"He was falsely arrested," said Nellie. "He should have sued them. But
he wouldn't do it. He didn't have to go to jail. He just went there for the
fun of it. He should have sued them for false arrest, but he was never that
kind of person." Boss "just got mad . . . and he apologized afterwards. And
he tried to get Harry not to go to jail, and Harry said no, I'm arrested, I'm
going to jail.

"It was all wrong. It was false. The whole thing was false."

"He was one that went by the law," said his daughter, Nelda. "He knew
law better than lawyers did then. He never did anything that he wasn't
supposed to, nothing illegal. He said he stretched the law . . . He would go

from border to border if you want to say that . . . Anything he did he knew it was legal but he was right there on the border I guess."

For the first time in his life, two months shy of his seventieth birthday, Harry Atwood was in jail.

Atwood's old friend, the journalist Bernie McQuaid, whose stories had helped create the Atwood legend, soon had the situation in hand. McQuaid, now editor of the *New Hampshire Sunday News*, assigned a reporter to cover this outrage. Readers picked up their paper one September morning and found a page-one, lead story with a photo of Harry Atwood standing triumphantly in front of the jail as if he were the warden and landlord and mayor of the county lock-up. Inside the paper was a photo of Atwood delivering a carton of Lucky Strikes as a gift to the inmates. The jailer, who met him at the door, looked puzzled. (The sheriff wouldn't allow them in the jail to take pictures and "ordered this newspaper not to print this picture.")

"The 10 days that Atwood languished in Hillsborough County jail had failed to dampen the old man's youthful enthusiasm for the scientific. He walked to freedom nattily dressed, his blue eyes sparkling, and as a remembrance of his stay in jail, sporting a prisoner's haircut," said the *News*.

The *News* was indignant. "The famed inventor-scientist" had returned to New Hampshire to retire, and even though Atwood's lawyer had "protested innocence," the judge "chose" to send him to jail. It was a disgrace to put such a man in jail—with his four hundred patents, "invention could be his middle name."

They spun the Atwood myth, the layered composition of truth and lie, and added new layers: landing on the White House lawn, setting early altitude records, building the Airmobile, working for Higgins. They discussed his theories of space flight, and introduced his ideas about atomic energy. As a student at M.I.T., they reported, he had irritated his professors when he had insisted that the atom would be split one day. And then there was "his 'flying saucer' scare" which "broke headlines all over the country. There were suspicions in Washington that Atwood was behind the strange aircraft. Government intelligence men came to New Hampshire and tried to track him down."

The famed inventor-scientist in jail. This was a story that could brighten the dullest cold-war Sunday.

"The irony of the police and sheriff causing Atwood to lose his freedom for ten days comes as he is on the verge of developing an invention which may, in future years, save the lives of countless of soldiers fighting in faraway jungles to preserve American freedom," said the *News*. "This is a bacteria-killing electronic device which sterilizes water whether it is taken from a brackish jungle bog or any roadside stream or rural well."

The blender used "a simple process of 'ionizing' germs electronically in such a way that they die immediately." This was as far as the *News* went in explaining the invention. A photo showed Harry and Nellie working the device, which looked like a science fair project: a box with dials, a light bulb, and a cup with an immersion coil.

Atwood claimed wide application for the blender. It stopped milk from souring and it could be used to purify a city water supply. "People can drink pure water instead of water diluted with an antiseptic," like chlorine, he said.

"He showed newspapermen this week a contract with a large and reputable Southern plastic manufacturer which promises $160,000 in royalties on his new bacteria-killing liquid purifier." He also claimed to have patent rights. "While Mr. Atwood believes the latest invention of his promises to give him the most success, both financially and as a contribution to science, it had already led him into the most disturbing episode of his career."

To finance the germ-killing blender, he had formed a partnership with some Berryville businessmen, he said. "The invention was nearing perfection when one of his partners . . . withdrew his support," without telling him. Some of the partnership's checks bounced. He made the "checks good from his own funds," Atwood said, "but by that time some of the hard-working Arkansas folks distrusted the Yankee scientist.

"There came a day when Arkansas men, riding horses and carrying guns, appeared at his tornado-proof mountain retreat and laboratory . . . they laid their guns under a tree, came into the house and warned, 'If you know what's good for you, get out of town in 24 hours.'

"Convinced that his life was in danger, Atwood abandoned the laboratory" and fled east with his wife and daughter.

Nellie, Nelda, and Boss said they knew nothing of this.

"He said that? Did the paper say that?" Nellie said surprised, years later. "He'd've never said that. No, ah-ah. He would not do that." They had lived there twelve years, she explained, as Yankees who were welcomed. "I mean we had friends everywhere you went. I don't know why he made that remark—I don't know if he did make that remark. Somebody must have misquoted him. We didn't leave like that. Nobody drove us away."

If something that dramatic had happened, said Boss, "he'd a said something, surely." He added, "I know that they got to where they didn't like him around town here, around Green Forest. He didn't get along with the president of our bank. They soon learned not to fool with him and I should have."

The last he ever saw Harry Atwood, "they's arguing about putting him in jail. I got the keys and stuff, and I took off and left him there."

With the witness heading home to Arkansas, the case was dropped, and Atwood was let go with a warning from the police chief to "keep out of trouble if you stay around Peterborough." He had heard about the bad checks in Arkansas, he said.

Back in Green Forest a lot of people had a good laugh on Boss. "They thought I was silly," he said. "I guess I was for ever taking off on a deal like that . . . I did get to see the Grand Ole Opry. So I got quite a trip out of it," as well as Harry's piano, which he had left for him.

Harry Atwood flew free. He always did. No one would help him with his new invention. He looked up Clarence Farr, who held a high post at a big Cambridge chemical company. He had not seen Farr in fifteen years, back when the Airmobile fell from sight. Farr held him off. "Try as I would, I couldn't possibly think of any way that I could get him into the laboratories," he said sarcastically. "I had been used before, I didn't want to be used again." The company "was too nice a concern for me to connect them up with a man whose scruples weren't better than Harry Atwood's."

Years later, Nellie said the "milk purifier" was more like a "toy." She doubted it could have worked on a large scale. But he had applied for a patent, she said, and there was a company interested in it. (In the 1960s, using the same principle, NASA developed a silver ionization system to purify the astronauts' water for the Apollo moon mission.)

Harry, Nellie, and Nelda left New Hampshire and found another small town in the mountains, Berlin, New York. The town sits down firmly in a valley by the Rensselaer Plateau of the Taconic Mountains. Coming from the north, one sees the spire of the Baptist church against the steep, hummocky hills. There is a small town hall, an inn, a big central high school, and a couple of lumber yards. Berlin is a mountain town, at once reminiscent of Greenfield, New Hampshire. The places Harry Atwood chose to live are all of a piece—mountain towns, out-of-the-way places. The nearest city, Albany, was about forty-five miles away.

Then Atwood did as he always did. He found a building site on a steep hillside with a good spring, a place with "plenty of water you could get without having to pump it or anything," as Nellie said. They built a plastic house with a pool inside, built it with plastic sheeting DuPont had sent. It was a solar house, humid inside, with lots of plants, like no house anyone in town had ever seen. He made models of plastic greenhouses, experimented with the pasteurizing blender, and built a heated press to make a wood and plastic veneer. He told some curious stories to the locals. Something about flying over Manhattan in a biplane. Stories in which he dropped names—United States senators, army generals, du Ponts. A few men in town took to calling him "Horseshit Harry."

The family departed quickly. In the middle of the night, neighbors said. They left owing money, a grocery bill in the hundreds. Nellie said they left because the snow was too much to shovel and Harry had a bad heart. "We needed to get away from that northern climate." Once more they went south.

⌇ Assumed Dead

Harry Atwood died the first time in the summer of 1912. A flyer named Harrison Atwood crashed and the public assumed it was the pilot they had read about the previous summer. That at any rate was a story Atwood had been telling since the late 1920s in Monson.

He had a knack for disappearing, for making a lot of headline noise one moment and vanishing the next. M.I.T., updating the register of alumni, had taken him for dead. They marked his card: "Assumed deceased . . . May 1955."

Through the years a group of early-bird aviation historians had been looking for him, and concluded that he had died in 1961 in New Orleans. Clarence Chamberlin told the historians that he had long ago lost track of "Harry Atwater."

His first daughter, Bethany Trask, was also looking for him. Her mother and Harry had separated when she was a little girl, back around 1911 or 1912, and she had not seen her father since. She was their only child. When she was growing up she was forbidden to mention his name. She had kept track of him in the newspapers and had last read anything about him in the 1940s. Katrina, Ruth, and Gene learned about Bethany only when their father died. They read about her in the obituary.

Where is my father? she had written to an old aviator who had known Atwood. Her father had wanted his privacy in the past, she understood, but now he might want to hear from his grandchildren and great-grandchildren. "He could be dead, I realize, but it would seem that our local papers would pick that up."

After *Yankee* magazine ran a story in 1964 on Harry Atwood's Washington flight, the editors noted: "Several people have written us saying they 'knew' Harry Atwood—but no one seems to know what became of him. Even his daughter wrote us to ask if we knew! We don't. Anyone?"

When he left New Hampshire in 1939, he had disappeared on Katrina, Ruth, and Gene. "We never saw him or heard from him for years," said Gene. In nearly thirty years, she only saw him twice. Sometimes he would call them, and even drop in, with no notice. If they asked about visiting him, he'd refuse them. "He would call me, but he wouldn't let me know where he was," said Katrina. "And if I wanted to visit: Well, no, and so on. And I got of sick of it. One night he caught me when I had company. And I'd had enough to drink . . . and I just told him—I hate to think what I told him: Well just don't bother me, you don't let me know where you are or anything. You're not going to come up and sell my daughter a bill of goods. I don't want her to know you." It was the last time Katrina talked to her father. Sometime after that she tore up a family photo album.

Hanging Dog

Hanging Dog, North Carolina, is not on the way to anything. It sits in one of the poorest areas of the state, deep in the Smoky Mountains. It is two hours by twisting roads to Asheville. The folks in Hanging Dog say that they are closer to the capitals of seven other states than to their own. Those who came of age after World War II can remember houses with dirt floors, stills making white whiskey tucked away in the mountains, and oxen yoked to the wagons around the town square in the county seat of Murphy.

It was here that Harry Atwood moved in the late 1950s. Just showed up one day with quite a story to tell. Hanging Dog met his usual requirements: a small, isolated settlement in the mountains, a hillside housing site with a good spring and a veneer mill nearby.

Land—if the old timers would part with it—sold for just a couple of dollars an acre. Most folks were related to one another—Dockerys or Kepharts or a few other families. There were only five or six families living in that part of Hanging Dog. "He was a new man in the country," said one neighbor.

This new man claimed that he had learned to fly with the Wright brothers. He said that he had over 250 patents—more than anyone else alive. And that in 1935 he was writing scientific papers on how a space capsule could reenter the earth's atmosphere without a heat shield. He said he had pioneering ideas that have never been credited to him. He talked one moment like a visionary, the next like a used-car dealer of ideas, a salesman about to sell some blue sky.

Many of his neighbors did not know what to make of all he said. He had sure known a lot of famous people, such as Thomas Edison and Amelia Earhart. But then, no one had ever read about him in a history book. They were not sure where he came from, had no idea why he chose Hanging Dog, were not even clear on why he did not go to church, unusual in a place where the ten commandments are carved in marble in the courtroom of the county courthouse, and in letters ten feet tall at a large hillside shrine. Harry Atwood had been in bankruptcy court more than he had been in church.

"Some of them down in there thought he was a spy or something. Because he didn't mix around with them very much," said a local doctor. "But he was always thinking about something, doing something."

"He was one of those fellows that kept you sitting on your seat all the time, always telling you something you didn't know he did," said one. The stories usually appealed for money. He had an invention and he was looking for investors. "He was going up the line in the business world and of course he'd take all his friends with him that wanted to go," said Olin MacDonald. "Harry Atwood talks a good story *all* the time."

Some in Cherokee County hated him. "He was a damn reprobate! A reprobate! He was nothing but a damned deadbeat—if you want to know my opinion of Harry Atwood," said Bess Alverson. She had not seen Atwood in twenty-five years. She worked herself up, her short stabbing pronouncements gathering steam, a locomotive leaving the station. "He was a sneak thief." He took her husband "for a ride. He certainly did." He had him paying his grocery, electric, and phone bills for one year and leasing a building for a planned factory. There were outrageous electric bills from his experiments. "I have nothing good to say for Harry Atwood. Period. Nothing. Period." She continued for almost an hour, managing only to outline her hatred of Atwood and his family. "I wouldn't trust any of 'em as far as I could throw a bull by the tail." Another said, "I just had the feeling that if I'd had a considerable amount of money, he would have taken everything I had."

"He was a con man, but such a nice fella'. A little fella'," said Dr. Charles O. Van Gorder, and then added a doctor's appraisal: he was about 140 pounds, five feet, seven inches. "He was a lot smarter than the rest of us. He had all kinds of schemes. He could sell anything. I don't know what he was doing poor."

Dr. Van Gorder knew just about everyone in the county, and when they greeted him, they told him their pains or told again how he saved them, back when penicillin was just a new drug come along.

After World War II, Van Gorder and his partner had set up a practice in Murphy. They were the only doctors around. Van Gorder had patients down in Georgia and over in Tennessee. He and his partner had served together in World War II as doctors. They had seen the invasions of North Africa and Italy. On D-Day, they landed with the glider troops in the early morning before the invasion and set up the army's first hospital in France. They were also with the glider troops in the invasion of Holland, landing just half an hour after the first assault. In the siege of Bastogne, they were captured by the Germans and sent to a camp in Poland, where they escaped. Two months later they made their way back to Italy. They were never separated.

"I came here after the war and thought maybe there was something I could do for the people," Van Gorder said. Back when there were no doctors and no hospital, Van Gorder's mother had died from a lack of medical attention.

Atwood "just come up to my office . . . and he said, Now doctor, I haven't got anything to live on. And I got to have a hundred dollars, fifty dollars. Whatever it was. And I felt sorry for him being eighty-three, no money, no Social Security."

Quite a few people gave him money, Van Gorder said. He knew people had covered the bills when the phone and power companies had cut Atwood off. Somehow Atwood had gotten a new car out of a nearby Chrysler dealer. The doctor said he would have felt "like a heel" if he didn't help. When Atwood got sick, Van Gorder paid his hospital bills, and didn't charge him anything. "You'd wish you had more money to give him."

"Everything he had done was so impressive, you didn't know whether your mind was playing tricks on you, or he was. He inspired a lot of confidence in his knowledge. I never did see a diploma or anything, but he'd known some of the big fellows. I'm not sure, but I think he knew Thomas Edison. But he wouldn't bring it up in a bragging way. He'd bring it up: Well, incidentally, you know—like that."

Atwood's house was as unusual as his stories. "You'd hear from one patient to another, talking about it: 'You heard about that man down there living in a plastic house all winter? No smokestack or anything. So how'd they heat?'" With each telling, the story was more curious; Van Gorder heard from another patient that this man had an indoor swimming pool he had wired up with electricity.

Van Gorder soon got to see the house. Atwood and his wife and daughter had built it out of plastic sheets, pine poles, and concrete. All the rooms surrounded an indoor pool which was fed by a mountain spring. The house was heated by the sun, something nobody around Hanging Dog had heard of before. There was a gravel floor and tropical plants and bananas growing. "You'd do a double take like you want to go change your bootlegger," said Van Gorder.

The plants grew wildly. "It took me 90 percent of my time to keep my plants cut back in my house because the moisture in the pool would keep 'em growing so fast," said Nellie.

The pool had varying amounts of electric current flowing into it. There were six or seven zones, each with an increasing charge. "It purified the water," said Nellie. "The water was pure blue." Atwood had taken the first plunge, just as he had tested the air currents over Manhattan. He had insulated the wires from the water with a fiberglass panel. The controls were in a cigar box. He handed the box to Nellie and said, "When I go in, if I scream, shut it off."

Van Gorder swam in it. "There was a buzzing, tingling feeling in the water," he said. "I got right out." (Thirty years later, municipal pools would experiment with similar ionizers to reduce chlorine use.)

After the house was finished, Atwood directed his wife, daughter, and one hired hand to build a high stone wall to the roof. He told his neighbor, Lester Dockery, "Oh this is just a tent that I threw up while I'm experimenting, something to get by with." Compared with his houses in Monson and Greenfield, it was.

"I was trying to keep it quiet that I was going out there to see him because I thought maybe he was a con man and I've been caught by one of them before," said Van Gorder. "I guess everybody has in time, if you live long enough. I don't know, but boy he had an interesting life if what he told me is true."

He told Van Gorder about flying cross country, and showed him some old newspapers. "I said, 'Well, Mr. Atwood, you didn't have any instruments or anything on your plane. How'd you know where to go?'

"He said, 'I followed the railroads.' They had a passenger train that was full of reporters. I guess you got to realize that this was some news. First semi-transcontinental flight. He would land in the field close to the railroad when he was running out of gas. And you know you had to fly about thirty to forty miles an hour back then—whatever day that was. He didn't have a compass or anything. Just weird—very interesting but enticing, weird story."

Sitting on the other side of the twentieth century, this old man in a mountain hamlet was saying that he once flew halfway across the country, without instruments or radio or airports, just sitting out on the wing following the railroad tracks.

It seemed improbable, as if someone had arrived to say they were there when the wheel was invented. At first people just pushed the wheel along for the joy and curiosity of watching it roll. It was entertainment. Then people began to see how far you could roll a wheel.

As a storyteller Atwood was an overachiever. He talked a good story *all* the time. In the back hills of North Carolina it would have been impressive enough to mention you had been to the Massachusetts Institute of Technology. Atwood said he had taught there. It would have been enough to say you had learned to fly at the Wright's school. Atwood said he was at Kitty Hawk and had designed the Wrights' airplane—or that is what everyone believed.

"The first time I was around, he mentioned something about being at Kitty Hawk," said James G. Lail, a building contractor in Chattanooga, Tennessee, about eighty-five miles from Hanging Dog, and a man Atwood wanted to impress. "And I thought, well, gosh, this fellow's old, but I'd like to hear more about that; I wonder if that story really checks out. He always stood by his story that he was there."

His daughter Nelda believed that her father had designed the first airplane for the Wright brothers and "then the Wright brothers got him to fly it." "It was the first airplane that was ever successfully flown." On a high school field trip to Washington she went to the Smithsonian Institution to see what they had about her father. There was just one little mention. "He was just the one behind the scenes," said Nelda, someone who did a lot of work, but didn't get credit.

When she was in the fourth or fifth grade, Nelda had to write a report on the Wright brothers.

"Mom what do I tell them?" she asked Nellie.

"Just put down what you know. Put down the truth," Nellie said.

"And so teachers made fun of her and said it was wrong and they got her right up in front of the class, you know, and made a lot of fun of her," said Nellie. "And she said, Well my daddy ought to know, he flew with the Wright brothers. And that made it all the worse. You know, who do you think your daddy is?

"So she sure came home crying. Her daddy went down and talked to the teacher, talked to the school, made the teacher, right in front of the class, made her get up and apologize to Nelda."

By upping the ante, Atwood threw everything into doubt. You just never knew where you were with him. Even those old newspapers he had—you could have those printed up at big city hotels or night clubs, folks in Hanging Dog said.

"I never could really figure him out," said Van Gorder. "That's why my curiosity had me going back there all the time, trying to figure out what the dickens is this man like. Or what is he made of? What's he thinking? How's his thought running?"

In his eighties, Harry Atwood kept the same schedule in his private laboratory that he had kept when he was in his late twenties, working twelve- and sixteen-hour days. He had worked all his life like a young man just starting out in the world, out for his fortune and adventure.

His schemes proliferated, the last hurrah for the plastic future. He was trying to leave something for his wife and daughter. "He was going most of the time," said Ralph Kephart, his hired hand. "From the time I got there he'd already be going and he'd stop at dinner and eat a little bit, and smoke a cigar, and get right up and go again. He had the most energy of anybody I ever saw." He moved faster than people twenty years younger. "He'd be here one minute and over there the next minute. He was really, really fast. Sure was."

His new inventions were earthbound. He wanted to create inexpensive, good housing that all could afford, and do for housing what he had tried to do with the Airmobile. The suburbs were booming, and William Levitt was celebrated for building his Levittowns.

Atwood's houses would be plastic, using few materials. He told Kephart that his own house weighed only eight hundred pounds. He persuaded two investors that he could build a house for five hundred dollars. He talked a steel fabricator in Chattanooga into building him another veneer and plastic press. To impress visitors, he would throw one of his plastic constructions in the pool. "How long will that last?" they'd ask. "Indefinitely," he'd answer.

Kephart helped Atwood make the plastic panels that were the basic building unit. "But you know that stuff don't last too long out in the weather," said Kephart. It cracked after three or four years.

With Nellie, he received his last patent (his forty-sixth) in 1960, for a housing construction system using square tubes joined in "multiples for the construction of the floors, walls, ceilings, roof, columns, joists, for framing the openings, making the doors and windows, skylights." The tubes could serve as conduits for wires, water, and heating and cooling. They could also house lights so the wall could glow. They were light-weight and strong, could be erected with a minimum of skilled labor, and required no painting and little maintenance, Atwood said.

He built a small, inexpensive greenhouse, but no manufacturers were interested. He had ideas to "revolutionize" home heating, ideas for solar buildings, doghouses, and chicken brooder houses used to raise thousands of chickens.

When James Lail, the Chattanooga contractor, visited, his host would "make sketches, talk about the things he thought he ought to be doing, and all he needed was the financing," said Lail. "He was always looking for money. That doesn't make him strange because 99 percent of the people are always looking for money."

He tried to interest Lail in his design for low-voltage, radiant heating with prefabricated flooring or wainscoting. Using a heating coil in a plywood laminate, Atwood said, he could heat a house for just pennies a day. "He felt that if he could get somebody to manufacture that thing for him, like a Georgia-Pacific or U.S. Plywood, or somebody like that, that it would revolutionize the residential heating systems."

Lail asked him if this setup would be firesafe. "And he said the National Building Science Institute has already given their stamp of approval. I never saw any documents." (They never tested the product; Atwood never contacted them.)

Still, Lail was curious. He brought Atwood a roll of Teflon to use in the heating panels, which cost him about $280, and Lail had become, in Atwood's eyes, a partner. "He used to say I was obligated to continue to bring him materials that he needed."

"One time when he came over to Chattanooga, I was involved in labor negotiations with six different unions. And I had more than I could possibly do or think about . . . and he came to my office and told the receptionist that it was a matter of life and death. He had to get in touch with me." His secretary pulled him out of the meeting. He had her send Atwood away.

"He left me a note saying that he was going back to North Carolina very disappointed. He was an eloquent writer; he could really spread it on."

Harry Atwood was always racing against a deadline to get an invention off the ground.

Atwood was seriously ill for the first time in his life. "He got to where he couldn't move his body, he couldn't turn," said Nellie. "I didn't drive, but

I rode with him, and he couldn't turn his body." She was his eyes. "For the last year, he was more comfortable sitting in the car behind a wheel than any other place. He was not comfortable laying down. But he still carried on all his meetings and discussions. And nobody knew it, like I say, except me."

He had tremendous willpower. In Arkansas, he had three heart attacks or seizures by Nellie's count. "I saw him a couple of times just refusing to die. Absolutely refusing to die. He'd lay there and he'd say I can't die now."

Swimming in the pool made him feel better, as if he had eight hours of sleep, said Nellie. "He was all rested up again, ready to go."

He was talking more about his past. In the 1920s and 1930s, when he was in his forties and fifties, his daughters never heard talk of flying that glorious summer in 1911.

Two businessmen flew in a reporter from Chattanooga. "We've never seen such a guy," said his visitors. Atwood told them about his hundreds of patents, his inventions and theories, from space travel to milk purifying. He had demonstrated the milk purifier before fifteen representatives from agricultural companies, he said. He took milk from a cow that had grazed in field of wild onions, and after a ten-second ride in his invention, the milk tasted perfect.

He showed the reporter the gold medal the president had given him on the White House lawn. Somehow, through all his travels and sudden departures, he still had that medal. He held it up to the camera and smiled. This was a different smile, not the sly smile of the twenty-seven-year-old aviator at his controls. There was something gentler in his eyes.

He said he had taught Hap Arnold to fly and had advised Amelia Earhart not to make her last flight. And he told them how he set his first record: "Orville had gone to town one day," Harry said, "and I decided I'd fly the machine. I had never been up but one time and then it was only for a few feet. But this time I got the thing off the ground and into the air."

It was 1967; in two years men would walk on the moon. The astronauts were the new heroes. The early bird flyers, before World War I, were forgotten. Already thousands of people had booked themselves on the Pan Am Clipper to the Moon, first flight tentatively set for the year 2000.

The flying stories of that fantastic era collapsed into one tale: Atwood's and Hap Arnold's and Charlie Hamilton's stealing that Curtiss plane and flying solo his first time. Who was going to question him? It was so long ago. Some of his stories had a longer life than some of the people he had known. Some stories were true, some false, but by now it was as seamless as a one-piece Duply Airmobile. Truth and lie were bonded tightly to form a new material, the fable of Harry Atwood's life.

"I had to learn to how to maneuver the stick and make the airplane fly. I simply got the thing into the air and didn't know how to get it down. It took about two hours for me to get the feel of it . . . After that it was easy and I had to figure out how to land it."

He was in all things, in flight, in invention, in talk, a skylark. He sang his song. That's all that mattered.

"I landed and found I'd been in the air longer than any other person. Everybody thought I was hero."

After they left, he collapsed. "But he'd keep going as long as anybody was there," said Nellie. "Nobody knew. He was dying from cancer."

In those last months, his first daughter, Bethany, found her father at last. He had not seen her for more than fifty years. She spent four days visiting the father she had never known. Her two sons also spent a weekend with their grandfather.

In Arkansas, Atwood had two brief reunions with some of his other children. Gene had visited. She was thirty-three; her half-sister Nelda was six. Her father had introduced Gene to Nelda as an aunt. She thought he was embarrassed to have her there.

Harry Jr. had also found him in the Ozarks. The minister and his wife who raised him after Mary Dalton died had told Harry Jr. that his father, too, was dead, said Nellie. Then one day Harry Atwood was in the news and the boy was desperate to see him. He spent a month with them, a con-fused, restless boy of sixteen or seventeen, said Nellie. One morning they awoke and he was gone. He had taken off in their jeep and enlisted in the armed services. When he was discharged, he said that he never wanted to hear from anyone in the Atwood family.

After Bethany had found her father, he learned that a group of avia-tion historians had been looking for him for years, and had thought him dead. He called one of the historians and said he would like to talk with them about that summer of 1911 and those days of flying before the first world war. He seemed to be "in exceptionally good health for his age," they said after their visit.

Harry had always wanted an electric organ. He had played an organ for a time, long ago in his sister's church. But an organ was expensive. He arranged to have a four-thousand-dollar organ delivered to his house.

Dr. Van Gorder arrived one day and there he was at the new organ. "And he was a whiz at playing it. I'd ask him to play some tune I'd like to hear, you know, Humoresque—Dvorak's Humoresque. He said, 'Now you want Dvorak's or the other fellow that wrote a similar Humoresque thing.' I said, 'Dvorak's.' Well he'd sit up there and run that thing off."

Harry asked him if he liked the organ. He said, "I had it sent up here from Chattanooga just for you."

"I don't want an organ. I can't even whistle," said Van Gorder.

"'I told them you're going to buy this,' said Harry.

"'Why did you tell them that?'

"'Because I thought you wanted an organ.'"

The good doctor was "astounded."

Harry Atwood could sell blue sky until his last day.

"When it got to the last, he'd take a raw egg—that was all he could get down," said Nellie.

The pain was too much. He would have to go to the hospital. He never went to hospitals. He always said if he entered one, he would never come out. Dr. Van Gorder was away on vacation and Harry refused to see anyone else. When Van Gorder returned, he sent an ambulance.

The medics carried him from the house. The last time anyone had carried him he was a young man. He rode on the shoulders of cheering crowds then: "All Hail the Conquering Air Hero."

Nellie rode with Harry in the ambulance. "I can't believe this," said Harry.

At eighty-three, it had been a short life. It had been enough life for five or six people, but in terms of infinity, as points on a line running on forever, it was nothing much at all, really. It wasn't dying he was afraid of. When you die you open a door and go on.

"I can't believe this," he said once more, and was silent.

Dr. Van Gorder operated for five hours, but Harry's liver was a solid rock. "He was just eaten up with cancer," said the doctor, and it had spread. There was nothing he could do for Harry. Van Gorder closed him up and went to tell the bad news to Nellie.

Six days later, Harry Nelson Atwood died, on July 14, 1967, fifty-six years to the day from when he had landed on the White House lawn. The headlines said, "Last of Wright Pilots Dies." Nelda chose a grave all by itself high on a hill. The man who believed in infinity had opened another door.

Family Reunion

Twenty-five years after Harry Atwood's death, there is a family reunion. Katrina and her daughter Trina meet Nellie and Nelda for the first time. Nellie has returned to visit New Hampshire after nearly forty years.

Unlike some family reunions, there are no overstuffed scrapbooks and family albums. No pictures on the wall, none of his trophies. On a coffee table there is a loose pile of family photos, maybe two dozen, and a folder with a few newspaper articles, and just one condolence note.

It is a tense meeting, at times an ice jam of awkward silences and side-long telegraphic glances, and many statements that just hang in the air, as if someplace mid–living room they had come up against a silent disbelief.

Each will say the other is not on the square, that this is not the way things happened. This is another Atwood monument, another house in which the rooms have been rearranged until the former inhabitants are lost. He played people, and is still doing it, long after he has died.

At dinner, on the first night, they confront each other. Katrina tests Nellie's love of Harry, and Nellie challenges her memory, saying, "Did you have *any* happy times with your father?"

"I think of all the good times. She thinks of bad times," Nellie will say later. And Katrina and Trina will note the hardship hiding behind Nellie's stories of life in the Ozarks and the Smokies. Nellie is careful in the stories she chooses to tell.

Nellie's entire face wrinkles into a smile when she talks about Harry. When she smiles, which is frequent, her face seems to be in its natural alignment.

Two times during the day tears come to her eyes. The first time we are outside, just us two. There is a stiff March wind, and at first I think maybe her eyes are tearing from the cold. She brings up Katrina's questioning of her love. "I had thirty-two years of wonderful life with him. When we buried him, I didn't have a dime, but I had wonderful memories." The second time we are sitting in Katrina's living room, and Nellie is talking of Harry's last days and the ambulance ride to the hospital.

"I know him from the fifties up," she says, by way of summary. "I wouldn't want to have been married to him when he was young. He changed as he got older. He got more mellow."

"I know your mother has a lot of hurt," Nellie says to Trina, "but he had a lot of hurt too." He was really hurt when Katrina told him off on the phone, says Nellie.

Talk turns to that afternoon in Monson, more than sixty years before, when he sent his daughters away, "skipped them," as Katrina says.

"It hurt him so, he was losing everything," Nellie says.

"Naturally we felt he didn't even like us," Katrina says.

A year later, Katrina is talking about her father. "I can see now how that hurt him to send us away. We thought he was just being hurtful." For the first time, she had been able to learn more about his life. All these years she and her sisters had been left with so little to go on. Her father had willed his life into fragments and they had only a few in their hands—a few years in Monson, a summer in New Hampshire. He had never told them stories about his record flights. Trophies, awards, letters, most newspapers—all had vanished. They had no way to judge his inventions, to put in context all the commotion. The central figure in their life's story was elusive.

But everyone leaves a paper trail. I had been sharing what I found with Katrina. Simple things like old newspaper stories, and more complex, layered documents like her father's FBI file. For Katrina that file was like a letter that had been lost in the mail for sixty years. The FBI agents had asked the questions she would have asked. They had covered the days she and her sisters had always wondered about. I summarized the file in a letter to Katrina.

She called immediately. "I can't tell you how much you've done. It's picking up a piece of life. You've brought something beautiful . . . I can't speak I'm so excited by your letter." She followed that with a long, excited letter, which began: "What a revelation . . ." She saw the bankruptcy in its totality: her father just ran out of dodges. "He couldn't afford us any-more."

When we met to talk now, her stories no longer led her to dark corners and troubled silences. She was past 80 and her emphysema was worse, but she was younger than when we had first walked together through the old stone house years earlier.

I love him again, she said. She is no longer lost in her father's house.

Her father may have flown half the continent, but this was a far more difficult and courageous journey.

⌒ Sources and Acknowledgments

Writing about a life as diffuse as Harry Atwood's required the help of many people. There is no one archive or collection to consult, and no previous Atwood book. Here, divided into the book's three sections, are the important sources.

I

Katrina Atwood Copeland and her sister, Gene Collyer, have been essential as storytellers and guides. Katrina died at age eighty-three on January 13, 1998. Gene died a few weeks later. They were rare spirits. I am fortunate to have met them, as well as Katrina's daughter, Trina Richardson. In the two years before Katrina died, I would go to her house to read her the manuscript that would become this book.

Katrina's last years were, I believe, a triumph. She had emerged from a long shadow, slain the darkness that was sometimes with her, and found peace.

I have found the historians of early aviation to be some of the most helpful and congenial people: Leo Opdycke, editor of *WWI Aero* magazine, an indispensable reference; Wesley E. Smith; Ken Hyde; Tom Parramore; Jay P. Spenser; Tom Crouch; Peter Jakab; Leo Boyle; Robert Parmerter; C. F. Gray; William Lewis; E. Henry Hinrichs; Stan Wacksman; and Wally Tripp. They provided exacting answers.

Bartlett Gould was most generous with his time, sharing his knowledge of Starling Burgess.

Glenn Messer, one of the last surviving early birds, provided a sharp recollection of flying the Wright Model B.

Without the aviation libraries and museums, often staffed with volunteers, this book would have been impossible. Thanks to: Larry Wilson, National Air and Space Museum, Smithsonian Institution; John William Ramsay, New England Air

Museum, Reference Library; Kirk House, The Glenn H. Curtiss Museum; Lois Walker, Wright-Patterson Air Force Base; David W. Dillion, Owls Head Transportation Museum; D. "Andy" Anderson, The Early Birds of Aviation, Inc.; Noel C. Shirley, League of WWI Aviation Historians; Lt. Col. Alan H. Clair, Maxwell Air Force Base; The American Aviation Historical Society; Emil Buehler, Naval Aviation Library; The Ninety-Nines, Resource Center; International Women's Air and Space Museum, Inc.; Iowa Aviation Preservation Center; Aviation Hall of Fame of New Jersey; G. H. S. Barton; Cross & Cockade International; National Aviation Museum, Canada; The Royal Air Force Museum, London; The Royal Aeronautical Society, London; and Musee de l'Air et de l'Espace, France.

I confess to having a research staff: my father, pilot and ace aviation researcher Pincus Mansfield, who always welcomes an excuse to visit an airport or flying museum.

I received invaluable assistance from librarians Pat Briggs and Judy Garabrant; Alan Lambert; Roger and Elizabeth Swain; Lea Poisson; Stephen Thomas; George Vecsey; Second Lt. Sue Bickford; and Cathie Zusy.

For the timely repair of a broken interview tape, I am indebted to Howard Eglowstein and Selinda Chiquoine.

Gil Speyer, of Phi Beta Epsilon, at the time a student, was a diligent researcher in the fraternity's archives.

Other sources for Atwood's early years: Columbia Oral History Collection; H. Hap Arnold Papers, Library of Congress; Llewellyn Howland III; Nadine Mitchell, Lynn Public Library; Quincy Historical Society; Roxbury Latin; Hall of History, Schenectady, New York; Middleborough Historical Museum; Barbara D. Arnold; Dorothy Vaughn; Vincent P. O'Brien; New Hampshire State Library; The Connecticut Historical Society; The Marblehead Historical Society; Roger Frazier; Daniel W. Pfaff; R. D. Layman; Office of the Registrar, Massachusetts Institute of Technology; Dr. Medhad Ibrahim; The Atlantic County Historical Society; The Historical Society of Washington, D.C.; Chicago Historical Society; C. E. Woerner; V. L. Barrett; E. S. Allen, local government historian, Castleton, New York; Fort Plain Museum; *Courier-Standard-Enterprise*, Fort Plain; The Cayuga Museum; Saugus Historical Society; Sally Dewey; Judith C. Herdeg; Ruth Owen Jones; and Edmund W. Cowan.

On Atwood's ventures in Ohio, Pennsylvania, and Delaware

Maura McEnaney aided an old friend by volunteering her Pulitzer Prize–winning reporting, and a day off to crank through reels of microfilm. Another old friend, robin brown, lent her reportial talents in Delaware. John J. Cianci kindly shared the labors of his Reading research.

Thanks to Janet Senne, The Erie County Historical Society; Toledo-Lucas County Public Library; Lucas County Clerk of Courts; Rutherford B. Hayes Presidential Center; Jean Gardner, Follett House Museum; Amherstburg Historic Sites Association; Phillips Exeter Academy; Everett W. Rubendall, Lycoming County Historical Society & Museum; The James V. Brown Library; Hagley Museum and Library; and Yale University Library.

On Atwood's years in Smithfield, North Carolina

Librarian Margaret Lee, The Public Library of Johnston County and Smithfield, was an invaluable help, and graciously arranged a group to meet with me when I visited: Mary Ellen Lawrence Dean, Benjamin F. Grimes, Nell Broadhurst Hooks, William S. Ragsdale, Jr., and Sallie Ives Robenolt.

Thanks also to Michael Hill, North Carolina Dept. of Cultural Resources; National Archives, Bureau of Aeronautics Collection.

PERIODICALS

The newspapers quoted in the book covered early flight with great verve. A reading of *Scientific American*, 1910–1914, offers a colorful record, as do articles in *American Magazine, Century, Collier's, Country Life, Current Literature, Harper's Weekly, Literary Digest, Nation, Outlook, Review of Reviews,* and *World's Work.* The aviation magazines of the era give a glimpse of the concerns of the early flyers: *Aero, Aerial Age Weekly, Aeronautics, Aircraft,* and *Aviation.*

BOOKS

Contemporary accounts of early flight

Arnold, H. H. *Global Mission* (New York: Harper & Brothers, 1949).

Beaumont, Andre. *My Three Big Flights* (New York: McBridge, Nast & Co., 1912).

Brewer, Griffith. *Fifty Years of Flying* (London: Air League of the British Empire, 1946).

Brewer, R. W. A. *The Art of Aviation* (New York: McGraw Hill, 1910).

Curtiss, Glenn H., and Augustus Post. *The Curtiss Aviation Book* (New York: Frederick A. Stokes Co., 1912).

Ferris, Richard. *How It Flies* (New York: Thomas Nelson & Sons, 1910).

Foulois, Benjamin D. *From the Wright Brothers to the Astronauts* (New York: McGraw-Hill, 1968).

Grahame-White, Claude, and Harry Harper. *The Aeroplane: Past, Present and Future* (Philadelphia: J. P. Lippincott Co., 1911).

Loening, Grover C. *Monoplanes & Biplanes* (New York: Munn & Co., 1911).

———. *Our Wings Grow Faster* (New York: Doubleday, Doran, 1935).

Ovington, Adelaide. *An Aviator's Wife* (New York: Dodd, Mead & Co., 1920).

Histories

Bilstein, Roger. *Flight in America 1900–1983* (Baltimore: Johns Hopkins University Press, 1984).

Borden, Norman E. *The Aviators* (Unpublished ms., New England Air Museum, n.d.).

Bruno, Harry. *Wings Over America* (New York: Halcyon House, 1944).

Casey, Louis S. *Curtiss: The Hammondsport Era* 1907–15 (New York: Crown, 1981).

Coffey, Thomas M. *Hap* (New York: Viking, 1982).

Crouch, Tom. *A Dream of Wings* (New York: Norton, 1981).

———. *Bleriot XI* (Washington: Smithsonian Institution Press, 1982).

———. *The Bishop's Boys* (New York: Norton, 1989).

French, Joseph Lewis, ed. *The Big Aviation Book for Boys* (Springfield, Mass.: McLoughlin Bros., 1929).

Gray, "Jack" Stearns. *"Up", A True Story of Aviation* (Strasburg, Va.: Shenandoah Publishing House, 1931).

Hallion, Richard P., ed. *The Wright Brothers, Heirs of Prometheus* (Washington: Smithsonian Institution Press, 1979).

Harris, Sherwood. *The First to Fly* (New York: Simon and Schuster, 1970).

Hughes, Thomas Parke. *Elmer Sperry, Inventor & Engineer* (Baltimore: Johns Hopkins University Press, 1971).

———. *American Genesis* (New York: Viking, 1989).

Jakab, Peter L. *Visions of a Flying Machine* (Washington: Smithsonian Institution Press, 1990).

Jewkes, John, et al., eds. *The Sources of Invention* (New York: Macmillan, 1968).

Lebow, Eileen F. *Cal Rodgers and the Vin Fiz* (Washington: Smithsonian Institution Press, 1989).

Leslie, Stuart W. *Boss Kettering* (New York: Columbia University Press, 1983).

Magoun, F. Alexander, and Eric Hodgins. *A History of Aircraft* (New York: McGraw-Hill, 1931).

Oliver, Carl R. *Plane Talk* (Boston: Houghton Mifflin, 1980).

Pacey, Arnold. *The Maze of Ingenuity* (Cambridge: MIT Press, 1975).

Renstrom, Arthur G. *Wilbur and Orville Wright: A Chronology* (Washington: Library of Congress, 1975).

Smith, Richard K. *First Across!* (Annapolis: Naval Institute Press, 1973).

Sullivan, Mark. *Our Times, The United States, 1900–25*, Vol. 2 (New York: Scribner's, 1927).

Trimble, William F. *High Frontier* (Pittsburgh: University of Pittsburgh Press, 1982).

Woodhouse, Henry. *Textbook of Naval Aeronautics* (1917; reprint, Annapolis: Naval Institute Press, 1991).

Vecsey, George, and George C. Dade. *Getting Off the Ground* (New York: Dutton, 1979).

Villard, Henry Serrano. *Contact!* (New York: Thomas Y. Crowell, 1968).

Vincenti, Walter G. *What Engineers Know and How They Know It* (Baltimore: Johns Hopkins University Press, 1990).

Wheeler, Allen. *Building Aeroplanes for 'Those Magnificent Men'* (London: G. T. Foulis & Co. Ltd, 1965).

Whitehouse, Arch. *The Early Birds* (New York: Doubleday, 1965).

Wollner, Joseph F., Jr. *The Aeronautical Experiences of Charles K. Hamilton* (Unpublished ms., New England Air Museum, 1985).

Young, David, and Neal Callahan. *Fill the Heavens with Commerce, Chicago Aviation 1855–1926* (Chicago: Chicago Review Press, 1981).

II

Many thanks to Grace Makepeace, historian, Monson Historical Society, for answering my questions and gathering those who met with me: Ken Carpenter, Jessee Smart Clark, Hank Miller, Lorraine and Mike Lanzetta, Sherwood Young, and Bernice and Phila Vaill.

Librarian Sylvia De Santis, Monson Free Library and Reading Room Association, took the time to dig for important information.

For their recollections, I thank Marcia Satterthwaite Sternbergh, Bill Stone, Herb Murray, Norman Nye, Francis Hickey, John Dudar, and Verner S. Dempsey.

Wally Konrad shared her considerable expertise as a business reporter to explain the wide-open pre-SEC days of the stock market.

Also helpful were Massachussetts State Archives; National Archives—New England Region; Connecticut Valley Historical Museum; Federal Bureau of Investigation; Commonwealth of Pennsylvania, Department of Health, Vital Records; Steve Young, Fairfield Historical Society; Beverly York, Windham Textile and Historical Museum; Mansfield Historical Society Museum; Isabel Atwood; University of Massachussetts at Amherst, Physcial Sciences Library; Boston Public Library, Science Reference Dept.; The Whitney Library, New Haven Colony Historical Society; Palmer Public Library; and Springfield City Library.

On the Airmobile

Clarence Farr's suitcase archive and his careful, detailed engineering stories illuminated the Airmobile effort. Aline Farr was a gracious host, and an honest witness to that era.

I thank Joe McQuaid, Bill and Patty Rotch, Mignon and Col. Bob Taylor, Bob Whittier, and Barbara Conway for giving me their time. I thank also David Heald, Paul Cummings, Bob Fay, Les Hibbert, Daniel Olney, Thomas Lord, Franklin Peart, John McQuaid, William J. Deane, Thomas Belt, Louise Lucier Brantley, James J. Kiepper, Joyce Seyer, Jim Tamposi, Sr., Connie Wheeler, A. Donald Vaughn, Roberta Window, Harold D. Barnes, Roger O. Leonard, JoAn Rand, Mary O'Hearn Armitage, and Stephen "Horace" Gilson.

It was a great pleasure to visit with the late Frederick Wetherbee.

Don K. Covington, Jr., of The Harbor Sales Company, and Robert Keller, Sr., of Keller Products were wise guides to the applications of wartime plywood.

Other helpful sources were Joseph Shipley Newell Papers, 1922–1951, and Institute Archives and Special Collections, MIT Libraries; Hillsborough County Court, Clerk's Office; Dartmouth Alumni Magazine; Dartmouth College Library; New Hampshire Historical Society; Manchester Historic Association; Wadleigh Memorial Library, Milford; George Holmes Bixby Memorial Library, Francestown; Steinway & Sons; Merton Smith; A. Hanford Eckman; George C. White, Jr.; Duke Iden; Calvin Arter, Piper Museum; Bill Piper; University of Wyoming; Federal Aviation Administration; John Meyer, AlliedSignal Inc.; Northern Indiana Historical Society; Peter Leatherwood; Tab Lewis, National Archives; Wellesley College Archives; Henry Ford Museum; Mearl T. Luvaas; Robert D. Moffitt; and Gore Vidal.

PERIODICALS

The Milford Cabinet, 1933–36, provided thorough coverage of the Airmobile and of small town life in the Depression. Other newspapers and magazines as quoted in the book.

BOOKS

Allen, Hugh. *Rubber's Home Town* (New York; Stratford House, 1949).

Bilstein, Roger E. *Flight Patterns* (Athens: University of Georgia Press, 1983).

Bough, James. *The Woolworths* (New York: McGraw-Hill, 1982).

Clements, Menefee R. *King of Stop and Go* (Unpublished: Bendix Corporation, 1970).

Corn, Joseph J. *The Winged Gospel* (New York: Oxford University Press, 1983).

Dade, G. C., and Frank Strnad. *Picture History of Aviation on Long Island 1908–38* (New York: Dover, 1989).

Earhart, Amelia. *The Fun of It* (New York: Harcourt, Brace, and Co., 1932).

Komons, Nick A. *Bonfires to Beacons* (Washington: Smithsonian Institution Press, 1989).

Emme, Eugene M., ed. *200 Years of Flight in America* (San Diego: Univelt, 1977).

Felaman, Hazel. *Poems That Live Forever* (New York: Macmillan, 1965).

Francis, Devon. *Mr. Piper and His Cubs* (Ames: Iowa State University Press, 1973).

Leary, William. *Aviation's Golden Age* (Iowa City: University of Iowa Press, 1989).

Lovell, Mary S. *The Sound of Wings* (New York: St. Martin's Press, 1989).

Meyer, Louis H. *Plywood, What It Is—What It Does* (New York: McGraw-Hill, 1947).

Monson Historical Society. *History of Monson Massachusetts* (Monson Mass.: Monson Historical Society, 1960).

Nichols, Ruth. *Wings for Life* (Philadelphia: Lippincott, 1957).

Page, Victor W. *Everybody's Aviation Guide* (New York: The Norman W. Henley
    Publishing Co., 1928).
Peek, Chet. *The Taylorcraft Story* (Terre Haute, Ind.: SunShine House, 1992).
Ramsdell, George A. *The History of Milford, N.H.* (Milford, N.H.: Town of Milford,
    1901).
Rich, Doris. *Amelia Earhart* (Washington: Smithsonian Institution Press, 1989).
Smith, Elinor. *Aviatrix* (New York: Harcourt Brace Jovanovich, 1981).
Spenser, Jay P. *Bellanca C.F.* (Washington: Smithsonian Institution Press, 1982).
Wright, Winifred A. *The Granite Town* (Milford, N.H.: Town of Milford, 1979).

III

Many thanks to Nellie Pickens and her daughter Nelda Atwood Stiles for their patience and enthusiasm.

On the Higgins Air Freighter and Atwood's Ozark years

Jerry Strahan and Augie Bellanca helped explain the Higgins operation; David Ellis, National Institute for Aviation Research, The Witchita State University, and J. F. Marchman, Virginia Polytechnic Institute and State University, explained the era's technology.

Thanks also to Gehrung Associates, University Relations Counselors, Inc.; Carroll County Historical and Genealogical Society and Heritage Center; Lester Boss; Jack Sweeney; Barbara McFadden, Jaffrey District Court; W. Robert Bentley; Katherine G. Wells; Wayne Curtis; and Tom Grazulis, The Tornado Project of Environmental Films.

On Hanging Dog

Many thanks to Dr. Charles O. Van Gorder and Red Schuyler for the day we spent visiting with Lester and Lucille Dockery, E. J. Greer, Carrie Kephart, and Ralph Kephart. Thanks also to Bess Alverson, Butler Carter, James W. Lail, Olin MacDonald, and Frank and Jeff Trask for their recollections.

Also helpful were United States Department of Agriculture, Forest Products Library, and the National Institute of Building Sciences.

Caroline Beyrau, Cliff Glickman, and their dog squad kindly put me up when I was in North Carolina. Beth Preston hosted me in Georgia.

BOOKS

Bowers, Peter. *Curtiss Aircraft 1907–47* (Annapolis: Naval Institute Press, 1979).
Cleveland, Reginald M., and Frederick P. Graham, eds. *The Aviation Annual of
    1944* (New York: Doubleday & Doran, 1943).

Craven, Wesley Frank, and James Lee Cate, eds. *The Army Air Forces In World War II*, Vol. 6 (Washington: Office of Air Force History, 1983).

Ginger, Ray. *Six Days or Forever?* (New York: Oxford University Press, 1958).

Knott, Richard C. *The American Flying Boat* (Annapolis: Naval Institute Press, 1979).

Leyson, Burr. *American Wings* (New York: E. P. Dutton & Co., 1938).

Miller, Ronald, and David Sawers. *The Technical Development of Modern Aviation* (New York: Praeger, 1970).

Neufeld, Michael J. *The Rocket and the Reich* (Cambridge, Mass.: Harvard University Press, 1995).

Page, Victor. *Modern Aircraft* (New York: The Norman W. Henley Publishing Co., 1929).

Rae, John B. *Climb to Greatness* (Cambridge: MIT Press, 1968).

Stout, William Bushnell. *So Away I Went!* (1951; reprint, New York: Arno Press, 1980).

Strahan, Jerry. *Higgins: The Man, The Boat, The Industry* (M.A. Thesis, University of New Orleans, 1974).

Simonson, G. R., ed. *The History of the American Aircraft Industry* (Cambridge: MIT Press, 1968).

Wooldridge, E. T. *Winged Wonders* (Washington: Smithsonian Institution Press, 1983).

For reading the manuscript I thank Elizabeth Marshall Thomas, Willard Williams, Dan Chartrand, Irwin Fisch, and Tasha Garland.

Many thanks and a deep appreciation are due my agent, Christina Ward.

Once more, my deepest thanks to my wife, Sy Montgomery, the best editor I ever had.